Praise for Aaron James's

Surfing with Sartre

"A beautiful book, essentially a dialogue with Jean-Paul Sartre about work and play. He's arguing that working less and playing more, especially in the surf, is not only an okay choice but a moral one."
—Jaimal Yogis, *Tampa Bay Times*

"Incredibly intelligent and compelling. . . . Provocative and pure. . . . Render[s] complicated ideas easily comprehensible by way of a context of surfing attitude."
—*The Maine Edge*

"Thoughtful and life-affirming. . . . Funny, enthralling and, above all, wise, *Surfing with Sartre* offers fresh insights into the human condition that will interest the academic theorist, the casual surfer and everyone in between."
—*Shelf Awareness*

"Carefully and conscientiously crafted and deeply thoughtful. . . . Addresses major questions in philosophy from his unique perspective as both a philosopher and former surfer."
—*Reason and Meaning*

"Provocative. . . . Entertaining. . . . [A] nimble set of essays on topics such as work and freedom."
—*Kirkus Reviews*

"[A] thoughtful meditation on surfing and philosophy. . . . Even for nonsurfers, James convincingly illustrates the ways in which catching a wave can change how people understand the world·and try to make meaning from experiences."
—*Publishers Weekly*

Aaron James

Surfing with Sartre

Aaron James holds a Ph.D. from Harvard and is a professor of philosophy at the University of California, Irvine. He is the author of *Assholes: A Theory*, *Assholes: A Theory of Donald Trump*, and *Fairness in Practice: A Social Contract for a Global Economy* and numerous academic articles. He was awarded a Burkhardt Fellowship from the American Council of Learned Societies and spent the 2009–10 academic year at the Center for Advanced Study in the Behavioral Sciences at Stanford University. He's a skilled, lifelong surfer and lives in Irvine, California.

Surfing with Sartre

Surfing with Sartre

An Aquatic Inquiry into a Life of Meaning

Aaron James

ANCHOR BOOKS
A Division of Penguin Random House LLC
New York

FIRST ANCHOR BOOKS EDITION, MAY 2018

Copyright © 2017 by Aaron J. James

All rights reserved. Published in the United States by Anchor
Books, a division of Penguin Random House LLC, New York, and
distributed in Canada by Random House of Canada, a division
of Penguin Random House Canada Limited, Toronto. Originally
published in hardcover in the United States by Doubleday, a
division of Penguin Random House LLC, New York, in 2017.

Anchor Books and colophon are registered
trademarks of Penguin Random House LLC.

The Library of Congress has cataloged the Doubleday edition as follows:
Names: James, Aaron (Aaron J.), author.
Title: Surfing with Sartre : an aquatic inquiry
 into a life of meaning / Aaron James.
Description: First Edition. | New York : Doubleday Books, 2017.
Identifiers: LCCN 2017000670 (print) | LCCN 2017021274 (ebook)
Subjects: LCSH: Philosophy, American. | Surfing. | Sports—
 Philosophy. | Sartre, Jean-Paul, 1905–1980.
Classification: LCC B936 (ebook) | LCC B936.J36
 2017 (print) | DDC 201/.679732—dc23
LC record available at https://lccn.loc.gov/2017000670

Anchor Books Trade Paperback ISBN: 978-1-101-97015-7
eBook ISBN: 978-0-385-54074-2

Author photograph © Skye Schmidt
Book design by Michael Collica

www.anchorbooks.com

Printed in the United States of America
10 9 8 7 6 5 4 3 2

For Tim, who believed in a surfer

To *ski* means not only to enable me to make rapid movements
and to acquire a technical skill, nor is it merely to *play*. . . .
I am changing the matter and meaning of the snow.

—Jean-Paul Sartre

By considering the body in movement, we can see better how
it inhabits space (and, moreover, time) because movement is
not limited to submitting passively to space and time, it actively
assumes them, it takes them up in their basic significance which
is obscured in the commonplaceness of established situations.

—Maurice Merleau-Ponty

Catch a wave and you're sitting on top of the world.

—Brian Wilson and Mike Love

Contents

Surfing with Sartre

This Book Is About Surfing, and Not

NOT SO LONG AGO, in the dark days before the forty-hour workweek, the average person worked constantly, without time to completely rest, let alone laze around, get creative, and maybe take up surfing. Fortunately, history brought something of a revolution. By the early 1940s, the labor movement had won limited workdays, weekends off, and periodic vacations for most workers. The postwar economy boomed. And many people hit the beach in this new leisure culture, finding new forms of meaning. Nowadays, in our more leisurely style of capitalism, the workaday surfer can be found at surf breaks the world over, stoked in gushing exuberance about the better waves of the day, feeling lighter about the stresses of work, acting as if the whole meaning of human existence can be found in the simple act of riding a wave.

And I mean, like, *super* stoked, at least in the peak moments. As in effusive, bursting forth in hoots and howls. As in feeling like things are easy. Fine. *Golden.* As though you can just relax and eat some nice tacos. As in you were worried about some things, but what were they again? Maybe the surfer gushes with profoundly vague slogans. "Only a surfer knows the feeling"; "Problems just wash off in the water"; "It's all connected"; "You just have to tap into something bigger, you know what I'm saying?" And maybe the honest answer is "Actually, what *are* you saying?" But, you know, whatever, because who cares? Can't the vague slogans just *express* the easy moment, without stating carefully defined truths? Surely complete thoughts aren't *always* necessary, if only because the world can never be mastered in language, even in the most precisely chosen words. When you're stoked about the waves on which every-thing totally came together, or when you got a serious, *proper* tube, and you rode inside the tube of the wave for what felt like *ages*, you don't need to get control of anything. You're stoked precisely because nothing else has to happen. Because nothing has to change. Because you can just be. Because right there at 3:15 p.m. on a Monday after a good surf session in Southern California, standing by the taco truck, under a fortunate sun, you are being.

Surfers aren't ungrateful slackers—at least not in any greater pro-portion than the general population. Most surfers work. They show up to work even when the waves are cracking, moved by that pained sense of duty that comes in acting contrary to the strong inclination to go surfing. The "workaholic" shows up to work eagerly, with a zeal for money and self-promotion that requires no thought of duty. But then whose work has greater moral worth? The one who is solemnly moved by duty, or the one who does as he likes?

For Immanuel Kant, the Enlightenment philosopher and moral rigorist, the moral worth of an action springs from its motives, and the workaday surfer who shows up from duty—maybe solely from duty—would be especially praiseworthy for doing what he or she really isn't inclined to do.[1] Yet the high-minded, über-rationalist phi-losopher (one of the big philosophers of all time, alongside Plato and Aristotle of ancient Greece) probably isn't the surfer's philosopher. Although Kant was apparently quite the party animal in his youth, he traveled little beyond his hometown of Königsberg, Germany. It was said that you could set your watch by his daily walk, while he

---

1. Of a sorrowful man who brings himself to help others "without any inclination at all, but solely from duty," Kant says here "for the first time his action has genuine moral worth" in comparison to a sympathetic person who just wants to help others. Here Kant surely overstated the point. But if working solely from duty is at least especially praiseworthy, the begrudging surfer would still get kudos. *Groundwork for the Metaphysics of Morals* (1785), sec. 1, at 398, or p. 11 in *Ethical Philosophy* (Indianapolis: Hackett, 1983).

presumably worked in deep thought. The hardworking genius was skeptical about happiness and hyperintellectual about morality and made much of strict conformity to law, and for those reasons alone a surfer might look elsewhere for help in articulating what is distinctively good about the surfer life.

Not that work these days is so terrible in itself. Most people can find some sort of meaning in a job taken to pay the bills. The time can fly while you get into a "flow state" (of which more later) while arguing about the new kitchen area policy, plowing through e-mails, or restocking a grocery store shelf. But most of us can't constantly pay close attention, especially not when the job turns mundane. The mind wanders, often to what one is missing. And so the surfer can often be found awash in daydreams of glorious wave-riding moments, at the keyboard, cash register, or roller brush, going through the motions, not quite into work with his or her whole being.

I once worked as a window cleaner for various restaurants. This paid mainly in flexibility, so that I could surf when the waves turned on. There was also joy in efficiently whipping the squeegee over the glass panes, without a drop left behind, and then, a moment later, opening the door for a customer with a pleasant greeting. The groove of fluid performance was intrinsically pleasing—not to mention time efficient, which put me on the road to surfing more speedily. Yet on the days when the wind would clock offshore, grooming the wave faces gently, with a solid six-foot ground swell running, when all I could think about was how *insane* the waves must be right this very moment, I could barely remember what I needed my small paycheck for. This wasn't the dim sense that life could be better, eventually, if I just worked for it. The whole meaning of life was happening *right now,* today, only miles away from Denny's restaurant, and there I was, at Denny's restaurant, suffering the pangs of lost time, a forlorn lover alienated from his beloved, forcing a smile for the nice people who'd eaten too much of the all-day breakfast.

The surfer daydreams of glorious wave-riding moments nearly always include a tube ride. As every surfer will tell you, riding inside the tube of a wave is an ecstatic, even orgasmic experience (almost, anyway[2]). "Time stands still in the barrel," they'll say. "It's just insane. Epic. Seriously, bro"—a thesis they'll corroborate by vividly retelling each moment of their best tube ever, even decades after the fact, as though they've just been reading Proust. They'll mention the *speed* and how *seriously deep* they were within the wave's churning bowels. They'll note certain drops of water flying by and how the spray of water was "chandeliering" at one point, with the water curtain *way* out in front of them. They'll note how they just *barely* squeaked under the heaving wave lip, or just how *super easy* it all was, given certain heroic adjustments, perfectly timed, along with some stance of preternatural relaxation, though they seriously did not *even* think they were coming out of that thing. They'll tell you of the giant sucking sound inside (accompanied by a sucking-sound demonstration), of the remarkable amount of wind swirling around, and maybe of a saucer-eyed guy paddling up the shoulder, hooting like crazy, who totally saw the whole thing and could totally verify all this if you aren't believing it.

Fortunately, you don't have to trust the surfer's telling, which can be as fantastical as a fisherman's. The towering, reeling deep-blue/green wall, with the surfer gracefully standing in the spinning vortex, is plainly its own thing of splendor, a feat of natural and human possibility, of attuned flow between person and wave.[3]

Surfers often have a certain natural lightness about being, about the meaning of their personal existence. Those more at sea existentially can certainly appreciate the surfer's good fortune. And it is hard to dislike people so thoroughly enthralled by living, even when their

2. In high school, surfer boys often compare the tube ride with sexual intercourse, noting any number of structural isomorphisms. They debate the relative merits as though they have to choose between them. Surfer girls aren't as impressed with the vague similarity.
3. Behold this truly epic tube clip of Koa Smith at Skeleton Bay, Namibia: https://www.youtube.com/watch?v=LG9ei558NEA.

personal shortcoming might invite distaste or criticism. Surely most of us could learn to live lighter, by sliding over life's problems. If we wished to "surf" through our daily business with easy efficacy, the surfer's way of being might even suggest something of a practical philosophy.

This is a book of philosophy. It asks whether the surfer might happen to know something about questions for the ages, about knowledge, freedom, control, flow, happiness, society, nature, and the meaning of life. It's a book about surfing, but also not, or not just, because what the surfer knows, or at least senses, without necessarily caring, turns out to be of world-historical moment, for nothing less than the future of work, the planet, and human civilization. Taken all together, what the surfer knows suggests that we should continue the leisure revolution that began in the postwar era, when we emerged from two world wars and economic depression. The trend toward working less has stalled lately, with work hours rising or steady, especially in the United States. Yet we presumably shouldn't be lazy about adapting our institutions in the current century. We should be ready to go along with the world-historical flow and get used to an even more leisurely, surfer-friendly style of capitalism, in which we all work, but a lot less, and work is to a lesser extent our reason for being. Or at least that is the overarching argument of this book, which I'll explain at length in later chapters.

This book is also my attempt at figuring out what my two life's preoccupations, philosophy and surfing, might have to do with each other. That inquiry brought me to Jean-Paul Sartre, the mid-twentieth-century philosopher and literary figure. This is a man who was so cool, so very French, that he declined the Nobel Prize in Literature in 1964. (He explained that he couldn't let himself "be transformed into an institution," while giving a few other equally slight or opaque reasons.) A theorist, dramatist, and public intellectual, Sartre spoke to his time, in an era darkened by two world wars, cold war dread, and a palpable sense of the absurd, the limits of reason, and the fragility of civilization. To many, he was the conscience of his generation, a courageous witness to its outrages and a voice to its anxieties. Sartre died in 1980, and although his views haven't ever been a major focus of the Anglo-American "analytic" style of philosophy of my profession, I've started conversing with him, as philosophers do with their greater forebears. If I could have a long chat with him in a café, or by the taco truck, this book is what I'd say to him.

Our inquiry builds up to matters world historical little by little, from deeper foundations, in the style of an olden treatise. Since that's just the sort of book we modern readers mostly don't read, for being too easily distracted (or too busy at work), I should probably say more up front about the surfer's peculiar role in world history, to suggest where the argument is headed.[4]

A few surfers should maybe get a job and make themselves more useful to others. Most of us, including most surfers, have the opposite problem: we work too much. Insofar as we do work too much, the surfer wisdom on the matter is that we should therefore work less. Meaning we should actually *do that,* actually work less. We can still work, of course, but more efficiently with less waste, for just enough money, in order to free up time for longer hours in the waves. It may sound odd as a serious proposition, and even many surfers haven't quite pieced it all together, yet nowadays working less and surfing more can be an ethical chore, another way to make oneself useful to others.

Work as we now practice it emits gases (carbon dioxide, methane, and so on) that are steadily warming the planet. So in our strange new condition of ecological scarcity, as long as we do something less consumptive of ecological resources than working, such as surfing (without too much driving, air travel, and so forth), we contribute to

---

4. Each chapter of the book is relatively self-contained, so the short-attention-span reader can skip around among the different topics, following his or her curiosity, going with the attentional flow, circling back to earlier or later themes as connections become apparent.

society by making the climate change problem a little less terrible than it would otherwise be.

Is this perhaps something of a surfer's rationalization for dodging work? The idea that working less is somehow a *contribution* to society—isn't that rather ridiculous, the warm beach baloney of some hippie surfer "philosopher," not to mention downright *disrespectful* of hard work, a cornerstone of civilization and personal virtue? Maybe so. But maybe not. The idea, as I'll argue, has a clear logic. The philosophical challenge, if you're down for fresh thinking, is to say where if anywhere the logic is mistaken.

Gone are the days of global ecological abundance, when a person could work for money like crazy and create greenhouse gases with no worries at all about the profound risks of ecological mayhem, with rising sea levels, droughts and floods, mass displacement, resource wars, and famine, among other dire results. Surfers aren't the most altruistic lot, but even aside from the barest concern for other people you'd expect them to worry about this for their own reasons, because rising sea levels stand to swamp the world's quality surf breaks. We should all *hope and pray* for an easy technological fix. Yet we can't blithely assume new technologies will make the whole problem go away, without our having to otherwise adapt. And as it happens, one useful adaptation among other urgent measures is to carry forth the leisure revolution that gave us the forty-hour workweek. If we all worked, but a lot less, in, say, a twenty-hour workweek, the climate crisis would be less terrible than it otherwise will be.

To this world-historical project, the surfer is an eager if unwitting contributor. For those not inclined to surf, there's also of course gardening, spending time with the kids, reading a book, or whatever you happen to be into at the moment. As long as the activity emits less gas than you would have emitted had you been working in the labor market, doing more of it, instead of working, mirrors the surfer's contribution to society.

The surfer is thus something of a new model of civic virtue. The real troublemaker is the workaholic, whose labor-intensive striving makes the problem of global warming worse than it has to be. I'm sure I speak for surfers everywhere in saying that it would be pretty uncool to scold people for an unfortunate inability to take it easy. Fortunately, not everyone has to do his or her full part in the new, limited workweek. Though for every workaholic who works above a new lower average, a surfer will need to be surfing, so as to "offset" the added emissions. This, as well as other weirdness, is what follows once we reckon with the new human condition of ecological scarcity.

The question is one of ethics: If climate science is even roughly correct, as I assume for the sake of argument, would it be morally okay for us to further enrich ourselves in work, without limitations, if many billions of living or future people are thereby put at grave risk of profound injury? Or are we obliged to adapt? Suppose our "sacrifice" in adapting is a matter of working less and spending more relaxing days with the kids and playing more sports. Would that be so tough? If we'd be happier, or even just no worse off, then continuing the leisure revolution would be not only an ethical imperative but something we could really get used to.

We would have to upend the Protestant work ethic, the quasi-religious ethic of hard work, discipline, and thrift, to which even the deeply secular remain firmly attached. Borne of the theology of Luther and Calvin, the ethic has become deeply ingrained in our lives, and it's a real question whether we could ever let go of it. Simply questioning the ethic can make people angry. The idea of living without it can feel deeply uncomfortable, even disorienting. Who am I if not what I do? Sartre, that great twentieth-century philosopher of being, thought we humans are not existentially suited to doing nothing. Being self-conscious and so free by nature, we are "condemned to choose" in perpetual self-creation. And on this point the quintessential Frenchman was fully in agreement with the old-guard capitalism that first caught on in Europe and then prospered in America. Being is just *doing*, which itself is a kind of work—the work of making ourselves into something, a *someone*, of a larger identity.

Sartre himself was a Marxist-socialist whose sympathies lay with the experiments in communism of his era. But the being-as-work idea was already well rooted across capitalist societies such as America, Canada, and Germany and remains with us today. One's identity, the product of one's self-creative work, is defined by what others will pay for one's time and talent from their own hard-earned money. We largely let the market decide how much we contribute to society, who can fairly claim public benefits, and how we appear in the eyes of others, and so to ourselves. Yes, the forty-hour workweek does afford a measure of free time, but as a strategy for optimizing productivity. Leisure's job is to "recharge the batteries" for work in our primary market occupations, the true source of our meaning. Time for being in leisure and lazing and relaxing and loafing and surfing is time for *recreation* rather than *vocation*.

The Protestant work ethic did nurture early capitalism,[5] and without the rising wealth of nations the leisure revolution would never have begun. For that the surfer owes a historical debt of grati-tude. That isn't to say the ethic is part of our very being, instead of a way of getting rich so as to free up time for activities other than work. Now that advanced countries are rich, could the old ethic be out of date? Surfers aren't exactly known for knowing things. Yet it could be—it isn't impossible—that they're on the right side of history.

That, anyway, is this book's main thesis: what the surfer knows, in knowing how to ride a wave, bears on questions for the ages—about freedom, control, happiness, society, our relation to nature, the value of work, and the very meaning of life. The surfer's answers to these questions suggest how we might adapt on a changing planet, given an unprecedented transformation in the human condition as

5. Max Weber, *The Protestant Ethic and the Spirit of Capitalism,* trans. Talcott Par-sons (New York: Charles Scribner's Sons, 1958).

our planet steadily warms. It's a utopian thought at the moment, as were most of the humane changes in our working conditions at one time. But this is what's great about philosophy: we can have such thoughts. We liberate ourselves from the daily machinations of politics, by looking beyond.

I realize all this might sound like some mash-up of surf camp musings and philosophical blathering in a Paris café. Be assured, the surfer offers fresh insight. Indeed, Jean-Paul Sartre, the prolific, incisive, provocative, chain-smoking existentialist philosopher, is my main intellectual opponent throughout this book. If I could chat with him about our twenty-first-century predicament in view of questions for the ages, I'd make my case that the surfer's knowledge undermines central tenets of his philosophy. Sartre brought deep questions about the human condition before us. He also left us in a bleak existential predicament. In searching for an exit, the surfer shows a way into the sunlight, a hopeful view of history, and intellectual permission for a more exuberant conception of being.

Part One

Epistemology in Action

1

What the Surfer Knows

A person who has a good nose for arguments
or jokes may have a bad head for facts.

—Gilbert Ryle, *The Concept of Mind*

A WAVE RISES FROM the deep, and a surfer surfs it, being carried along by the wave's natural momentum.

When an ocean swell is mounting over shallowing sand or reef, its wave face will steepen and crest and then plunge into the wave trough. If the wave is any good for surfing, a sloping shoulder will pull up into the cresting curl, and a moving wave face will run along the beach, tracking the contours of sand or rock below. Assuming one is up and riding (no easy feat, and I'll come back to tips for beginners momentarily), the surfer glides along the wave face, in or around the wave's breaking curl. Then a lot of different things might happen. The wave may shift. Or shoulder. Or wall up. Or race along. Or tube.

Whatever is happening, the surfer has to sense it and adapt. The surfer has to sense what next moment is approaching and adjust as the coming moment asks, before the wave's curl passes one by.

They say it's good to "go with the flow," in walking a city street, in a work project, in the day's tasks, and as a general way to live, with less anxiety, less striving, and a certain graceful success. "Going with the flow" is a pleasing metaphor for *something*—but what? The surfer *literally* goes along with a flowing natural phenomenon, often on a daily basis, in a way of life devoted to just that activity. So if we wanted a better sense of what truth lies behind the metaphor, we could do worse than look to what the surfer knows.

How to Surf

As an ocean swell approaches, mounting over shallow reef or sand, you'll want to catch it before the wave face peaks and pitches. With careful positioning, you paddle yourself under the vaulting peak, so as to be caught up and carried along by the wave's natural momentum. Then quickly move to your feet, pushing yourself up, pulling your body into a sideways upright posture, all while keeping a crouch and low center of gravity.

As you drop into the wave's quickly steepening face, suddenly picking up speed, you can start sensing how the wave might develop, how it might shift or inflect. Then try to respond as the wave is asking, pausing if it is shouldering or becoming less steep, or instead racing ahead if the face is walling up, because the wave section is about to pitch and crash. You keep adapting in each new moment, with a keen eye for the wave's next offer or request. With enough practice, you'll eventually be carried through from each moment to the next, flying along the whole wave's length, linking wave sections together, with effortless speed, fluent power, and stylish fluidity.

The beginner will wonder about basics. "Respond" how? What maneuvering might be "asked" of you? In which "moments"?

Unfortunately, here philosophy can't provide a definitive answer. It is much as Aristotle said of moral virtue, which he likened to an exercise of skill in sports. What to do next depends entirely on the wave situation before you, which can only be known in practice. Even on waves of the most machinelike predictability, there are just too many possible wave moments, each with its own apt reactions, for any rules or principles to tell you ahead of time how to go on in any definite way.

Still, one could come into a general sense of the variety. So consider a few key surfing moments.

PUMP: Sometimes you have to hurry down the line of the wave, and so you'll pump the surfboard up and down like a steam engine, because the wave face is walling up and might leave you caught behind a breaking section.

FADE: Or maybe the wave section is slowing, but about to rebuild, in which case you have to downshift, like hitting a down-beat note in a jazz riff, by fading back into the curl of the wave, in order to be well positioned as the wave steepens again.

SNAP: Unless you're already in exactly the right position, in which case you just unload your best turn! If the wave face is steep and hanging there for you, like an eager dance partner in waiting, you can place the surfboard right up in the wave curl's pocket, verti-cally, and snap it back to six o'clock, while pushing the surfboard's tail through the rotation.

CUTBACK: If you're in a mellower mood, you might just project out onto the wave's sloping shoulder and lay down a long, carving turn, burning your speed, gradually unloading your strength, as you track through the arc of the turn, like a bar of soap slipping around in a bathtub.

ANTICIPATION: In any case, when you're in transition out of one of these other maneuvers, you want to be ready for the next section, sowing seed for the next harvest. While keeping an eye on what's going on down the wave's line, you quickly get back into a low, tight crouch, out of which you can spring into the next moment of release.

TUBE RIDE: Most important of all, if you're lucky, or the waves are just really good on that day in particular, the wave lip might suddenly be throwing out, while the wave trough is sucking up. You then tuck yourself under the curl in a balling crouch as the pitching curtain engulfs you in a spinning, roaring, snarling cylindrical vor-tex. Inside the tube, don't get too excited. But do go fast. Watch the lip line out in front of you so as not to get clipped when you could have tightened your crouch and kept going. Keep your weight for-ward. Pump or ease forward if you're getting drawn too deep in the tube, so as to sustain your momentum. Don't get caught up on the foam ball behind you, which can lift your surfboard fins and spin you into whitewash oblivion. And otherwise just wait for a chance to exit, which might well come, if the wave gods are showing you favor.

So, you know, like that. Depending on what is happening, you respond as the wave asks, which is to say, appropriately.

That is still not especially helpful. Appropriately how? Appropriately when? Those are the questions you'd have to know how to answer to actually surf a wave, and you can't answer without having a wave actually before you, which is telling you what move comes next.

If a complete book of surfing's rules could be written, it wouldn't necessarily help unless you could also learn the "know-how" that comes in faithful practice. You could read and understand all of its instructions, grasp them intellectually, and still not know how to put any rule into action. As a new wave situation presents itself, you have to know *how* to go on in the next moment. To borrow from Ludwig Wittgenstein, the enigmatic early-mid-twentieth-century philosopher, if rules were all you had to go by, they couldn't tell you how to "go on" from what came before, even with suggestive coaching.[1] Given only rules, with no further sense of how to apply them in a fresh particular moment, you'd have to look to *further* rules to tell you which rules to follow and when. But then you'd also need rules for applying *those* rules, and so on, without end, ad infinitum, all the way up. Which is absurd, or impossible, or just not what we do in learning to surf.

So there must be a different way of engaging one's situation, which isn't simply dictated by knowing rules, but somehow the *basis* for following and interpreting them. Here Wittgenstein says, "If there has to be anything 'behind the utterance of the formula' it is *particular circumstances*, which justify me in saying I can go on—when the formula occurs to me."[2] And so one must have a way of knowing what one's situation is. There must be a different, more

---

1. *Philosophical Investigations*, trans. G. E. M. Anscombe (New York: Macmillan, 1953).
2. Ibid., sec. 151.

"intuitive" way of knowing how to sense and adapt to a new moment, which isn't simply grasping a rule's content intellectually.

For Martin Heidegger, the early-mid-twentieth-century German philosopher who revived Aristotle's appreciation for the ordinary, our basic orientation to the world is not that of knowing things to be true by thought, reason, or perception. It is that of "handiness," of knowing how to use things: "The nearest kind of association is not mere perceptual cognition, but, rather, a handling, using, and taking care of things which has its own kind of 'knowledge.'"[3]

His central example is a hammer. You "know" it not by *thinking* about it, or *staring* at it, but by *using* it. You know the object as "for-hammering," with a sense of how to pick it up in your hand and pound a nail. And so it is for nearly all of human experience, which is made up of all manner of ordinary know-how, supplied by the material culture that organizes all of our choices.

So life is less thought than action, or rather thought *in* action, without too much thinking. Philosophy, as the saying goes, doesn't bake bread. So of course it can't teach you to surf. Surfing, in a word, must be lived.

This might explain certain dissatisfactions with modern routinized work and why it is often contrasted with living. Following Heidegger, Matthew Crawford explains, based on his own experience in motorcycle maintenance, that "craft knowledge" in our ever-refined division of labor is broken down into "minute instructions" that replace experience, "animated by the worker's own mental image of, and intention toward, the finished product."[4] This contrasts with the older way of the tradesman:

> The physical circumstances of the jobs performed by carpenters, plumbers, and auto mechanics vary too much for them to be executed by idiots; they require circumspection and adapt-

3. *Being and Time,* trans. Joan Stambaugh (Albany: State University of New York Press, 1996), 1.3.15, p. 63.
4. Matthew B. Crawford, *Shop Class as Soulcraft: An Inquiry into the Value of Work* (New York: Penguin Press, 2009), p. 39.

ability. . . . The trades are then a natural home for anyone who would live by his own powers, free not only of deadening abstraction but also of the insidious hopes and rising insecurities that seem to be endemic in our current economic life.[5]

The intuitive know-how of trades work goes beyond mere "knowledge that" because, much as with surfing, it's "always tied to the experience of a particular person. It can't be downloaded, it can only be lived."[6] A machine such as Deep Blue, the chess-playing computer that beat the grandmaster Garry Kasparov, only *simulates* the tacit, intuitive knowledge of an embodied, living person. Because this living know-how is the source of work's human meaning, to replace it with narrow rule following is to degrade a person's work, to compromise or corrupt its value. There is still genuine and enthralling knowledge work, but it is increasingly concentrated in the hands of an ever-smaller elite. Even in white-collar work, dealing in the stale abstractions of routinized spreadsheets and cost-benefit calculation is not the same as thinking. And at low or medium wages, "creative" work is mainly an illusion cultivated by upper management, who tend to "push details down and pull credit up."[7] (Think of "employees" versus "associates.") Crawford thus encourages a return to trades work. In chapter 9, I'll suggest a different upshot: we should move to a shorter, more flexible work-week that leaves more time for engaged leisure, whether in surfing or motorcycle repair.

Surfers Do Know Something

Surfing came into its own as a cultural phenomenon in the 1960s, when it became iconic of and to the counterculture. Surfers seemed

5. Ibid., p. 53.
6. Ibid., p. 162.
7. Ibid., p. 50.

to be onto something, something that exposed the limitations of a stagnant conformism.[8] Timothy Leary, the 1960s-era acid-dropping, hippie-boosting psychologist, tried to explain. Surfers, he said, are "truly advanced people" who are "evolutionary" for their general appreciation of waves and change. "Many, perhaps most, surfers have become almost mystics," he claimed. For the surfing act is "almost Taoist poetry. Almost Einsteinian."[9]

Only "almost," but even that may be a lot to expect from profoundly vague contemplation over tacos. Very few surfers are completely oblivious, let alone disrespectful and constantly stoned.[10] And few are hippies nowadays; most work, and anyway aren't after the sort of freedom that licenses anything whatever, while going wherever. The times, they are still a-changin', and Leary's "question authority," "turn on, tune in, drop out" countercultural era has passed. Change brought the triumph of capitalism over surf culture or, rather, enterprising surfers into big business, the surf industry, with clothing and wet suit sales, branding, and professional surfing. These days, most surfers are neither neo-hippie heroes nor deadbeats but conformists, more or less. Just as many non-surfers live for their work, serious surfers live in dedicated pursuit of excellence in a particular exercise of skill, by way of faithful daily practice, before or after work.

Surfers do know something, even if they couldn't be consulted for the oracular wisdom of the Stoic sage or the Zen master. The main preoccupation of the surfer is not wisdom but *waves* and *surfing them,* and the last swell, and the swell coming in the next days, whatever this might ultimately mean. A few surfers are charming

8. As Pink Floyd's 1973 song "Breathe" put it, "For long you live and high you fly / But only if you ride the tide."
9. "The Evolutionary Surfer," *Surfer,* Jan. 1978.
10. The stereotypical case in point is Jeff Spicoli, the epic surfer dude played by Sean Penn in the 1982 film *Fast Times at Ridgemont High.* Of a more recent surfer dude, who speaks of getting "pitted, just so pitted" in a widely viewed video clip, one wants to query, you high, bro? (You really are joking, right?) https://m.youtube.com /watch?v=d0mpUKnh9yo.

and silver-tongued, like Shaun Tomson, a former world champion. And of course there's Kelly Slater, the undisputed best surfer ever, who despite two decades of win-if-I-feel-like-it competitive dominance, his nth world title, and steady progression into his forties, long after most pros retire, also happens to be a thoughtful, articulate, nice guy. Yet zoologically speaking, the global tribe of surfers is motley and carnivalesque. It's a mix of kids, professionals, beach people, and working-class types, united only by the zealous love of waves, with varying interests and aptitudes in everything else.

Still, the love of waves is a lot to have in common, and all the time in the water does engender a shared sensibility about life and existence. So it makes enough sense to speak of *the surfer,* at least for purposes of asking what the surfer might appreciate above and beyond the technicalities of wave riding.

What might the surfer know? Leary, who apparently surfed himself, offers the tube ride as a metaphor for "the highly conscious life":

> At that point moving along constantly right at the edge of the tube . . . think of the tube as being the past, and I'm an evolutionary agent, and what I try to do is to be at that point where you're going into the future, but you have to keep in touch with the past . . . there's where you get the power; . . . and sure you're most helpless, but you also have most precise control at that moment. And using the past . . . the past is pushing you forward, isn't it? The wave is crashing behind you, yeah? And you can't be slow about it or you [get picked off].[11]

Totally; but what does this mean? If I may introduce myself as a relevant data point, I'm a lifelong surfer and a philosopher by profession, and though I could be too literal-minded, I don't quite follow Leary's meaning.

11. "Evolutionary Surfer."

So, okay, we're in the present. But things are changing, as they of course do. And we shouldn't forget our past, which is "pushing you forward," but somehow go forward and find power in light of it? Or what, exactly? Surfers do say you have to "stay in the pocket," the moving power source of the wave. Miles Davis says, "The good drummers don't play all that in-between stuff, only the bad drummers do to break up the time. Because they can't lay in the pocket." The attuned surfer and the attuned jazz player both mix passive waiting with active, present sensing, in a spontaneously adaptive activity founded on good timing. But this, too, is the sort of thing a philosophy should illuminate.

To be fair, the meaning of surfing isn't obvious to anyone. Few professional philosophers surf. And most surfers are more interested in *surfing* than talking or writing about the idea of surfing, let alone strenuously philosophizing about it. Socrates exaggerated wildly when he said that the unexamined life is not worth living, as though you could sanely choose a pensive life and early death over a pleasant, long, but unreflective life of surfing. If Socrates was expressing his do-or-die passion for philosophy (he did die for it finally), his sentiment was a lot like the surfer's surf-or-die passion for waves. Both activities can organize a meaningful existence.

Yet doing the one doesn't necessarily help with the other; the practical and intellectual skills in each don't necessarily transfer over. To again take myself as an example, I've devoted my whole life to regular surfing and to serious philosophical study. But before I thought about writing this book, I wouldn't have been able to say what exactly the two have to do with each other.

This illustrates an ancient problem: How if at all can practical know-how bring theoretical knowledge? Why should having the physical ability to skillfully make such-and-such bodily movements at certain right times on a wave bring any insight into the ultimate truths of philosophy?

In Anglo-American philosophy, much of "epistemology," the theory of knowledge, doesn't look to "know-how" for insight. The focus is usually on "knowledge that." Can it be defined (for example, as non-accidentally justified true belief)?[12] Or is it a primitive, indefinable notion?[13] Knowing-that might then have no connection with mere know-how, much as Plato suggested long ago. A mere "knack" born of repetition, as Plato put it, could never bring true knowledge, which comes only through intellectual contemplation. In the mid-twentieth century, the Oxford philosopher Gilbert Ryle convinced most philosophers of a basic difference between the "knowing how" of a craft or skill, such as archery or surfing, and the "knowing that" of a proposition that can be true or false, of the sort wanted in science or math or philosophy.[14] The nerd, as they say, is not fashioned for sports, no matter how steeped he may be in baseball sabermetrics. And just as the dumb jock won't know much about history, the surfer won't know much about bathymetry, let alone the finer points of geometry or moral theory. At least not without *studying*, or spending time in thought. (For Plato, true knowledge comes a priori, in reflection, which one can do in the waves.) In this perspective, we shouldn't expect any special insight into philosophy's great questions from a surfer, not per se, anyway.

On the other hand, "knowing how" and "knowing that" could be different and still have some deep relationship. According to a more pragmatic tradition, which runs through Martin Heidegger and Ludwig Wittgenstein in Europe, William James, John Dewey, and C. S. Peirce in America, and then all the way back to Aristotle in ancient Greece, ordinary know-how can be at least partly *explicated*, as propositional claims to truth. The know-how of dexterous

---

12. On having a true belief justified by accident, see Edmund Gettier, "Is Justified True Belief Knowledge?," *Analysis* 23, no. 6 (June 1963), pp. 121–23.
13. Timothy Williamson, *Knowledge and Its Limits* (Oxford: Oxford University Press, 2000).
14. *The Concept of Mind* (Chicago: University of Chicago Press, 1949), chap. 2. Ryle's "anti-intellectualism" has been questioned lately by Jason Stanley and Timothy Williamson, "Knowing How," *Journal of Philosophy* 98, no. 8 (2001), pp. 411–44; and Jason Stanley, *Know How* (Oxford: Oxford University Press, 2011).

hammer use, for instance, might be articulated as claims about how "one ought to use a hammer," which is to say, claims that can be true or false and the object of belief and knowledge-that. As even Ryle might say of the builder, the surfer, and the intelligent reasoner, "He applies in his practice what Aristotle abstracted in his theory of such practices."[15]

Some winemakers believe that wine should be made at every stage from a philosophical conception of its value. For the South African winemakers Eben Sadie and Johan Reyneke (who are also surfers), the liquid in the glass should speak for or express its earthly origins—much as a wave expresses structural contours of the sand or reef below when it draws off the bottom and breaks, peeling off in a particular shape and direction. The value of a batch of wine lies not in qualities such as color, taste, and body scored on a 100-point scale, let alone the resulting social score in a wine (and winemaker) status contest. What matters is its ability to holistically capture the distinctive qualities of soil, sunlight, temperature, moisture, and elevation from whence its grapes came. Beyond all the chemistry and technicalities of production, this shared understanding guides every stage of the growing and fermenting process, even down to the harvester picking each grape from the vine. In a biodynamic craft that approaches a form of art, fully understanding wine and how to make it thus means knowing its distinctive value and enacting it.

Surfers are actually pretty good at wave bathymetry; they intuitively know how any number of wave types will interact with the bottom topography of their local breaks. As a given swell approaches, they'll know how it will shift and break over the bottom just below. A lump of swell is approaching, and, *zooop*, the surfer is off paddling,

---

15. *Concept of Mind,* chap. 2. Even here "applies" wouldn't necessarily mean that the builder or the surfer grasps a proposition in action, or that he could verbally explicate one if asked, even on reflection. This can come after the act, perhaps only by reflection in certain cases, as a matter of "constructive interpretation," as I suggest below.

darting in the direction of a cresting wave that suddenly appears. "Wave knowledge" varies with ability, but the best surfers have an almost magical attunement.[16] This isn't simply a "knack" for hydro-locomotion; surfing isn't just a matter of moving the body around on a wave so as to keep going. A surfer surfs *from* a sense of the value in surfing, of his or her own particular way of enacting it, in this or that turn, line, or approach, at just this particular wave moment. The surfer draws a line *through* a wave's sections, in a way that reflects his or her own understanding of what is worth going for, in view of the very point of surfing, in something of a performance. Each surfed wave interprets a wave's moments and a larger surfing practice, which the community is constantly remaking in daily wave-riding actions, from shared ideas of surfing's distinctive value and meanings. The surfer's unspoken question is, "Check this out. Here's what I got for you. Am I wrong?" When an especially good turn or tube ride goes down, the rest of us watching nod and answer, "Yesss. Right ON! You've got it."

That's plenty for something of a philosophy. Like all animals, human beings come into the world knowing something about how to adapt to their natural surroundings and to other people. Young children know how to navigate social relations from an innate sense of fairness, a "tacit competence" that shapes their feelings and actions, which can be articulated as a principled theory of justice.[17] So maybe wave riding reflects the heightened development or full expression of pretty basic mammalian and human capacities, a "second nature," as Aristotle called it, that still expresses our first nature at birth. Just as we can construct a theory of our sense of justice, perhaps we can draw out and articulate what's implicit in

16. The former world champion Tom Curren is legendary because it was as though the best waves would come to him because he was waiting for them. His influential style, refined in his youth in the point breaks around Santa Barbara, California, was all about attuned anticipation.

17. John Rawls's landmark theory of justice, in *A Theory of Justice* (Cambridge, Mass.: Harvard University Press, 1971), seeks to articulate our "sense of justice." He compares his project to Noam Chomsky's famous psycholinguistics, which undercut Ryle's behavioristic view of the mind.

surfer competence, in what philosophers would call a "constructive interpretation" of the surfer's practical knowledge.[18]

How might that work? We must first put off asking what philosophical claims are true, given all the arguments, as philosophers usually do. We instead ask straightaway what the distinctive value in surfing is. The question is then which philosophical viewpoints fit best. Surfing *has* a distinctive kind of human value, I would argue, so the question becomes which possible philosophical views best explain or capture it. We can consider any big question we like. What is it to be free? To be effectual? To be happy? How are we to relate to nature? Should we change our style of capitalism? On a given question of interest, we consider different possible answers, surveying the best that philosophy has to offer. We then select the theory or theories that, if true, best fit surfing, seen in light of its distinctive value and the sensibility about life it engenders and reflects.

We are, in short, looking for the *surfer's position* on the topic in question. If, upon considering a given proposal, the average surfer would say, "Yeah, that!" "That's what I'm all about!" "Stoked you put words on it, brother!" we can say we've articulated what the surfer knows "implicitly." So while I'll be making various philosophical suggestions, I'm not offering them simply as my own opinions, as expressions of my personal sensibility (I'm only part surfer). I'd like to speak on behalf of my fellow surfing tribesmen and tribeswomen, in view of what all or most of us seem to understand. That's still my own interpretation of our common knowledge, of course, and if most surfers would feel conflicted, or confused, or simply disagree, I wouldn't bang the table and insist that, lo, I am the surfer's mouthpiece. But I would like to suggest, dear reader, that we—*you and I*—can learn from what the surfer knows in knowing how to ride a wave. We can glean a philosophical perspective that fits with

18. I argue that Rawls's theory of justice relies on constructive interpretation in "Constructing Justice for Existing Practice: Rawls and the Status Quo," *Philosophy and Public Affairs* 3, no. 33 (2005). I run the method for the global economy in *Fairness in Practice: A Social Contract for a Global Economy* (New York: Oxford University Press, 2012).

and expresses a surfer way of looking at things, which we ourselves might find attractive, and maybe even true.

The Philosophy of Aquatic Sports

Aside from all of his pondering and pontificating and smoking in the Café de Flore in Paris, Sartre wrote some of his major works while a soldier at war, and even as a POW. Despite the dread of World War II, mass bloodbaths, and the insane possibility that Hitler could close the curtain on free civilization, the indefatigable Sartre found a moment to ponder water sports.

Deep in the pages of his masterwork, *Being and Nothingness,* Sartre has a long and wonderful discussion of snow skiing. Snow skiing, he says, exemplifies the free person's path above and through material reality. But skiing turns out to be just one kind of "sliding over water," and at one point he says that other forms of sliding exemplify human freedom even better. The "ideal limit of aquatic sports," as Sartre puts it, is "sliding on water with a rowboat or motor boat or especially with water skis."[19]

To which the surfer will reply, waterskiing? I'm sure water-skiers have a good thing going, but I know I speak for surfers everywhere in saying that the act of surfing a wave has no equal, in aquatic sports, solo sports, action sports, and maybe any sports whatever. Surfing is the zenith of all human endeavors; it's up there with the arts, friendship, love, music, and even sex (or maybe not quite up there with sex, at least for many surfers, who perhaps agree with the promiscuous Sartre and his lover Simone de Beauvoir on that point[20]). Sartre never encountered surfing, but I'm thinking that for all of his obscure genius he would have graciously agreed that "sliding over water," in the sense that reveals the human condition

19. *Being and Nothingness,* trans. Hazel E. Barnes (New York: Washington Square Press/Simon & Schuster, 1956), p. 746.
20. Their famous carousing suggests a sporting attitude toward the activity. For their story, see Edward Fullbrook and Kate Fullbrook, *Sex and Philosophy: Rethinking de Beauvoir and Sartre* (New York: Continuum Press, 2008).

of freedom, is beautifully expressed in the natural act of riding a wave.[21]

A wave rises from the deep, and a surfer surfs it, being carried along by the wave's natural momentum. Moment by moment, the surfer is sensing what next moment is approaching and, without too much thinking, responding with his or her body as the coming moment asks, so as to be carried along by the wave's propulsive forces.

The surfer, in a word, is *adaptively attuned*. The surfer is *attuned* to a changing natural phenomenon, so as to sense how it is changing over time. The surfer is *adapting* as it changes with his or her body, so as to be carried along by the wave's propulsive forces. And the surfer finds this dynamic relationship purposefully, valuing it for its own sake—for instance, because it's a sublimely beautiful thing to do with one's limited time in life.

That, I propose, is the essence of surfing. To *surf a wave* is

1. to be attuned to a changing natural phenomenon,
2. so as to be carried along by its propulsive forces by way of bodily adaptation,
3. where this is done purposefully and for its own sake.

So defined, surfing a wave has a distinctive kind of value. Being adaptively attuned to a changing natural phenomenon, in part by not needing to control it, is at once a kind of freedom, self-transcendence, and happiness. Or so I will argue in later chapters. To a surprising degree, I submit, what is valuable in human life is a matter of being adaptively attuned—a way of "surfing," in an extended sense.

21. I'm sure Sartre would have agreed had surfing come earlier to the exceptionally good waves in the southwest of France, around Hossegor and Biarritz, in time for him to read about it in Paris or see it for himself on vacation. After all, there's only so much a philosopher can figure out from pure reflection, sitting in a café, without laying eye upon the surfing act—even for Sartre.

To *surf*, in general, is to be adaptively attuned to a changing phenomenon beyond oneself, for its own sake. In a *social* form of adaptive attunement, you could "surf" through a conversation, a meeting at work, or a crowded city street, going along with the flow of conversational or meeting or traffic dynamics, by staying attuned to other people and responding fluently in each new moment of cooperation. Whatever else you might hope to achieve, you'd do that purposefully, with a certain awareness of its intrinsic value, partly for its own sake. You'd give up seeking control, perhaps in order to keep cooperative relations sweet, for the feelings of harmonious social connection and the consequent sense of peace.

Surfers often wonder in completely earnest puzzlement what in the world non-surfers are *doing* with their time. They seem to be spending a lot of time working for a bit more money and are definitely not doing a lot of surfing. Surely they simply don't know what they are missing, short of being simply nuts, in which case the surfer feels profoundly fortunate to be in on the secret. ("Only a surfer knows the feeling" is a real saying.) No one thinks surfing, or any one activity, could be absolutely everything (though one ideal limits things to "Eat. Surf. Sleep. Repeat"). And of course once-serious surfers do sometimes lose faith. But being a surfer myself, I do believe that surfing is uniquely and even supremely valuable among things to do with one's limited time in life. Maybe it's even the final end of world history, or what all the blessings of wealth and leisure after the Industrial Revolution are ultimately *for*.

It's surely better than American football, as well as skiing, water-skiing, baseball, golf, and, dare I say, even *fútbol*/soccer. But I won't quibble over petty comparisons. Anyway many surfers have a strange fondness for golf, and I myself think ballet and jazz improvisation rival surfing in important respects. So I'll settle for an inclusive thesis: whether or not it is the best of all activities (which it may well be), surfing has a *distinctive* kind of human value, which other activities can share in (though often not in the same straightforward way, and to a lesser degree). At the very least, the value of surfing helps us more clearly appreciate the value in many other and related things. So maybe sailing, for instance, can in some moments count as wave surfing in the literal sense. We could call it "surfing" in the extended sense as well, now with a better sense of its distinctive value, the value of being adaptively attuned.[22]

Rational Groping

In my view, surfing naturally invites philosophical reflection. I myself was a serious surfer well before I became a philosopher by profession—long before I read about the gloomy Nietzsche and Sartre and encountered Schopenhauer's dictum that "life is suffering." (On the contrary, "life is surfing" seems more apt.) Oddly, my first attraction to philosophy lay in the control I seemed to gain over what I believed, even though in life as in surfing control is what you have to let go of, so as to flow. Only gradually did I find a way of doing philosophy that fit my surfer sensibility. Yet for all the benefits of being less inconsistent in my main life pursuits, I never spent a lot of time on the surfing/philosophy connection, not as a sustained topic of inquiry.

Everything is connected to everything, so sure, you can always find examples of big philosophical issues in odd places. Surfing can nicely illustrate fundamental insights that don't really depend on surfing, which I occasionally noted in my studies.[23] My experience

22. But then why not just call surfing "sailing," in its own extended sense? To my ear, that doesn't sound especially apt. Windsurfers and kite surfers are perhaps surfing both the waves and the wind. A conventional sailboat might "surf" the wind and ocean in an extended sense. But the conventional board surfer isn't "sailing" along the wave in any sense, literal or extended, if only because wind isn't needed and because the adaptation is of an essentially bodily nature.
23. I wrote a second-year paper in graduate school on something called the "supervenience" of value, which my adviser, T. M. Scanlon, took to be in some sense really about the value-making features of waves. The paper derived from my senior undergraduate thesis at Westmont College, which I included in my application to Ph.D. programs, and used surfing to illustrate a key distinction. Professor Scanlon, who was on the Harvard admissions committee that year, reported to me that this confirmed my originality as a philosopher. Surfers aren't so common in the profession, which assuaged fears of plagiarism. All this could easily have gone a less happy direction.

and travels as a surfer definitely influenced my choice of intellectual projects. I wrote a book about fairness in the global economy, and although it isn't specifically about Indonesia, my sense of the place, and the economic buzz and bustle of developing countries generally, came from my regular surf trips to Sumatra. And in an enjoyable side project, certain irritating surfers inspired a philosophical theory of the asshole.[24] But for all that, when people would ask, "Don't surfing and philosophy naturally go together?" I'd say, "Not as much as you'd think. Philosophy is more like math than poetry."

That's especially true in the Anglo-American analytic tradition, which becomes more formalistic and less poetical with each passing decade. The analytic approach puts a premium on clarity; it insists on defining terms and uses logic to carefully structure and clarify rival positions and arguments.[25] This brings certain risks: if the surfer is onto some deep insight, obsessing about analytic clarity might stand in the way of grasping it. Ludwig Wittgenstein famously declared, "What can be said at all can be said clearly." He then added, "And what we cannot talk about we must pass over in silence." Of that which is beyond our clear grasp, we should not speak, calling it simply "manifest," or even "mystical."[26]

Yet must we be quiet simply because the optics are blurry? The continental schools (as in continental Europe) certainly aren't worried; they'll just let it rip in very abstract phrases, which *feel* big and deep, but maybe can't quite be clearly and precisely articulated, or even sound unintelligible.[27] My education in analytic philosophy

24. *Assholes: A Theory* (New York: Doubleday, 2012), and for special political dynamics, *Assholes: A Theory of Donald Trump* (New York: Doubleday, 2016).
25. A proud saying among graduate students at Stanford University's department of philosophy goes like this: "We're putting the *a* back in 'anal-ytic' philosophy." Perhaps relatedly, I once heard a joke about an MIT graduate student in philosophy of language who was asked to teach a course on "the meaning of life." The first day of class he wrote those words on the board. He then announced that they would begin with "the," then turn to "meaning," and then discuss "of." But "life," he x-ed out, because there just wouldn't be time for it. (I'm sure this was just a joke-rumor.)
26. *Tractatus Logico-philosophicus* (London: Kegan Paul, 1922).
27. Heidegger famously wrote of nothing, "Nothing itself noths (or 'nihilates,' or 'nothings')," suggesting that nothing is something, a something that nothings, which

gave me only passing familiarity with Sartre, from an appreciative but reluctant distance. No one doubted his depth; as with many continental figures, the main trouble is that he can be hard to read. Witness this doozy of a passage: conscious beings, rather than mere objects, "are what they are not and are not what they are." Does Sartre mean this, or is he just *messing with us*? The obscurity can be irritating to the analytic stickler. What is he actually claiming?[28] Yet his method has an admirable motive: ideally, the grand, impressionistic language would let us come to see life from a clarifying distance, to gaze upon big, deep things we'd be missing in our everyday preoccupations. The analytic style of philosophy shares that aspiration, in a more plodding method, which one *hopes* will add up, eventually, to something larger.

Anyway, we are all trying to understand, even as philosophy is never final and probably can't be. It's sort of like backing up a few feet from a particular spot on a pointillist painting, in order to see a gentle scene or image emerge—though not exactly. No, you're trying to cram a wild and bumptious reality into a theory or system and then step back and see it all at once, before it explodes all to pieces.[29]

Should we then look only to science for knowledge? Science has been enormously successful as a human institution, so one can at least understand the hubris occasionally on display when a good scientist blathers on about the irrelevance or unimportance of philosophy (often while *doing* philosophy, badly). Philosophy often begins

---

is to say, that somehow acts. To which one should ask, huh? To be fair, in his defense of what looks to me like nonsense, he did feel that conventional modes of speech and grammar couldn't express his central tenets, which broke radically from the received philosophical tradition, and so he invented his own rather unusual language. For help in comprehension, I look to Hubert L. Dreyfus, *Being-in-the-World* (Cambridge, Mass.: MIT Press, 1991).

28. Scholarly debates about Sartre's text are partly driven by his fondness for the dramatic zinger. Are those remarks mere rhetorical ploys and not what he really thinks? Or are they his real view, provocative as they may be? The latter is the standard way Sartre is read, and I'll follow suit. The more forgiving approach can bring Sartre closer to the surfer position (of which more later).

29. The brilliant Robert Nozick once said something like this.

in what the sciences haven't yet captured, and perhaps can't ever capture fully. It's the mother of all the sciences (psychology only moved out of the house a hundred or so years ago), and could she have *suddenly* become barren, despite two thousand years of generating healthy offspring since Aristotle pioneered physics and biology? Still, many do have the sense that philosophical speculation is relatively unimportant. If our *only* hope is that it might eventually birth a science and coach it to maturity, maybe adding a few pointers, then science will still be the real source of knowledge.

This is itself a *philosophical* position, so it isn't exactly the rejection of philosophy. It's a scientistic epistemology, a theory of knowledge much like the one that originally inspired the analytic approach to philosophical problems. In the early twentieth century, the "positivists" or "logical empiricists" of the Vienna Circle (which included Moritz Schlick, Otto Neurath, Rudolf Carnap, and Hans Reichenbach) proposed theories of logic and language to explain how the empirical sciences were possible. Any other supposed source of knowledge, whether of ethics or religion, went out the window.

The group wasn't simply hostile to the impenetrable prose of poor Heidegger,[30] and to all hairy metaphysical systems, including the German "idealism" of Kant or G. W. F. Hegel.[31] The problem wasn't just difficulty of comprehension. Meaningful claims, the positivists insisted, can be *verified*. They can be tested in sense experience, in a laboratory experiment or an immediate observation, with the five senses. For some reason, the positivists weren't especially bothered by the fact that this thesis is self-refuting. "Meaningful claims are always verifiable." *This claim* can't be tested by the five senses. But it seems plenty meaningful: it implies that any ethical or religious claim that can't be verified experimentally—whether "surfing is worthy of one's time in life," "happiness is good," or "God exists"—

---

30. Isn't his claim that "nothing noths" really just BS? On this theme in light of some recent continental philosophy, see G. A. Cohen's "Complete Bullshit," in *Finding Oneself in the Other* (Princeton, N.J.: Princeton University Press, 2013).

31. According to one joke, only two people understood Hegel in his lifetime: Hegel and God.

isn't cognitively meaningful, and at best is an expression of feeling. Not simply unknown or mistaken. But *meaningless* as regards truth or falsehood, much in the way the claim "the number 2 occurs on Tuesday" is. And if there is therefore at least one meaningful claim without verifiability—the thesis of verification itself—why not *two*? Or three? Or nine! Any limitation would seem pretty arbitrary. So while verification might be needed in a laboratory, why not just generally use our best methods of reasoning to sort out what the truth is? That works well enough in mathematics. Why not do it in ethics?

The Vienna Circle finally broke up, and Carnap and Reichenbach fled the war in Europe to join the philosophy department at UCLA in sunny Southern California. I gather they didn't try out surfing when it went mainstream in the late 1950s and the 1960s. The two towering figures who later did the most to undo logical empiricism, W. V. Quine of Harvard and Donald Davidson of Northern California's UC Berkeley, apparently did dabble in surfing. I've never heard that it informed their more pragmatic view of scientific inquiry, which favored a more holistic method. But maybe it loosened them up a bit. At any rate, the new pragmatism opened the door to rational inquiry into value.

How does one inquire into value? The standard answer these days is, by rational groping. That is, we begin from our intuitive sense of things and then fashion our ethical "intuitions" into a body of knowledge through reflection. Say we ask the question, is time in leisure good in itself? I'm inclined to answer, "Yes, intuitively speaking; it does seem so." Which is to say something like "Yes, it seems so, but I don't yet claim to have an explanation why this would be true, and I might change my mind if I can't find one." But then I can try to think up principles or theories that would explain my intuitive reactions. I can adjust and prune either the intuitions or the principles or theories, until they all fit into a coherent system. I can keep tinkering until the overall fit seems holistically satisfying, much in the way scientists gradually refine theories. John Rawls, the twentieth century's most influential political philosopher (and Quine's colleague at Harvard), called this the search for "reflective equilibrium." It is always a search, in both ethics and science. We never just coast along without the Socratic labors of reexamination. But the search has a destination. We can gain in understanding and confidence.

Still, why go to all this trouble? The unexamined life is certainly worth living; an unreflective surfer should keep on surfing until the last of his or her blessed days. Why then devote a life to formulating answers to questions that may not have what people would readily call "answers"? For me at least, the value in philosophy and in surfing is not so different. Both are fun! But more to the point, waves and ideas are often sublime, or beautiful, or both, and in patiently attending to them, you see and feel ever more of what is easily missed. You gain ever deeper understanding, ever greater attunement, in your thinking and your actions. The superficiality of life, the mania for status or money or power, along with its contagious anxieties, then fades away into the background, becoming white noise in a peaceful life lived by its own joyous music.

Theses for Sartre

So this book takes up a natural occasion for philosophical inquiry, which is especially pressing in the present century. The labor of philosophy is to soberly articulate what would otherwise be obscure. Here Sartre's "phenomenological" method is especially useful: we can just *look at what our ordinary experience is like,* in our ordinary activities. Once it is sensitively depicted, we may discern deeper principles, maybe even a quasi-universal "logic" that is "implicit" in the ordinary know-how we take for granted. I still say clarity is a good way of keeping our bearings; we know what we are saying, at least for starters. From there we can follow the inquiry where our groping leads us, grasping in words for the ineffable. (Wittgenstein abandoned his own dictum about silence eventually.) This goes beyond science, but it isn't unscientific. Much like the scientist, we need only attune our inquiry, in sober wonderment, to a world we can never master. And if we can so ponder the cosmos, we can surely pursue Sartre's themes of life and being, by considering the surfer.

Sartre would be the first to welcome a phenomenology of surfing. And I've come to accept that continental figures such as Husserl, Heidegger, Sartre, and Merleau-Ponty can tell us much about its meaning. Indeed, as I explain later, it was the French phenomenologist Maurice Merleau-Ponty who most clearly explained, almost as if speaking for the surfer, how bodily attunement could be a primary source of human meaning. He and Sartre studied together at the École Normale Supérieure in Paris, they worked together at Sartre's magazine *Les Temps Modernes,* and they were longtime friends—until their friendship soured in a disagreement over communism. They had common influences and a similar method, but Merleau-Ponty's concerted focus on the body ultimately makes him the surfer's philosopher.

Our task then is to describe what the surfer knows, implicitly, in knowing how to be adaptively attuned, in a life organized around its distinctive value. We begin in Sartre's existential predicament. Freedom, in his view, is willful self-determination, a laborious project of self-creation in the face of absurd options. The first step is to give up such willful controlling, which only makes it harder to get into the flow. Freedom, for the surfer, isn't radical self-determination but a kind of achievement, in adaptive attunement. It's a way of being efficacious without control, precisely by giving up any need for it.

Neither then is the surfer akin to the Stoic, who controls his mind in order to maintain a steady tranquillity and detachment. Surfers are deeply attached to a life of surfing, and not so cautious about loving without reservation, despite its risks. Betting one's happiness on nature's caprice does bring certain frustrations. Yet life is not so terrible, even for the occasionally bummed surfer, who must then play guitar or do philosophy while waiting for waves. The challenge is just to keep faith, giving up any need for control, even over one's own mental state, so as to settle into a more flowing way of being efficacious through the ebbs and flows of nature's rhythms.

Surfers go along with the flow of a wave by intuitive sensing, by attuning to their surroundings with their whole bodies and not simply their brains or eyeballs. This turns out to be the highest expression of human perceptual capacity, the human's way of at once being and doing. Thus finding flow is more than an enjoyable state of experience. It's more than finding the much ballyhooed "flow state" of heightened experience in peak performance, which is often elusive, even for the best of surfers. The surfer's flow is a more ordinary mode of being, which is achieved even in ordinary waves, in the sublime beauty of one's daily surf.

This is a relatively easy route to self-transcendence, thank goodness. Attunement comes by faithful practice, but without the Buddhist's hard road to enlightenment, the abnegation of desire, any radical loss of the self, and without all the effort in constant "mindfulness," or in striving for personal perfection. The surfer just goes surfing and with relative ease transcends him- or herself in a dynamic, attuned bodily relationship to the world outside.

Society of course brings its own discontentments, especially in the grave dangers of status consciousness. Even out in the waves, surfers often have to compete for right-of-way and status, given scarce waves, and so can become irritated and extremely bummed, sometimes resorting to violence. Yet as the tide ebbs and flows, a shitty mood passes, and surfers spontaneously attune to each other and to a changing common wave environment.

Theirs is an adaptive "anarchical society," a microcosm of different societies adapting together on a changing planet. Given our warming planet and rising sea levels, surfers themselves have to actually do something to keep the world's surf breaks from being submerged. Yet we all, surfers and non-surfers alike, can help attune society to the changing human condition in a new kind of social contribution: working less and taking more leisure instead, in a much shorter workweek. And if work and material possession can't mean so much to us any longer, simply being in, and staying in, the attuned moment can be nearly the whole meaning of life, in the creative project that is human history.

2

Freedom

DIMITRI: I have to admit, Tasso, sometimes
    I wish I were more like you.
TASSO: But you can be! Existentially
    speaking, you are a totally self-originated
    being! You are who you create!
DIMITRI: That's terrific! Because I always
    wanted to be as tall as you.

—*Plato and a Platypus Walk into a Bar . . .*[1]

SURFING IS FREEDOM. Or so the surfer will tell you. Sartre would disagree: freedom is a more anxious condition, one of taking control of ourselves and our fortunes in the face of absurdity. Which raises the perennial question: What is it to be free?

Freedom as Anguish

For Heidegger, to be, to exist, is to be *somewhere,* situated, in a concrete place, mixed up in a "life world" of ordinary know-how, an everyday "significance" by which our culture defines our very existence, our very possibilities of meaningful action. I know how to tie my shoes, how to walk a crowded street, how to have a conversation, and how to be or betray a friend. I know how only within a thick cultural matrix, which gives my choices meaning, leaving me with

1. Thomas Cathcart and Daniel Klein (New York: Penguin Books, 2007).

no intelligible possibility of going for something completely different. What Aristotle thought of as the man of practical wisdom, who always does the appropriate thing at the appropriate time in the appropriate way, is but a cultural virtuoso. Even acting *against* one's culture is a move within it.[2]

This may explain why Heidegger supported Hitler's rise to power in 1930s Germany. Hannah Arendt, the twentieth-century political philosopher, a Jewish exile, and his former lover, charitably thought he merely had an "escapade." He was just being careerist, under some bad influences, and anyway oblivious—which you might expect from someone who believes there's no seeing beyond one's life world. And even if he was just an anti-Semite who longed for the old days and blamed the Jews for Germany's problems, his views don't *entail* sympathy for the Nazis. Heidegger, the man, could have simply been worse than his theories, in which case we must ask for ourselves what if anything we might learn from them.[3]

It's a cramped-sounding existence, if you ask a surfer. Even with the Nazis vanquished, the rebel surfer of 1960s lore couldn't hack the thick expectations of postwar Southern California, a life of work and marriage and family that doesn't leave a lot of time for things like surfing. Surfing, and an unconventional life devoted to it, have thus come to symbolize freedom in our culture.

When Sartre read Heidegger, he must have had that surfer feeling, of wanting to bust out of cultural expectation, to get free. For Sartre, I am free in my very person, whatever my history, however confused my noisy culture, before any "life world" tells me what things mean, or who I must be. I'm free to blow off work and bail for Mexico or Indonesia. Not simply with an "absence of external impediments" on my movements about the planet, as in Thomas

2. For discussion of how or how far culture might be transcended for Heidegger, see Hubert L. Dreyfus, "Could Anything Be More Intelligible Than Everyday Intelligibility? Reinterpreting Division I of *Being and Time* in the Light of Division II," MS.
3. Or was something more German at work? The (sadly late) philosopher G. A. Cohen once spoofed the "German conception of freedom" as absolute subjection to an ironclad, unjust law.

Hobbes's thin definition of freedom. If I were merely free to move, I'd bring my unfreedom with me in my travels, with my baggage. Full freedom comes from *within*, whatever my location, from the internal structure of my own mind and consciousness.

An addict gets loaded against her own will, finding herself disgusting. A homeless man roams the city, deranged, with no sense of person and purpose, free to move but going nowhere. Both watch themselves making awful choices, alienated from their own motives, but too knowing to just enjoy the wanton freedom of a wandering dog blissfully rummaging through fresh garbage cans. This poses the basic question of freedom: What are such souls lacking? What would it take for them to be free? What, that is, makes a person the morally responsible author of his or her actions, who can be aptly blamed or thanked for them?[4]

For Sartre, to be a person is to be a minded, conscious being who experiences the world from a distinctive perspective. A person (a "for itself") is fundamentally different from a mindless object (an "in itself") such as a stone or a tree. I have thoughts, about all sorts of things, including thoughts of myself and what I myself might be or become in an open future. But I am not simply a passive observer of what might just happen to me. I am the *agent* of my choices, which, taken all together, make up who I will finally be. Maybe I've been cowardly about quitting my job. But I am not yet a coward, because my future has yet to be decided, and it is always still up to me. So maybe I'll just quit in the coming week, defining my whole self by today deciding my future.

I wake up in the morning. At some point, I cross a line between drowsy waking and wakeful awareness. Now I must choose. The question is not Hamlet's "To be, or not to be?" It is, "To lie here, or to get up and going?" I *am* there in bed, already, in the moment of waking. So shall I lie here, or get going?

4. A locus classicus here is Harry Frankfurt's "Freedom of Will and the Concept of a Person," along with Gary Watson's reply "Free Agency." Both appear in *Free Will*, ed. Gary Watson, 2nd ed. (Oxford: Oxford University Press, 2003).

One option I won't have is to just *see what happens,* as if I were watching someone else in bed, or as a sleep scientist might observe a test subject's waking and rising in an experiment. (Gregor Samsa, in Franz Kafka's *Metamorphosis,* woke to consciousness as a beetle and took just this observational attitude toward his predicament; Kafka's point was that his was an alienated perspective.) If I get up, because my job expects me to be somewhere, I've chosen to *get going.* But even if I lie there in self-conscious waiting, that will eventually have been my chosen option: then I'm *waiting.* Either way, I will have chosen. Just in naturally waking into consciousness, I am, as Sartre puts it, "condemned to choose."

This is the human's predicament. A dog, drooling over the sight of pizza, is thinking something like *"Fooood."* I, too, see the pizza, but I can back up, asking myself, "Should I really eat the pizza at which I'm leering?" I have a remarkable power to self-consciously ask myself what I ought to do. I can answer by my own powers of reason and then follow through in action, for one reason or another. Simply being so constituted, I count as my own, as responsible for my chosen actions.[5]

My behavior isn't then a simple reflex reaction, part of the impersonal causal order of scientific study; it's *my* behavior, my free action. I've chosen my conduct, anew, despite what has come before in my history, whoever I've been before this present moment. And for Sartre, I am in this way responsible for myself. "For human reality, to be is to *choose oneself.*" I choose myself, in the totality of each choice I make. Whatever might come to me "either from outside or from within," I have to decide what to "receive or accept," and "without any help whatsoever" I am "entirely abandoned to the intol-

---

5. Can't a dog do rudimentary reasoning, for example, about how to get to the pizza if it's under a box? Many nonhuman animals, especially higher primates, even seem aware of themselves (for example, in looking in a mirror, they don't confuse the image for another animal). Sartre can assume the difference from humans lies on a spectrum. If Homer Simpson would mainly be thinking "beeeer" while leering at a six-pack, the idea would be that if he's a human creature (is he?), he's at least capable of asking for himself whether he really should drink it. He may never or rarely in fact ask the question.

erable necessity of making [myself] to be—down to the slightest detail."[6]

It can happen that the surfer finds herself working a crap job (here defined as a job that consistently requires missing good waves). For all her love of waves, in a spell of what Sartre calls "bad faith," she sees herself as just another object in the world, like a coffee cup on a table, or a flirt being courted, whose hand "rests inert between the warm hands of her companion—neither consenting or resisting," as though a mere thing.[7] She acts as though her behavior were predictable by the laws of causation, open to control and manipulation, but not fully her own. Maybe she won't step back and question her circumstances, seeing the job as now for her to choose or reject for her future. It's only those *other,* luckier people who take a pay cut, travel, and score perfection in Indonesia or Tahiti. In this case, for Sartre, she is in fact free but not owning up to freedom's responsibility—its weighty demands for "authenticity."

For Heidegger, you haven't lived until you've lived in the shadow of your impending death. To be authentic, I embrace this moment, in this *very sip of coffee,* because the sips of experience are sooner or later ending. Here Sartre was more upbeat (and more American in optimism than you might expect from a Frenchman). I act authentically, in good faith, when I myself see my present and future as not simply a given fact of the world but *up to me*—under my control. Such is my "absolute freedom": nothing else determines my actions. What is simply given, in my history, body, and the present flux of sensory perceptions, never settles my future. Myself and my future are up to me. So in my crap job, I can always step back in reflection, and ask myself, "Who am I, and what shall I do now?" In my simply *asking the question of possibility,* any constraint I might have felt on

6. *Being and Nothingness,* pp. 568–89.
7. Ibid., p. 97. Likewise note Kanye West's alienated way of speaking of himself in the third person: "I was asked my opinion and I was given a platform. And when given a platform, it's very hard as we know—and I'm going to talk in third person like I'm a crazy person—but it's very hard for Kanye West to not be very true and vocal to what he feels."

my choices (such as my waiterly duty) is "negated" or "nihilated" into "nothingness" a moment later. My future self and doings are open (I see that I can quit).

In *The Graduate*, Benjamin Braddock threw off the unsolicited advice to go into "plastics." Braddock couldn't go with the cultural flow, despite the glories of conventional postwar prosperity, of washing machines, suburban houses, and lush lawns. Like the generation of Americans that hit the road with Kerouac, he proved to himself his freedom, but anxiously, without any particular direction. For that's the thing about being on the road, being free to roam: you are constantly condemned to ask, "Now what?" And despite our powers of constant self-creation, Sartre's depressing answer is still this: nothing of any real meaning or value, or at least nothing that could fully determine what is right for me without my having to simply choose.

As a free person, one has no "essence" (beyond one's freedom). The waiter has no duties of service by nature, not by virtue of being either a waiter or a woman. To choose is to choose not from what one already is but from nothing, ex nihilo, with no real reason to do any one thing rather than another. No option really is any better than any other, beyond my choosing it, more or less arbitrarily, even under the guise of one's abstract values, which still must be determinately lived. And yet we remain fully responsible for what we make of ourselves. We are condemned to choose from nothing, under the weight of authenticity, in the despair that Sartre calls "anguish."

All of which leaves us with the question, could anything then justify the surfer's lightness of being?

The Ideal Limit of Aquatic Sports

According to the foremost philosopher of freedom in all of Western history, the free person's place in the cosmos is expressed in certain sporting activities, in "sliding upon water," as done in the sliding sports. Much depends on the H_2O sliding substrate, the material basis for lateral momentum. Ice-skating, Sartre explains, is "very inferior," because it "scratches the ice and finds a matter already organized." It contrasts with snow, for instance, which is "light, insubstantial, and evanescent." In snow skiing, but not ice-skating, I can imagine that I'm "not making any mark" in the snowpack while I'm barreling down the mountain. With the blanketed expanse running beneath the ski tips, I can imagine myself free from an "already organized" material reality, as though I have no traceable path in my history, no past that limits or could predict my future.

For if I *was* determined to take one or another direction—given my history, essential nature, past character, or a divine plan—I would not be free to choose my course and future. For Sartre, any such determinism is simply incompatible with my freedom. But here as I slide along, my trajectory through an impersonal cosmos really does seem up to me. I seem free, free to tell the cosmos how things are going to be, as goes my trajectory. The world shall be thus and so, just by my say-so, in a godlike act of creation, as I throw down a turn. As Sartre puts it, my turning actions come from nothing, ex nihilo, without being determined, except by me.

How is free sliding possible? Well, *speed* is crucial. Our bodies are part of our given physical reality (our "facticity," as Sartre calls it). Gravity pulls us into the snowfield, leaving us less free to move. Yet with a bit of speed, the snow suddenly becomes supportive. I gain new powers, to choose this or that direction, to accelerate, slow up, or *carve,* according to my style and fancy. As Sartre explains, in snow sliding, "It is I myself then who give form to the field of snow by the free speed which I give myself."[8] My path in and through an impersonal material reality becomes *personal,* or my own, because I am choosing self-consciously to go this or that direction while speeding along.

The skier thus approaches the speeding "continuous creation" of

8. *Being and Nothingness*, p. 744.

the unique person's free consciousness. What am I? Not any particular thought of this or that—of the Swiss Alps, of Sartre styling ski boots and a flowing scarf, having made the trek over from Paris. (He writes as though he had himself done some skiing.) I, myself, I am the *someone*, the person, who is conscious of all such momentary and fleeting mental happenings. I am the singular locus of experience, wherein light, insubstantial, evanescent thoughts, feelings, and experiences flow along together, in the windstorm I speed through in my continuing existence. So flows my consciousness, freely. I act on relatively few of these ideas, thank goodness; any given thought or perception is present and gone an instant later, preserved only in the occasional act of remembering. My flowing minded activity leaves little trace behind, with almost nothing by way of a discernible history. Where did my thoughts from last month disappear to? I search to recall my thinking of two days prior, but most of my experiences have passed out of a temporary existence, once felt and quickly forgotten. As I now remember, I am also *refashioning* my then experiences into something fresh, leaving my "memory" something that never quite happened.

But alas, if skiing *feels* like freedom, for Sartre this is finally an "illusion." How disappointing it is, Sartre explains, to look back upon the snow tracks left behind. "How much better it would be if the snow re-formed itself as we passed over it!" I suppose not everyone succumbs to existential disappointment while gazing back up the slopes upon one's snow tracks. Yet the top American skier Dave Rosenbarger gets the point exactly when he praises vertical-drop skiing (as in dropping down a chute or off a cliff): "Marginal conditions call for marginal style. I'm interested in skiing . . . untracked."[9]

Freud thought we act from libidinous "drives" for sex and pleasure, as warped by our upbringing, by family birth order and early attachments. For Sartre, our freedom in action means we transcend any such history. If you're dogged by an old inferiority complex, it is still *now chosen* in your present action, "as a turning back of the future toward the present."[10] Your complex will be up for interpretation in a therapy session; what will matter is not your "memories" but what you now choose to make of them, in your present act of retrospection and refashioning.

This is why Sartre found sliding upon liquefied water more promising than snow sliding as a model of freedom. Liquefied water is "without memory," for its supple quality of reformation. So sliding along liquid "leaves no trace behind." The displaced spray droplets settle roughly as they were before, being reabsorbed, with no trace of a history that could tempt one to deny one's present freedom to turn and carve afresh, whatever one's personal history.

Sartre calls motorboating and especially waterskiing the "ideal limit" of aquatic sports. Water sports exemplify freedom, and those styles are in this regard the closest to perfection. Yet surfing involves the same general kind of sliding (*glissement* was Sartre's term for the overall category). Though he never encountered it, I'm sure Sartre would have been duly impressed by surfing. Would he have conceded that his radical kind of freedom therefore isn't necessary? Perhaps not. Yet I submit that surfing does exemplify freedom equally well, or even better, than motorboating or waterskiing. It has the requisite aquamarine properties but also lacks features that make motorboating and even waterskiing relatively unfree.

For starters, the surfer's spray flies off the surfboard into the air and then rains into the ocean medium, being reabsorbed completely. In an especially good carve or snap in the wave pocket, the spray will erupt in a fanning plume, with an existence as evanescent as a passing fancy. There's "no trace left behind" that could predict and limit one's present turning action or future direction.

Moreover, speed is crucial, especially for proper carving. As I glide along the wave face, I may have to rush down the wave's line. With the wave face steepening, and the section running ahead, with a cresting lip hovering, I'll fly right under it if I go even faster, if I keep trimming along the high line, holding it, and then holding it for

10. *Being and Nothingness*, p. 591.

longer, waiting, pumping, hanging high and tight, until I know I'm making it and the next section relents. Then with speed to burn in the slowing section, I might celebrate the moment of release, laying down a sweeping cutback, my full weight pressed into the rotation, my body extended and then drawn into a focused center-weighted compression, ideally in a carve that would redefine carving, with a fan of spray punctuating my freedom in attunement.

And because surfing is adaptive, it exemplifies the free flow of consciousness. Just as my passing rush of thoughts or sensations is soon forgotten, the surfer flows *through* different wave moments, moving *from* one moment to another and then to the next, which is quickly coming. And just as each span of a person's whizzing wind of experience is unique and non-repeatable, each wave is its own complex moment, calling for a fresh adaptation of flowing ability, bodily movements, and stylish self-presentation.

So far, so good. Surfing is at least on the same footing as motorboating and waterskiing. Weirdly, Sartre also says sliding along a surface is a way of *using* it, in a kind of "appropriation" for one's purposes, as though you *own* the surface, as part of your acts of self-definition. He means not simply that you're having fun with it, or leaving your personal mark in a skillful movement, as you might in doing a stylish snap in the wave pocket. He means you're *mastering* or *possessing* it, as a slave is mastered or possessed by his or her owner.[11] For the same reasons, he explains, people climb a mountain and *claim it,* "appropriating" the mountain in triumphant conquest, "being victor over it."[12]

Such "appropriation" isn't part of the freedom in surfing. Is surfing less free for that reason? No way! What follows instead, according to the surfer, is that Sartre's radical freedom is not really necessary. Had Sartre appreciated what is distinctive in surfing, he might have admitted more clearly that one can be free and, in a deep way, bounded in embodied, situated reality, all at the same time.

11. Ibid., p. 747.
12. Ibid., p. 587.

In mountain climbing, I suppose the casual hiker occasionally does say, "Yup, made it, to the very top. *Check me out.* I took this bitch out." Yet surely the hard-core mountain climber suffers no such pretensions of mastery or possession in reaching the summit, except as a megalomaniacal joke. Of his 1688 crossing of the Alps, John Dennis said that his perils produced in him a "delightful Horror, a terrible Joy," which left him "infinitely pleased, I trembled."[13] Sartre's climber who claims victory over the mountain seems rather lacking in what Immanuel Kant called "the mental attunement that befits the manifestation of [a sublime] object," which, he says, "is not a feeling of the sublimity of our own nature, but rather submission, prostration, and a feeling of our utter impotence."[14]

In the face of awful, awesome waves, twenty feet and up, the big-wave surfer is definitely aware of his impotence.[15] The English philosopher Edmund Burke proposed that experience of the sublime comes with feelings of "delight" in what is terrible, as though from a safe distance (for example, while watching from a deep channel). Yet the surfer's delight comes while he or she is right there in harm's way, just beyond the impact zone, where a "sneaker set" (of larger than average set waves) might take you out. It's terribly easy to drown, as did Mark Foo in 1994 at Mavericks, in Half Moon Bay, California; and Todd Chesser in 1997 on Oahu's North Shore. (Mark Foo presciently said, "It's not tragic to die doing something you love.") You just accept that you *will* get pummeled, as in flipped and trounced, and maybe bounced, sooner or later. Yet while you're waiting for waves or paddling over a monster, the feeling is less one of terror than of *paying your respects* to sublime rolling ocean moun-

13. John Dennis, *Miscellanies in Verse and Prose* (London: James Knapton, 1693), pp. 133–34.
14. *Critique of Judgment* (1790), trans. Werner S. Pluhar (Indianapolis: Hackett, 1987), p. 122.
15. "Big" wave surfing means paddling into waves up to around twenty-five or so feet, at places like Mavericks, California; Dungeons, South Africa; and Jaws/Pe'ahi, Maui, or getting towed into waves up to seventy feet or more at a place like Nazaré, Portugal. This is doing something with the wave, but no sane person can or would think he was "appropriating" such an awesome aquatic manifestation.

tains, which will finally crash asunder, after heaving, and pitching, in a moment of cresting order. When you do finally surf a giant wave, the feeling is hardly one of *domination* or *owning*. What you feel is joy, or momentous gratitude, for great fortune.

Maybe skiing down a mountain is a better example of mastery or possession in Sartre's special sense. But are you "appropriating" the mountain for your sporting purposes even then? To me, skiing still seems mainly a matter of *coping* with the mounds and ledges as they come at one by the ineluctable force of gravity. It's exhilarating as far as one can manage, and freer in snow powder, but still more managing than mastering. And the mountain isn't even moving (though I suppose one could ski/surf an avalanche).[16]

Sartre does say that motorboating and waterskiing are even closer to the ideal limit of aquatic sports. Both have an element of controlling or owning. Yet are they not *less* free for that reason? The boat's buoyancy naturally supports it against the downward pull of gravity, and it slides along the water only by artificial propulsion, a combustion-powered motor. The surfer, by comparison, slides over water by the wave's natural momentum, with no slogging, gas-guzzling motorboat tugging one along, artificially. If waterskiing is supposed to exemplify freedom even better than motorboating for all the extra sliding and carving, I guess we're supposed to ignore the motorboat controlling the water-skier's direction, speed, and future, which looks less like freedom than bondage (complete with ropes and vulnerability and whipping motions).

The surfer isn't "possessed" or "mastered" by some boat driver but free from the will of another. It's just the surfer and the wave—and maybe a pelican, or a dolphin, gliding along the wave face. The floating is of course artificial; one needs a surfboard, short of going completely natural and bodysurfing (but then with certain trade-offs for speed and possibilities of carving). But the crucial element

16. A Swiss friend and advanced skier, Enzo Porcelli, grew up just below the Alps but later took to surfing and moved for most of the year to the Canary Islands. He says the after buzz in surfing is way better, by which he means that the surfing activity is better.

of speed comes naturally, as one taps the wave's natural momentum, by one's own attuned pumping and carving, in one's own natural, free bodily activity.

So surfing bids fair to be the true "ideal limit of aquatic sports." The surfing kind of sliding is a full, maybe the fullest, expression of the free human's natural state of being.

Embodied, Embedded

Sartre's view of freedom is often said to be too "dualistic," too much like Plato's or Saint Augustine's or Descartes's view that mind and body are distinct but somehow interacting. He posits no detachable soul to explain how something that is still *you* could survive the grave, as in traditional dualism. Yet Sartre still says we at least aspire to a godlike, disembodied freedom. "Man," he says, "is the being whose project is to be God."[17]

To the surfer, even the aspiration sounds too disembodied, too alienated from the bodily relationship to one's external environment that is freely riding a wave. If one had the powers of Poseidon, to bend the waves to one's will and whim, one couldn't be a good surfer.[18] There'd be no occasion to flow freely, in heightened adaptive attunement to what is beyond one's control. The state of grace is necessary for surfing. Why not be content with it?

Moved by this very thought, almost as if speaking for the surfer, Sartre's longtime associate Maurice Merleau-Ponty explains freedom as an "exchange" between our conscious bodily engagement and the situation that carries us along:

> [In the] exchange between the situation and the one who takes it up, it is impossible to determine the "contribution of the situation" and the "contribution of freedom." I am never a

17. *Being and Nothingness*, p. 724.
18. The closest we humans get is a watercraft assist. This is now seen as impure unless it's absolutely necessary, as in twenty-five- to seventy-foot waves that move faster than a human can paddle a surfboard.

mere thing and never a bare consciousness. In particular, even our initiatives, and even in the situations that we have chosen, once they have been taken up, carry us along as if by a state of grace.[19]

So maybe I decide to rush down the line, instead of laying down a deep cutback. I could have done either. I passed on the cutback, and that was my free action. But it is equally my free surfing action when I really *have no choice but* to gain speed and rush down the wave's line, because of an approaching fast section. Either way, I'm surfing freely, with wave and surfer each making its contribution to the surfing moment. Am I *less free* for being dynamically bounded as each new moment presents itself? I am still surfing freely, of my own free will and free powers of movement. As an embodied, embedded human being, I'm freest not when I'm imposing my will on events, like Poseidon, but when I'm responding attunedly to each next moment of the wave. Freedom is not simply the basic condition of my conscious being but an *achievement* in action, not "bare consciousness," but a reciprocal relationship, the successful "exchange" between my initiatives and the circumstances that carry me along. I'm free in surfing just because I'm successfully flowing, adapting as appropriate, for being attuned to each next wave moment, in a state of grace.[20]

---

19. *The Phenomenology of Perception* (1945), trans. Donald A. Landes (New York: Routledge, 2012), p. 480.
20. Simone de Beauvoir thought this was basically Sartre's view and that Merleau-Ponty presented a false contrast ("Merleau-Ponty and Pseudo-Sartreanism"). Sartre himself seemed to concede a difference, which he found instructive ("Merleau-Ponty Vivant"). He even mentions waves: "Merleau felt sufficiently involved to have the constant awareness of restoring the world to the world, sufficiently free to objectify himself in history through this restitution. He freely compared himself to a wave, a crest among other crests, and the entire sea pulled upwards by a hemstich of foam" (p. 570). Both pieces appear in *The Debate Between Sartre and Merleau-Ponty,* ed. Jon Stewart (Evanston, Ill.: Northwestern University Press, 1998).

Conditions for the Possibility of Surfing

The sea is all around us, sublime in agitation and repose.[21] The ocean itself, including the day's wind, tides, and swell, is of course completely beyond our powers of influence. You definitely notice this fact while being sucked along a swift current, pushed ever closer to exposed rocks or reef, or flipped over by plunging breakers, repeatedly, while being scraped along the ocean bottom. (One is advised to act like a "rag doll," using one's arms to protect the neck and head, waiting for a chance to push up to the surface for air. Also, relax. Don't think about death, or don't worry about it.)

Big waves are awesome, in the olden sense of "awesome"; they are an apt object of awe, in fear or respect, admiration, wonder, or apprehension. But of course a wave is but one passing expression of the ocean's great constant forces. You feel them even in gentle seas, while waiting atop the pulsing, shifting expanse, being lulled along by a rolling swell, an easy current, and the slow tidal flow, as the whole planet's oceans are drawn along by the rotating moon's gravitational forces. Even in easy breakers, the surfer has no trouble giving up any pretense of mastery or possession, being palpably aware of the ocean's sublimity and our relative powerlessness before its waves.

This isn't the *utter* powerlessness of the paralytic. One can paddle and swim, and so move an arm, kick a leg, with direct control over one's body. Yet there's no getting one's bearings as on terra firma, as in Heidegger's land-loving "life world" of practical meaning, where hammers are "ready to hand" in part because they don't sink. Surfing is a primordial or at least otherworldly experience. It calls upon extraterrestrial powers of mammalian water navigation along with rather exotic tool use (the surfboard is made for no other purpose).[22]

---

21. Much of what surfers feel instinctively about the sea, beyond wave riding, is beautifully captured by Rachel L. Carson, *The Sea Around Us* (1950; New York: Oxford University Press, 1989).

22. For the science of such things, see Neil Shubin, *Your Inner Fish* (New York: Pantheon, 2008). The dawn of surfer reason seems to have first occurred either in

To just sit there holding balance on the wobbly surfboard requires constant slight adjustments in one's weight, even before one learns to catch a wave, stand up, and be taken along by the wave's natural momentum. If surfing is to happen in the normal range of human powers and limitations, you have no choice but to learn how to go along with what the ocean offers, accepting it as a given, with no pretense of the will for imposition and mastery that Sartre calls "appropriation."

Our relative powerlessness before the ocean and its waves is not just a fact of the human condition. It is a fact we must firmly *accept*, even embrace, in order to surf. An attitude of acceptance is *constitutive*, if you will, of the mentality needed for the very possibility of performing the surfing activity: without that sensibility, you can't surf a wave.

Surfing is less a matter of asserting one's will than of transcending it, by standing ready to revise one's best-laid plans, according to what the ocean is offering. And unless one surfs *from* a sense of one's relative powerlessness, one simply can't attunedly adapt to each coming moment of wave. One won't be ready to respond, immediately, at the right times, in the right places, in the right ways, unless one is present with the ocean in front of one, watching and waiting, paying close attention to *this wave,* and *this coming moment,* in light of the waves like this one over the last hour. This is why the blowhard whose controlling nature becomes especially visible in sport will find surfing hard to learn. If the guy can't see the point of not imposing his will upon the waves, of not trying to control as much as possible, perhaps from a manly desire for possession or domination, then, well, he might do well just to sit and watch. He could start by learning to sense the sublimity of ocean waves and the act of surfing them and the manifest beauty in being effectual

---

Peru or in various islands of the South Pacific, before becoming central to life and society in Hawaii. I've never heard of a definitive anthropological study of early surfing, but for a terrific general history, with special concern for technology and the postwar boom, see Peter Westwick and Peter Neushul, *The World in the Curl: An Unconventional History of Surfing* (New York: Crown, 2013).

without control. Then, but only then, would he be ready to learn something about being attuned.

This is partly just a matter of human aquamarine possibility: whatever your aspirations, if you don't keep adapting, you fall off. Not falling off requires innumerable basic attunements that present the main task for the beginner. As a beginner or novice, one can follow general rules, so as to at least feel "in control." "Gently kick your feet for counterbalance while you sit on the surfboard." "Keep a low crouch after standing." But such rules gradually become either unnecessary or inappropriate; one won't still keep a low crouch when one needs to extend the front leg through a top turn or to stand upright in a tube. Progress often means "letting go" of any sense of control that such maxims once afforded. One learns to focus on the coming moment, and what next response might be apt. The real challenge is to gradually pick up a bodily sense of one's situation, which allows one to spring into action with smoothness and flexibility of a sort that wouldn't be possible while thinking very self-consciously about rules or control.

To be sure, one can't feel completely "out of control." Depending on the day's conditions and one's skill level, one needs to feel that surfing is worth really trying, perhaps despite *a lot* of paddling and duck diving through heavy breakers. But at no stage will the waves you catch or how you surf them need to be fully or even mainly "under your control" in any general sense. What's needed is not Sartre's radical self-determination, appropriation, or mastery of events but just bodily coordination, the efficacy that comes from attunement, or both.

Bodily Control

For you to have basic control of yourself, your actions do need to be *your* actions, and not your mere behavior, or some autonomic reflex. So maybe your surfing involves certain gyrations, with peculiar lizard-man movements, but this is part of your own distinctive approach and not just a sad something happening to you, like being born hideously deformed or being struck by lightning. You need only *own* the lizard-like motions as your own. Just do them knowingly, purposefully. As Aristotle suggested, that is the basic mark of *action* rather than mere behavior. You won't receive a compliment, except from the nicest of friends, but a wonky style, of concocted contortions, can sort of get the job done.

Bad style does have limits. "Speed, power, and flow" are key judging criteria in professional surfing, and advanced surfing almost always aims at stylish, flowing performance. These are more than counsels of excellence. While they aren't quite a condition of surfing's very possibility—ugly surfing can still be surfing, badly done—a good measure of speed, power, and flow is necessary even for basic surfing. To harness the natural power of a wave, you have to call up a complicated ensemble of constant, efficiently coordinated bodily adjustments in fast succession. The guy with a "stinkbug stance" (who surfs in the manner of a slow, butt-in-the-air stinkbug) might get through a few basic maneuvers by moving around the arms, legs, core, and torso, in some of the right ways, at some of the right moments. Yet your style can be *too* clumsy, or funky, or sorely lacking in crucial fine-grained adjustments. If your weight becomes shifted too far back or too far forward at the wrong moment, you'll simply fall off, often suddenly, in a way that may invite scorn, questions of competence, and personal embarrassment.

So the beginner must learn a kind of basic unconscious control that contrasts with bodily flailing. The limbs and weight have to coordinate in lots of small, attuned adaptations, which must gradually become automatic, and if one is thinking about controlling one's movements, one is still in an early stage of learning. It's usually best not to consciously aim to *try to control the body,* unless one suffers some special body control problem—a peculiar gyration, for instance. Better to "let go" and let the apt movements come to you as a result of steady practice. Which is to say, try to sense what bodily positions create a rapport with the wave, watch what the pros do, visualize making those movements, and then practice them over and over, refining your own surfing according to what seems to work. Try for greater attunement, by paying close attention and by looking for possibilities of perception and movement. Which you will see because you are waiting to see them.

Control as Heightened Attunement

Even at advanced levels, fluid surfing has no need of control beyond the possibilities of bodily movement given by each moment of the breaking wave. Any general plans ("I'm thinking I'll nab the swinging set waves"; "I *gotta* get tubed") can be filled in on the fly, with snap intentions and spontaneous bodily adaptations. No plan can be very determinate beforehand. The surfer will find a fluid, flowing efficacy only by being ready to adapt afresh at each new moment, with no set plan. It's crucial to *not* try to bring the wave or its moments under your willpower through specific standing intentions, if you're to adapt attunedly. You never "force things."

"Good control, man" is occasionally offered as a compliment for a particularly good display of heightened attunement in technique and timing. The surfer managed to set a rail, or stall, or crouch, or recover from a tail-wafting snap, or do some crazy rotational aerial, at just the right moment of the wave. Or maybe a forceful carve or snap "threw buckets" of spray, which happens only because one is going along with a wave's powerful bowl in a sustained way. Yet no maneuver can be done at will, or on command, not without just the right, fleeting wave circumstances. Even manly "power surfing" isn't remotely like the delusional dreams of men who go on about "making your own weather" in politics or "creating your own luck" in business. The powerful surfer lays into a turn or carve, pushing through the rotation, with unusual force and command, but he could never pull this off in a less attuned state. "Power surfing" comes not from willpower, or mere force, but from perception, intuition, and anticipation—from one's sense that the ocean and its waves are to be not controlled but respected, and so read and answered, in an adaptive relationship.

In the best moments, a surfer's cumulative powers of intuitive sensing and bodily adjustment will coalesce with wave fortune, and he or she will suddenly "bust out" of the usual conventions, with impossible speed, radical and rotational maneuvering, and/or expressive, soulful styling. Is this not the spontaneous, radical freedom that Sartre took as the very nature of being? That's a tempting conclusion. Yet these are simply moments of grace, the fullest expression of adaptive *flowing*. The aim is not to somehow become unbounded, or to gain ever more control over what was uncontrollable, but a kind of efficacy—efficacy without control.

So there is in the human condition a way of being efficacious in action without having control of events. In view of the surfer, one might say, "Don't force things. Go with the flow. Things will come together. Just do each next right thing."

Surfing (and Life) Are Not So Terrible

Blaise Pascal, the seventeenth-century French mathematician and Christian philosopher, said that "the natural misfortune of our mortal and feeble condition is so wretched that when we consider it closely, nothing can console us."[23] For Sartre, it was Pascal who put reason in its place—in what became a typically French romantic disappointment caused by a scientist embrace of reason. Dostoyevsky wrote, "If God does not exist, everything is permissible." Sartre agrees fully, ruling out any anguish-free embrace of secular morality. "Indeed, everything is permissible if God does not exist, and man is consequently abandoned, for he cannot find anything to rely on—neither within nor without."[24] If Pascal wagered on God's existence, Sartre the atheist concluded that we are abandoned to choose from nothing, in the absurdity of life with no meaning beyond our self-construction project.

What then of all good surfer vibes? Is the surfer just blissfully

23. This line is quoted by Sartre in his "Commentary on *The Stranger*," in *Existentialism Is a Humanism,* trans. Carol Macomber (New Haven, Conn.: Yale University Press, 2007), p. 75.
24. "Existentialism Is a Humanism," in ibid., p. 29.

oblivious of the sickly, anxious state of the human person, of the manifest misery of the human condition? Or maybe guilty of escapism? Or of being in denial? Or, worse, is the surfer intent on shirking existential responsibility, just *lazy* in blowing off the slogging task of endless self-creation?

To this the surfer will answer, but is not surfing the whole point of freedom, or even its perfect culmination? Whether God exists or not, surely not *all* things are permissible. Killing for fast cash. Betraying a friend. Bailing on work to go surfing (without certain exemptions[25]). These acts are morally impermissible. For that, they need only fall short of the principles by which we can justify our conduct to others.[26] You couldn't justify to your friend spilling her confidences to someone else. If she were to look you in the eye and ask, "How could you? What were you *thinking*?" you'd have no reasonable answer. (Wouldn't God also give just that reason why betrayal is wrong? You couldn't justify it to the betrayed. If there's also a wrong against God, the community, or all humanity, it's because you'd be wronging *her*.)

By the light of surfer reason, it also is not permissible to lie in bed when the waves are pumping. Unless you really need rest, or you'll surf later, just lying there can't be justified to oneself. For surfing wasn't *simply* chosen for no reason in a radical act of self-creation, nor could it equally be un-chosen for no reason on a blah morning. It was always *worthy* of being chosen, or "choice-worthy," in Aristotle's phrase, in the first place. Unless one really does need to recover and laze, surfing is still worth a few hours in one's morning. Why? Just for its own sake. Because it's super fun. And because being attuned to a wave is sublime. And beautiful. And so a very good thing to do with one's limited time in life.

The depressive won't say so on a bad morning, of course. But surely a psychic disorder or downward mood swing is not a para-

---

25. My father, who grew up on Maui and surfed before he broke his back in a surfing accident, made me this deal while I was in high school: if I kept my grades up, he'd call in sick for me when the waves were on.

26. T. M. Scanlon, *What We Owe to Each Other* (Cambridge, Mass.: Harvard University Press, 1998).

digm of full freedom. If the depressive surfer is having trouble being moved by his or her own truest values, that raises the question of what is valuable. Is there not reason enough to keep on rising each morning? Today, hopefully you'll surf with friends, relax, get some work done, listen to music, read a little, and go to sleep in happy recollections. Maybe you'll do the same tomorrow. Yes, freedom means we have options, but some are better than others. Good waves are better than bad waves, and bad waves are better than nothing. It is worth surfing for its own sake, worth giving away a wave occasionally, ceding one's right-of-way, so as not to be greedy. It is good to help a stranger, just for his or her benefit, by giving him or her directions or a little money. Maybe you try to do something for society, you know, to give back. There's always good enough reason to check the waves and get coffee. Maybe this year you aren't quite up for a surf safari to Namibia in a quest for perfection in an otherwise dark human condition. Yet some simpler things can be simply worth doing for their simple reasons. Not because life is simple, but because value, at bottom, is.

However, could even such simple "value" be an illusion? In theory, surfing could have no simple *intrinsic* value at all, because its only value is instrumental. Rest or leisure might be needed only because it is needed for doing something respectable with oneself, in alignment with getting even more money, or spending a day in e-mail exchanges or meetings. Yet even workaholic Americans aren't so fetishistic about production to the point of officially rejecting freedom. And if freedom has genuine value, what would its value be if it isn't freedom to *go surfing,* or do something of comparable importance, just for its own sake? After all, even the money hungry often play golf. They do it, I gather, because the greens are peaceful. And because you can work on your swing. As they say, isn't that what all the work and money is *for?* But then golf or surfing does have value, and not simply because it is instrumental for work and money. If it isn't simply of instrumental value for anything else, that's just to say it *has* intrinsic importance, as worthy of one's limited time in life, for its own sake.

Surfing is of course part of life, so it partakes of life's absurdities. What is the absurd? As the philosopher Thomas Nagel explains,

> In ordinary life a situation is absurd when it includes a conspicuous discrepancy between pretension or aspiration and reality: someone gives a complicated speech in support of a motion that has already been passed; a notorious criminal is made president of a major philanthropic foundation; you declare your love over the telephone to a recorded announcement; as you are being knighted, your pants fall down.[27]

Or a guy paddles into a wave with stink-face seriousness, with everyone going, "Okay, bro, . . . if you're *sure* you've got it, we'll yield." As the wave jacks, he eats it, in inhuman bodily contortions, as the others miss out on what would have been an epic tube. Or maybe two men splash and quarrel about right-of-way ("You snaked me, bro! No way, you go fuck yourself, bro. Let's take it to the beach, bro!"). Meanwhile, waves go un-ridden, even as both have traveled thousands of miles over many days in exhaustion to surf the sublime perfection reeling off before them.

But as for the act of surfing itself, the simple act of a person successfully riding along on a wave, can it be absurd? It can't. It has no grand pretensions or aspirations to fall short of. When surfers say you can "surf just for surfing's sake," they mean that done just for its own sake, it lays no claim to cosmic meaning, beyond being a sublimely beautiful thing to do with one's time in life. It has no pretense that could be thwarted even in larger cosmic happenings. If a meteor bound for Earth was about to bring humanity to a sudden, seemingly absurd end, you could still meaningfully surf with a few friends for the hours remaining, with the clearest of conscience.

So Sartre seems mistaken: You aren't yet fully free lying in

27. "The Absurd," in *Mortal Questions* (New York: Cambridge University Press, 1979), p. 13.

bed in an existential conundrum. You are freer getting up, step-ping into the water, actively doing something worthy of the life you are leading. Freedom is that achievement, that way of success in action.

We've now taken a first small step out of Sartre's existential pre-dicament. We've got out of bed. We have yet to justify the surfer's lightness in living, however. For all we've said, it might be a product of certain special activities, which not all of humankind engages in. Speaking of mountain climbing, Sartre himself mentions that the climber's fatigue is "lived in a vaster project of a trusting abandon to nature." But, Sartre adds, such acquiescence is itself chosen as a project, or "consented to," so that "the dust of the highways, the burning of the sun, the roughness of the roads may exist to the full-est," being "felt at full strength."[28]

So maybe one can freely abandon one's freedom, if only tempo-rarily, so as to be intensely engaged, for sporting purposes. Then surfing could be the ideal limit of aquatic sports, but still only a sport. It wouldn't be especially *representative* of the general plight of the human person, which might otherwise be mainly miserable, for lack of sufficient meaning.

We have yet to address this genuine source of anxiety. Sartre and other existentialists wrote in the wake of world war, chaotic events, economic depression, and the seeming failure of Enlighten-ment reason, with an uncertain future. The French existentialist Albert Camus portrayed Sisyphus as shouldering a boulder up a hill for eternity in *protest*, in an act of willful defiance.[29] Though cosmi-cally absurd, Sisyphus's plight allowed for at least that much simple meaning. But Camus's point was that this would hardly be suffi-

28. *Being and Nothingness*, p. 587.
29. "The Myth of Sisyphus" (1955), in *The Myth of Sisyphus, and Other Essays* (New York: Vintage Press, 1983).

cient. He said the first philosophical question is whether to commit suicide, because we face a serious question "whether life is or is not worth living."[30] The simple meanings there are may or may not be enough to make living worthwhile in the final reckoning.

So we have yet to really answer the bigger questions: What is the human's condition? How is it to be managed? Can it, as it were, be surfed? This is the subject of the next few chapters.

Carried Along by Necessity

The human condition also raises a question of freedom if or to the extent it is deterministic. Suppose my getting out of bed, or not, has been settled long ago, by the unchanging laws of physics and the big bang's initial conditions. Would this mean I'm not free to rise in the morning, of my own free will?

In asking whether to lie in bed or to get going, I do have to "act under the idea of freedom," as Kant put it (writing before Sartre, without really explaining). I can't act as though my actions are already decided. I can't just say to myself, "We shall see if I get up. The matter is already decided." That *is* bad faith, what Sartre would call a cowardly "determinist excuse." It is treating oneself as a mere object, instead of a person, who, being free, can decide in action what his or her future will be. If I'm not a coward, I accept that the decision to rise in the morning is mine to make, for my own reasons.

Now consider a super physicist with a godlike ability to predict the course of events from a complete knowledge of the laws of nature, past physical events at all levels, micro and macro, and what the laws and past facts imply for the future. She talks to a surfer, assuring him that, yes, you'll always have a life full of surfing. In point of fact, she says, things *cannot be otherwise, regardless of your choices.* Given the laws of physics and the universe's initial conditions (or the controlling hand of the Creator, if you prefer a

30. Ibid., p. 3.

theological variation), the whole history of the world is meticulously determined, sealing the surfer's fate as a surfer, the waiter's fate as a waiter, the butcher's fate as a butcher, and so on. Given the assumed determinism, now we can ask, would said surfer be free?

Sartre's answer is no, he's not free. His choice to surf would not then be his own. Freedom for Sartre is radical freedom. Freedom is *incompatible* with the deterministic world suggested by macro-level physics (or Calvinist predestination theology). As many philosophers would agree, we *can't* be free if every event and action is meticulously determined to happen just as it does in fact happen from the beginning. For then we could not have done otherwise than what we are in fact doing. So if we *are* free, as we usually assume, the world must not be deterministic, but more wild and random and open than a deterministic physics à la Isaac Newton.[31] We must be able to act somehow *into* the causal order from outside (perhaps through the slack provided by quantum indeterminacy[32]). We would indeed have godlike control, being able to master or possess the world, by telling it how to be. It would be thus and so, on our say-so, just as Sartre says!

Surfer freedom is not so controlling. A person can be free simply for being able to do what is worth doing, because he or she values it, for good reasons. I rise in the morning in order to go surfing, and I surf for its own sake. Those are my reasons, my view of my actions, and why the actions are my own. And that, by itself, could well be

31. The "libertarians" who take this view affirm freedom and therefore reject determinism. You can instead go "nihilistic," by affirming determinism and so rejecting freedom. The two conclusions share the assumption now in question that freedom and determinism are incompatible.

32. Confused physicists sometimes go on about how quantum mayhem (perhaps in the brain) is the only way we might have freedom, without realizing they're assuming an incompatibilist position in the free will debate. Even the college sophomore philosophy student learns quickly that there are many "compatibilist" positions. David Hume even thought that freedom *requires* determinism, because otherwise we'd be too unpredictable to count as sane and rational. An undetermined agent would be more like a lunatic than the free author of an action for which he or she could be praised or blamed.

part of a deterministic universe.[33] Freedom and determinism are indeed compatible, because we can surf for what we ourselves see as intrinsically good reasons, even if every event, past and future, is, as it were, already decided. History would carry us along by necessity, but we'd still be freely surfing, in a state of grace.

Think of it this way: If every event in history were already decided, would the surfer thereby be unfree, because he or she couldn't have been a *waiter*? Most surfers I know wouldn't say so. They'd simply count themselves fortunate that they wound up free as surfers.

John Locke, the English early modern philosopher, asked us to imagine being in a locked room. Maybe you have no wish to leave, or didn't even know you were locked in. Still, it seems you are not free to leave, simply because you can't do so, whatever you might prefer or choose. Likewise, maybe the surfer has no wish to be a waiter. Yet the mere fact that she *couldn't have been one if she wanted to* means that she isn't free. The surfer is "locked" into being a surfer, and so unfree.

A locked room does sound pretty confining, especially compared with a more spacious place such as Indonesia. Suppose I'm already there in the dry season, the best season for waves. Without knowing it (maybe the island or boat isn't getting reliable media), I become unable to leave the country. But suppose I anyway don't and wouldn't *want* to leave, because I'd miss the next swell, which is expected to be epic. Then it seems fine to say that I'm *staying freely,* happily surfing. I don't know I can't leave, but even if I *did* know this, why would I wish to? Reason tells me to stay, tells me that waiting for the impending swell is certainly most worth doing. And in following my reasons, doing what is truly worthy, I am free, living my life by my own good purposes.

---

33. For such compatibilist views, see Watson's "Free Agency" and T. M. Scanlon's "Significance of Choice" in Watson, *Free Will*; along with J. M. Fischer and Mark Ravizza, *Responsibility and Control: A Theory of Moral Responsibility* (Cambridge, U.K.: Cambridge University Press, 1998). Fischer and Ravizza call responding to reasons a kind of "control," but what's meant is a compatibilist kind of attunement.

For this I do have to get out of bed, purposefully, for my own reasons, because I find it worth doing. Yet I don't have to think the grand metaphysical structure of the cosmos is particularly *relevant* in the momentous, self-determining question of whether to get up and pee. Wetting the bed is disgusting and unhygienic. Does one need a better reason for rising, which is thus done freely? As long as surfing is choice-worthy, surfer freedom is easy, being compatible with either determinism or indeterminism, or even some macro-micro split between them (depending on the area of physics).[34]

So suppose a certain surfer skips work to go surfing, lying to his boss about what he's doing. The grand metaphysical structure (or lack of structure) is then simply *beside the point*. Let's assume the lying surfer has done something morally wrong. He's rightly blamed for this, and so did it freely. Whatever the value of surfing, the question is then, is he rightly held morally responsible for that free decision *only* if he happens to be radically free in making it, because the world is nondeterministic? If the world *were* deterministic, would he be off the hook? Or is the metaphysical structure of the cosmos neither here nor there, simply *irrelevant* for purposes of blaming him?

We can answer by considering potential excuses. What might the derelict surfer say to his boss? He might say that, yeah, I'm sorry, I know, but, man, the waves were freaking epic, and so could you maybe understand a little? On the other hand, if he really couldn't have done otherwise, because the world is deterministic, and because Sartre is right about the need for radical, undetermined freedom, then he could also just point this out and absolve him-

---

34. Is determinism itself a surfer position? It seems fair to say the surfer would prefer a measure of indeterminacy, so that even perfect waves would have moments of genuine spontaneity, or a leaf could meander along in a quad on a path through space-time that isn't even in theory predictable. Likewise, the surfer won't mind if the atom decomposes into a particle/wave dualism. If there's a temptation to decide that it must be one or the other, the wave would certainly be preferable. It would even be preferable, as a matter of metaphysical aesthetics, to the supposedly unifying "strings" of string theory, despite the attractions of wavelike harmonies between different strings.

self of responsibility. He could say that he's reading this book about modern physics and that the macro-physical world is pretty much a deterministic system in which he (being a macro object) could not have done otherwise but go surfing, given the laws of physics and the initial conditions of the universe, way back to the big bang. So, he might conclude, holding him morally responsible is a mistake. *He couldn't have done otherwise,* so he's not to blame.

No one would be morally brazen enough to actually say this. Silly as it may sound, nothing would be wrong with the argument on our present assumptions. Determinism *is* an excusing condition, and so our surfer wasn't free. To rebut the argument, the boss would have to challenge the surfer's physics (that is, deny the alleged determinism). But that should seem strange. As the boss, most of us would just say to him, yeah, yeah, whatever, dude. You promised to be here, and I think I'm comfortable holding you responsible for your choice not to show. What the physicists are saying just isn't relevant in these matters.

If that's right, then determinism doesn't undermine freedom, because it isn't relevant to these ordinary ways we hold each other responsible.[35] And Sartre's radical freedom isn't then necessary for free surfing. A person can be carried along by necessity, going with the flow of the universe, and yet free.

---

35. This argument from irrelevance was made famous by Peter Strawson in "Freedom and Resentment," in Watson, *Free Will,* one of the most cited papers of the later twentieth century.

3

Control

What, then, is to be done? To make the best of what is
in our power, and take the rest as it naturally happens.

—Epictetus

To SURF IS TO ACQUIESCE in a wave's shifting moments, so as to go
along *with* its flow. How does the surfer do this? In part by giving
up the need for control. By throwing off a central preoccupation of
modern society, which is to stay in control, to master nature, and to
tame an uncertain future, the surfer finds a beautiful way of being
effectual in relative powerlessness before a sublime ocean.

Plato and Aristotle were the great philosophers of ancient Greece.
But in late antiquity, around the first century, the Stoic school
emerged and offered what has become the most distinguished practical philosophy of how to live. Born a slave and later freed, the Stoic
philosopher Epictetus knew something about powerlessness. He
explained how to be happy: "Make the best of what is in our power,
and take the rest as it naturally happens." I am powerless over my
circumstances, and so I should just accept them. But for the Stoics,
I do not abandon control entirely. I can accept my circumstances
and find happy equanimity only by controlling my own attitudes,
the domain of life where my fortunes are up to me.

Should I want pie at dinner? It depends. What are the chances
my fellow diners will forget to leave a slice for me? Before I even

form a desire, however secretly, I should wait and see, until such time as the plate is passed around the table and within my graceful reach. If I find myself desirously gazing, I should avert my eyes. By a simple act of will, I can pay attention to one thing rather than another. What I attend to will change what I judge to be true or worthy of doing or feeling or wanting. My desires then follow my better judgment.

In this way, I can adapt my desires to my circumstances, *whatever* they may be. If my child has died, I should remind myself in my grief that she was a mortal; I could never have expected her death not to happen. If I embrace my living spouse, I secretly take note that she is mortal as well, in order to prepare myself for her passing. If I'm virtuous enough, I can be content even while being stretched upon the rack.[1] And if some desire is recalcitrant or "irrational," persisting despite my better judgment, I can choose to disregard it as beyond my control, as something just happening to me. So It Goes. But come what may, I stay in control of myself.

The surfer, by comparison, isn't so cautious about all-out wanting, or even daily wave lust. Like the Stoic, the surfer embraces his or her lack of control over a naturally changing wave. But the surfer also gives up any need to control his or her passing thoughts and feelings, for the happy efficacy in being adaptively attuned. A disciplined mind comes not by control but in attunement to what lies beyond.

Perfection Beheld

If there's an epicenter of surfing nowadays, it is Indonesia, the relatively new democracy in which generally good people still take bribes and occasionally issue the death penalty against Westerners for drug trafficking. Whipped up by Indian Ocean storms around

---

1. The military teaches Stoic techniques to soldiers, which are invaluable to POWs. Those who perfect them often come home chronically disengaged from normal living.

the "roaring 40s" (the 40th latitude), powerful, ruler-drawn swells march into the thousand-mile-long archipelago and reel off with easy magnificence along the shallow coral reefs. Welcome to Surfing Disneyland. More so than anywhere the world over, the waves are *rippable,* and I mean, like, *crazy* rippable, which is to say about as suitable for surfing as waves can be.

The backstory for Indo surfing begins with Bruce Brown's 1966 film, *The Endless Summer.* In an era of Gidget and beach blanket bingo at Malibu, the newly discovered waves inspired a generation of surfers to leave California, Hawaii, and Australia in wide-eyed quests for new surf breaks.[2] By the early 1970s, they stumbled into perfection, first in Bali, then in Sumatra and Java, and, in time, all along the archipelago. The waves weren't just better than anyone ever imagined; they were *a lot* better, and with photographs and films filtered through the surf media, surfers formed a new concept of surfing perfection.

To pay for all the expenses in the early days, many of the first explorers ran drugs.[3] Others did what surfers still do—get by on the cheap.[4] In time, a legitimate surf industry began to prosper (eventually with revenues estimated at $13.2 billion). The quest for Indo perfection became a fixture in the serious surfer's schedule, especially during its May through September dry season. Treasures have turned up elsewhere in the world (Tahiti and Fiji are highlights). The famously tubular "Banzai Pipeline," on the North Shore

2. Although on the South Africa leg they famously just missed the now legendary Jeffreys Bay, which would have been pumping on the day they got the great footage of Cape St. Francis, which by itself spurred the surfer gold rush.
3. The documentary *Sea of Darkness* tells the tale. For a preview, see https://www.youtube.com/watch?v=tqBLuGOyRdE.
4. William Finnegan's epic *Barbarian Days* (New York: Penguin Press, 2015) faithfully describes how he scraped by at what have become the usual go-to spots around the world. Things are easier for my later generation of surf travelers, with improved infrastructure and various surf camps, sometimes with luxury accommodations. For the rich worlder, exchange rates are still great. And there's still plenty of less well-charted territory to explore if you're willing to take a chance and miss waves at the reliable known breaks.

of Oahu, Hawaii, will always be a key proving ground for professionals. But Indo is where most surfers go, or really *want* to go, often year after year, in some sort of half-sacred pilgrimage.[5]

Like a lot of South Asia's tropical zone, the place is stunning. The locals are delightful. Things are pleasantly unruly. There's plenty of cool culture to check out. Bali is a good place to settle in before setting off southward to Lombok or Sumbawa or northward to Java or Sumatra in hopes of less crowded waves. Alas, the gorgeous cliffs and beaches along Bali's Bukit Peninsula, including the famous Uluwatu, one of the first great discoveries, have become a circus. The Rio-style *favela* piled atop the magnificent cave at Ulus is definitely a sight to see, anthropologically speaking, perhaps before checking out the monkey-strewn temple perched upon the dramatic cliff and then surfing a less crowded break.[6] And yet not far away from Bali's traffic, just across the Lombok Strait, we find what is by almost all accounts one of the single best surf breaks on our fine planet.

In the southern part of Indonesia, freshwater flows from the Pacific into the Indian Ocean through the various islands and waterways of the Indonesian archipelago. The Indonesian Throughflow, as scientists call it, is an essential part of the "heat conveyor belt" that encircles our planet, regulating the average temperature of the atmosphere, which in turn influences the weather in L.A. or Lisbon and the farming in Peru or Mozambique. And right there

5. The celebrated Hawaiian Islands have big and powerful but much less perfect waves, a few exceptions being Oahu's Pipeline and Maui's Honolua Bay. Still better for size, power, and perfection is Tavarua, Fiji. But perhaps only Tahiti has Indo beat overall, for a wide variety of waves that are raw in open-ocean power but equal in perfection. Even so, Indo spots are more varied and numerous.

6. The 1971 film *Morning of the Earth* captures the wonder of the early Bali explorations. (See https://www.youtube.com/watch?v=4e_2SrcjJLY.) In *Barbarian Days,* Finnegan reports that by the time of his visit there in the late 1970s, Bali was already "overrun, and the collision of mass tourism and Indonesian poverty was grotesque" (p. 237). I still felt its charm on my first visit in the late 1990s, when Kuta Beach was busy but Ulus was still in its natural state except for some bamboo structures for food and massages. The wave itself is still super fun, if you're up for crowd surfing.

in the Throughflow itself, which partly runs through the Lombok Strait, between the islands of Bali and Lombok, we find Desert Point, or "Deserts."

The spot works only on very low tides, so it will be one of the first breaks to be swamped forever if sea levels rise very much. (Only a few extra feet of water over the reef would do the trick.) As the lore has it, this is the remote and barren outpost where a feral surfer got his arm hacked off by local marauders with machetes. (Though I've heard from someone who was there that famous night that the guy stupidly attacked first in self-defense, instead of just parting with his stuff.) It's been a while now, and these days, when the place is set to turn on, surfers descend like locusts upon the harvest. The lines of swell appear from deep in the strait, mount as crystalline green walls, and then rope down the reef, the tube unspooling with faster and slower sections. When the right conditions come together, the prosaic imperfection of the human condition takes a reprieve, and the most coveted act in surfing—riding inside the tube of the wave—becomes possible to an otherworldly degree.

To put this in perspective, in California, a mere three seconds in the tube can make the surfer's day or week or month. At Deserts, on the right day, with an ultralow or lowish tide, ideally pushing upward, the skilled surfer can ride for *ten* seconds, and in principle twenty seconds, inside the heaving, snarling tube, by weaving and adjusting and stalling, while leaving a chance of exit, before emerging after an eternity, maybe never being touched by the spinning water cave, and then collapsing in joyous delirium.

For advanced-world surfers, the longings for perfection begin back home in the mediocre waves they surf around their everyday life and work. One has to be grateful for the wealth and comforts of advanced-world living but maybe not so pleased with the unnerving volatility and the breakneck pace of change. Amid the fever to keep up, or not fall behind, at least not by too much, amid all the loud news of the rising fortunes of winners in our winner-take-all economy, a few hardy souls might work up immunity to the discontenting messages. For most of us, though, tuning out the noise takes constant taxing effort.

None of that matters in Indo, where even the first days of culture shock allow you to feel human again. Surfing perfection suddenly seems attainable, even easy. On the good days, the best surfers become demigods of Greek stature and power. But even the average surfer can occasionally score a big barrel and, for a moment, reach to the sky, exultantly claiming a place in the pantheon.

I'm one of Indo's many surfer sojourners. Mainly I go for the waves. I also go to remind myself that perfection, of one sort, is actually attainable in a human condition that is otherwise a dodgy and tragic place.

Even in Indo, you need a bit of luck. It's relatively easy to get good waves. Yet it will still bum you out if you could have scored the epic, otherworldly, possibly life-altering perfection that is regularly served up, and yet you missed it by a week. Surfers aren't knights gallantly in the quest, ready to die in honorable chase. They want to *score,* to actually surf perfect waves, not just hear about them.

Bad wave luck can be mitigated somewhat. In the area around one well-known place, a nice little wave serves as the surfer's saving grace. After a motorbike ride through a foul-smelling town and along the coastal road that winds beneath the deep green and black jungle canopy, you start to see waves plunge into the reef through the crisscrossing palm tree trunks, until you arrive at a cheerful seaside village. The surf break itself sits just beyond a few cinder-block and tin-roofed homes, which means the reef can be busy, and not just with the occasional roaming goats, octopus fisherman, or church service. The reef is also something of a shitting area, which is naturally cleansed with each high tide, with clear and shallow water, and coral heads visible just below the surfer's dangling toes. The locals are fortunate for having their waste conveniently run out openly into the fresh splendor, when you consider that in some of the other, much poorer villages not far off, you find yourself in the unhygienic situation of doing your business in the stream from which everyone drinks or venturing out into the nearby woods, where flies buzz back from the lightly buried shit piles to the village food and eating areas, causing untold early deaths, from sickness and diarrhea. Here at the seaside village, you can keep yourself and your family from needless death while having a moment with your body amid the fresh roar of the cracking waves. And most important for surfers, the wave out front is reliably fun even with minimal swell. An approaching wave becomes a focused, wedging peak, which shoves you into fun sections that you can repeatedly shellac with snapping turns, maybe while nabbing a quick, bowly cover-up. And it doesn't take much by way of swell energy for the thing to become a full-on drainpipe—in the best possible sense, of becoming a crystalline, peeling tube. You can catch the wave from the peaking wedge and then get nicely barreled at any number of points along the fifty- or seventy- or so yard stretch of the break. When the wind swings just the right direction, you can get drained across the whole reef in a crazy ten-second tube ride.

Indonesia, in this respect, is a wonderful place. Even when you're not expecting waves for lack of serious swell, a moment of perfection can burst forth from a human condition that can be a foul mess.

The Ordinary, the Mundane

Plato thought perfection isn't part of our worldly, sensuous experience. We can grasp an abstract concept—of a Circle, of Justice, of the Good—in pure thought. But no material object can be perfectly circular, no real society just, and no person completely good or virtuous. Perfection belongs only to the eternal Forms or Ideas, and our material world of sensory experience is at best a shadowy, pale copy of their eternal existence in their own heavenly realm (or perhaps in God's mind, as for the Neoplatonist Saint Augustine).

Indonesia is an earthly heaven, where perfection and imperfection bathe the surfer's senses. The sublime and the beautiful are all over the place, immanent in ordinary experience, right there, in the tube grinding off across the inside reef. I drew archetypal waves on my schoolbooks as a kid, having seen magazine photographs of a gaping tube and exploding foam set against the black-green jungle at Lagundri Bay on Nias Island in Sumatra. But now there you are, with a schoolbook barrel grinding off right in front of you. The waves really can get perfect, for all of surfing's purposes. (And do we have a better concept of perfection?) If a young child didn't yet have a concept of the sublime, or of the beautiful, those ideas might be *revealed* to her in sensory experience, in a glimpse of Desert Point when it's working. You could simply point and say, "Now *that's* sublime, and beautiful, right there; do you see it?"

The "gnarly," in surfer speak, is one form of the sublime. This is the source of endless mealtime discussions of such topics as sharks that eat people; the recent shark attacks; what to do, if anything, about shark attacks (poke 'em in the eye? Punch like crazy?); the guy who just face-planted the reef; the poor guy who just *died* face-planting the reef at Hollow Trees in the Mentawai Islands; the guy going "over the falls" in utter helplessness, but who somehow lived, on that crazy, crazy, sucking-underwater death wall at Teahupoo, Tahiti; or just any number of "slab" surf breaks, of grotesque size, hollowness, and power, especially Teahupoo.[7]

When a wave, or wave moment, is dangerous, terrifying, or just really heavy, it is not necessarily said to be beautiful as well. That much squares with Edmund Burke's preoccupation with the sublimely gnarly in his 1757 treatise on the subject (*A Philosophical Enquiry into the Origin of Our Ideas of the Sublime and Beautiful*). Burke distinguished the sublime from the beautiful, but too sharply. He invited the unfortunate notion that they are opposed. It's true that the sublimely *gnarly* and the beautiful are opposed. The gnarly is never beautiful. But the *sublimely beautiful* is possible and real, and the music of the surfer's worldly experience.

What is beautiful for Burke is what induces feelings of enjoyment. What is sublime is what induces terror, but from a safe dis-

7. Here's raw footage, with plenty of carnage, from a solid 2015 swell: https://www.youtube.com/watch?v=gLg6qxkQ94A.

tance, along with a sense of pleasurable "delight" in being relieved of pain or fear (often of death, by perhaps unspecifiable means, in such things as darkness, obscurity, high mountains, the stormy ocean, outer space, the ungraspably vast and formless, the absolute power of God, grand buildings, public executions, war, and the ruin of civilizations[8]). Burke's idea was to define both concepts by the feelings they induce, in "pleasures" of opposed sorts. Kant followed Burke's view and explained in this way: The beautiful is pleasing. But in our being alternately attracted to and repelled by the sublime, "the delight in the sublime does not so much involve positive pleasure but admiration or respect."[9]

When Kant spoke of our "mental attunement" to a sublime object, and its attendant feelings of "submission, prostration, and . . . utter impotence," he overstated the point. The sublimely beautiful floods and bathes the surfer's whole being, but not with utter impotence. The Beach Boys song "Girls on the Beach" put the genuine insight ironically: the beauties lying around, "with tans of golden brown," are "all within reach," at least "if you know what to do." The average Joe has no idea at all what to do, how to be so bold as to make *that* approach. So Joe must behold the sublime sight from a distance, in admiration, awe, and a certain paralysis of the will. Yet he's not *utterly* powerless; he knows full well he could strike up a conversation, if he just had the courage, if he could just find the attuned bons mots. Which is why he lambastes himself later for not just walking over, rising to the awesome challenge. And of course the girls on the beach are very beautiful, which means the beautiful and the sublime can splendidly mix. They mix in the low drama of everyday life, in a place as ordinary as a summer beach. Or in beholding an undulating sea. Or in whales breaching just offshore, ever so slowly, in flopping antics. Or in the unruly bustle of a place like Indonesia, amid the wafting smell of burn-

8. Here I'm indebted to Luke White's brief online history, at http://www.lukewhite.me.uk/sub_history.htm.
9. *Critique of Judgment,* sec. 23.

ing coconut husks and a milky-turquoise wind-groomed Sumatran wave.

If the olden use of "awesome" refers to the sublimely gnarly, a newer meaning in surfer-speak refers to welcome and surprising breaks from the mundane in ordinary life.[10] There's no need for humble feelings of utter powerlessness, as though one stands before a violent or vast ocean, a humongous wave, or God Almighty himself. A mildly sublime break from the usual mundane happenings calls only for a moment of pleasing wonder, and maybe a laugh or a hoot. What's not spoken of but felt is the sense of dependence upon and harmony with what lies mainly beyond one's control. The sublime becomes familiar in the everyday ordinary. This is what the Beach Boys called "good vibrations," the heightened harmonious dependence that saturates the life of stoke.

Even in ordinary activities, perhaps after a surf, this sense of favorable connection sweeps away the mundane, the drab, the blah, the why-am-I-even-here melancholy that can get a person bummedly asking existential questions about whether all the tedium, humdrum, and monotony could really, *really* give anyone enough reason to live. As Kant put the idea, though we often worry about our "property, health, and life," the sublime "calls forth our strength" to regard such concerns as "small" or trivial.[11] As surfers often put the point, "Problems wash off in the water."

Thus it often happens that life is full of wonder, on a completely ordinary day, on this very afternoon, whatever else might happen, simply for being in the water, for surfing this wave. It is good to be

10. I take this newer use of "awesome" to apply to natural phenomena such as waves. So this is a broader meaning than the essentially social concept defined by the philosopher and former pro in-line skater Nick Riggle. "Being awesome," he explains, involves creating social openings, by breaking out of the usual roles, going off script, as with a fun joke, so as to express one's individuality and open a door for mutual appreciation. "Being down" is taking up such openings; "being game" is doing so enthusiastically. To refuse them is "to suck." For Riggle's full system, see *On Being Awesome: A Unified Theory of How Not to Suck* (New York: Penguin Books, 2017). For an overview, see his "High Five!," *Aeon*, https://aeon.co/essays/how-being-awesome-became-the-great-imperative-of-our-time.

11. *Critique of Judgment*, p. 121.

here, alive, sumptuously present, seeing plainly what matters, and what matters not, what is trivial, and what is truly worthy of one's time in life. I can accept my being again, wholeheartedly, without worrying too much about that thing, whatever it was again, that so occupied me, absorbing my attention, sapping my energies, damming the floods of stoke. For the surfer at least, the human's condition can itself be an object of appreciative wonderment, a sublime mix of the beautiful and the grotesque, the meaningful and the absurd, the fair and the foul, the just and the unjust, much as the French poet Victor Hugo said: "The ugly exists beside the beautiful, the unshapely beside the graceful, the grotesque on the reverse of the sublime, evil with good, darkness with light."[12]

"He Had Bad Luck"

Indo surfing can be seriously gnarly, even woeful, given the considerable risks of death, paralysis, or other permanent injury from such misfortunes as regular earthquakes and occasional tsunamis (especially in the northern parts, up in the northern Sumatra area); frequent collisions with sharp and shallow coral reefs (in some cases leading to total paralysis, and delayed rescue helicopters, which must tend to all the similar accidents of the day along the several-thousand-mile chain of islands); malaria beyond Bali (which is permanent if not fatal, depending on the strain you contract); ferries that sink from disrepair, killing most of their passengers (though some surfers have grabbed their boards and paddled to safety); plane crashes (although some of the local airlines have newer planes, posing an interesting choice between technology and pilot experience); daily motorbike injuries and deaths (with shoddy clinics and hospitals). Thankfully, there's not a big problem with sharks.

Surfers keep showing up in droves anyway, fanning out to all manner of remote outposts along the archipelago. The risks are

12. Preface to *Cromwell*, at http://www.bartleby.com/39/41.html.

refreshing, a healthy corrective to the advanced-world myths that our lives are firmly under our control, such that we are to be credited for our good luck and blamed for the bad things that happen, because it was in our power to have chosen to make things different (with sufficient planning, hard work, adequate insurance, and so on).

A certain amount of planning is of course necessary, to get around, meet one's basic needs, and be ready to surf when the waves are cracking. Planning is the main way the human agent shapes his or her future actions, so as to realize temporally extended projects.[13] Planning now needn't presume anything like "control" over future events, let alone give one reason to expect things to work out according to plan. If one now fully expected the same outcome given past similar efforts, one would be wrong to feel entitled to the future being like the past. In shedding the illusion of control, along with the hope of attaining it, one can stand ready to revise one's plans, on the fly as necessary. Best-laid plans do often go astray. Because why wouldn't one have to adapt? As in surfing, in life. As with vast numbers of people in the developing world, the risks, mishaps, and unpredictability leave no illusions that mere planning would have any magical reach of control into the coming future. So, yes, one has to plan, in view of the risks and prospects as they stand at the moment, but without the rich worlder's temptation to expect to not have to revise or change course ("because I get what I want," as some put it). For the coddled advanced worlder who is accustomed to reliable electricity and plumbing, on-time flight schedules, but now stripped bare in Indo, one lives a bit more like one's fellow humans live all across the developing world, firmly accepting the reality of our limited powers before fortune.

Luck differs from fortune. It is lucky to win a lottery, because this might easily have not happened. It isn't *lucky* when the sun

---

13. See Michael Bratman's *Intention, Plans, and Practical Reason* (Cambridge, Mass.: Harvard University Press, 1987) on how intentions rather than desires unify us in action over time.

rises in the morning. The world would have to be radically different for this not to happen. But the sun's rising this morning is still *fortunate*. One will rightly feel blessed, or even grateful, in either good happening. The world is going one's way, and why not celebrate? Yet when our benefit is simply fortunate, we aren't as tempted to take credit. When we are lucky, and the outcome could have gone either way, our agency can seem to have made the difference, or at least improved the probabilities. So we may feel less blessed than right or good, praiseworthy or deserving, and maybe even entitled to the fruit of our meritorious efforts. And in our self-congratulation, we may presume the less successful are not simply unlucky but also responsible: surely they must not have done what might or would have made the difference, as they could have had they been trying. And if certain poor souls are such that luck can't or won't reliably work in their favor with a bit of effort, well, that's just unfortunate for them. We shouldn't hope to improve their condition when we celebrate our own blessedness.

So goes a fair bit of advanced-world thinking. Which is why I go to Indo yearly, to remember the meaning of life. I try to stay off the motorbikes that are everywhere. (The middle-class family usually has one and can't afford a car.) Yet I occasionally find myself riding along on one with Damien Wao, a local on Nias Island, Sumatra. Named "Democracy" by his government worker father under the rule of Suharto ("Damien" is an English transliteration; his brother, Raffiel, was named "Revolution"), Damo runs the *losman*, or guesthouse, at Lagundri Bay where I spend my visit. He's an unusually careful driver—"slow but sure" is our watchword—and he's otherwise warm, good-natured, and reliable. He laughs constantly and often speaks solemnly of his responsibilities as we motor along, crawling through the buzzing, crisscrossing traffic madness, with teenagers recklessly weaving as they fly past, as whole families pile on a single bike, with two or three kids sandwiched between momma and poppa, while momma rides sidesaddle in a gorgeous dress on the way to church or mosque.

It isn't that the locals aren't aware of the many accidents. Damien knows he's supposed to wear a helmet. Yet, hard as I try, I can't get him to wear one reliably. While riding along, with the asphalt of the narrow road speeding by below, I ask him to consider what would happen if we dropped a melon at this speed. As I hold out my hand, feigning a melon release, I say, "Just like that, it would be your head. You don't want that, right? Think of your kids!"

"Ha ha ha, that is funny. Okay, fine," is his usual reply. He then puts the helmet resting in his lap onto his head. Until, only five minutes later, he takes it off again.

"I don't like it." He says this taking comfort in the warm wind. Besides, he hasn't had an accident yet, even as he knows he might. He often adds, "If I crash, that's bad luck."

This is of course contrary to key counsels of Modern Western Man (and Woman). Being one to offer such counsels when they are not being observed, I say, "But you can prevent it, right now. Or at least minimize the risk." To which he replies, "Ha ha, you're funny, Air-ron."

Damien did finally get into a motorbike accident. He hit his head on the ground going pretty fast. Thankfully, he was wearing his helmet that time, and so suffered a bum leg and a few months on his back instead of a busted melon. Score one for the wisdom of Modern Western Man.

On the other hand, when something unfortunate happens to a person—when one's child dies, or one falls ill, or one's pig (a major capital good) dies before it can be sold off—the locals on Nias Island, where Damo is from, will kindly, stoically say just what he said, that "he had bad luck." By which they mean that the bad luck is the end of the matter. It wasn't the suffering person's fault. It was bad luck. Period.

Modern Western Man does say "well, shit happens" about a fender bender. Then, once afflicted by a serious and incurable disease, or the death of a child, he also says, in all sincerity, "How could this possibly happen to me?" As if life were supposed to be perfect, or mostly work out, and you aren't getting your due when it doesn't. Despite having Done Everything Right. As if life in advanced society really is always mostly under someone's control, so that what happens is always to someone's credit, or someone's fault, and barely or in no way subject to luck and chance, except of course in Vegas, or the stock market. Hence one can blame those who suffer. They've made bad choices. They did not create their own luck. They did not work hard enough.

Whereas, often, when someone suffers a major setback, what we should say, because it is true and sufficient, is that "he had bad luck." We can leave it at that.

Score a big one for the Indonesians.

Indo surfers often suffer bad luck, even with the advanced-world benefits of travel insurance, access to a good hospital, and other safeguards. You're still there, present in body and flesh, physically exposed, vulnerable to violent harm or death in a thousand ways, with constant dangers of a serious reef bounce, of being splayed out on the street in a motorbike wreck, or, in really hard luck, of sudden death by whizzing coconut, with a clock to the head. Surfers do worry; they are not fine with early death, because they won't be there for it, as Epicurus suggested: "Death . . . the most awful of evils, is nothing to us, seeing that, when we are, death is not come, and, when death is come, we are not." True enough, but the *risks* of death while alive and vulnerable are surely worth considering, if only for all that one gives up for being unnecessarily dead. Even if you don't die of malaria (as some surfers do), you might still wind up a quadriplegic (as some surfers have). A surfer recently fell off a boat into the night without catching anyone's notice. There he was in the dark with no land in sight, treading water for some twenty-three hours, fending off seagulls nipping at his nose. He tried three times to drown himself, but couldn't swing it. Which was lucky, as it turned out. Amazingly, he was finally discovered, when the boats somehow spotted his bobbing head in their search of the Sumatran seas. I myself saw a guy instantly paralyzed after hitting the reef at G-Land, Java. His friends pushed him to shore on his board, and then duct taped him to it for rigidity, where he spent the night waiting. The rescue helicopter landed late in the day, due to delays from similar accidents, which, according to the pilot, are extremely common along the archipelago. He was lucky to be evacuated the next morning.

While waiting for waves at Nias, I sometimes get caught up in terror-filled daydreams of another big tsunami, like the two that hit in late 2004 and early 2005 (one of which everyone saw on TV). I imagine what must have actually happened. The whole sea sucking out; a heaving monstrosity of a wave bearing down on the main surf break; a walloping for the ages for any hapless surfers who would have been propelled into the dark jungle, to be impaled on a tree. (In a different tsunami nearby, surfers clung to the tops of palm trees and survived.) During the actual events, Damien was at home and suddenly found himself chest deep in water. The family had managed to evacuate, only to realize that their daughter was still back atop the bunk bed. With the poise of a surfer, Damo waded back to the house, grabbed a surfboard, slung his daughter on his back, and paddled to higher ground, getting pushed along by breakers. If the next tsunami hits at night, you might wake up to find yourself "surfing" a mattress along the storm surge into the rice paddies—which, actually, might be rather exhilarating as long as it lasted.

All this is part of the charm of the place. You take note of the rumored deaths or mishaps and try not to do anything too stupid. Stupidity still happens, despite one's best efforts. One can't control outcomes, and this must be firmly accepted, so as to gracefully adapt as the risks change. Then, as the ancient Stoic wisdom of Epictetus suggests, just "take the rest as it naturally happens," for worthy surfing purposes. When your luck is working out, as it often does (tsunamis are fairly uncommon), there is a quiet joy in being completely fine, and alive, right here, right now, whatever might happen next. In contrast with superficiality and groundless anxieties of advanced-world life, you're off the Matrix, unplugged, palpably exposed to Reality. But unlike in the movie, real life is fine, and actually great, or complete. Nothing else has to happen, as long as the waves keep pumping.

Extending Grace

Yet put down a few points for Modern Western Man when I'm discussing Damo's giving me a ride to the Nias airport, in an uncertain two-and-a-half-hour trip, and he wants to leave only two and a half hours before, giving us no margin for error. I'll say to him, "Can't we leave a bit earlier? What if I miss my flight and all the connections because the road is blocked, like that time a palm tree fell and obstructed the road? If we hadn't been on the motorbike [which we lifted over the tree], we'd have been stuck for hours." To which he answers, "Well, that'd be bad luck."

The grace the Indonesians extend to others, we can surely extend to ourselves. When events go awry, we can say, "I had bad luck," and leave it at that. Which is all well and good when one's luck has *already* gone south. The sentiment is less apt when a decision has yet to be made, or can still be changed, when one is now trying to figure out what risks to take or allow, *ex ante*. As Sartre would say, then doing nothing is a decision. When my house is already on fire, I merely try to get out alive. But beforehand, I can certainly buy a fire extinguisher and fire insurance. Society can set up a fire department to keep mishaps from spreading from house to house, paid for with taxes, by socializing our risks, in the socialism found in every advanced country. Even the death toll by coconut-clock-to-the-head can be mitigated with a bit of organization: someone might regularly pick the ripe coconuts above any walking paths, before they become dangerous. If we can carefully manage the risks to which we are exposed with prudent foresight, reducing the chances of suffering bad luck, why give ourselves over to fate unnecessarily?

Does that mean adverse outcomes *are* within our power or control after all? No, it doesn't. Therein lies the advanced worlder's confusion. I can move my arm or hand, which is usually within my bodily control. Our modern powers of planning work only indirectly, by shaping *how likely* it will be for a bad outcome to "naturally" come about down the road, given the options we now have and the evidence now on hand, which may of course change.[14] Beyond misfortune in what is relatively fixed, bad luck befalls even the best-laid plans, when things could easily have gone differently. All the how-could-this-happen-to-me, I've-done-almost-everything-right fretting only keeps the precious advanced worlder out of the flow. It's a way of not really accepting what has happened and so not really being on the lookout for an attuned adaptation.

Epictetus reassures us that "some things are in our control and others not." He offers fine examples of what is indeed in our control ("opinion, pursuit, desire, aversion, and, in a word, whatever are our own actions") and what is definitely not ("body, property, reputation, command, and, in one word, whatever are not our own actions"). But the difference is one of degree, and the whole question of risk management is where to place ourselves on the probability spectrum. As long as the outcome is not completely certain, chance also decides what finally happens, however prudent our actions.

The ancients lacked our modern resources for risk management. We moderns can *shape* our luck, by managing our risks with increasing efficacy as technology progresses (as in ever more accurate weather and surf forecasts). We can mitigate misfortune (for example, by buying insurance), but the very fact that we have that option is a reflection of our good fortune, and even then our powers of mitigation work only on the margins of probability. The techno-utopianism of Silicon Valley isn't wholly misguided megalomania: social planning and technology are powerful forces, which is why it is so tempting to think our fates are in our hands. Now so more than

14. Thomas Bayes's formula for "updating" one's credences given new evidence is so very surfer as a theory of rationality. See Andy Clark's *Surfing Uncertainty: Prediction, Action, and the Embodied Mind* (New York: Oxford University Press, 2016).

ever, they *are*—at least until, suddenly, they aren't, and we see that our feeling of "being in control" is an illusion.[15]

Consider our toilets. We have toilets, along with excellent sewer systems and roads, grand buildings, telecommunication networks, and financial markets, all of which advanced worlders take completely for granted. We have them only by any number of fortuitous developments in history, largely in the modern era, including such high points as developments in mathematics, especially the emergence of probability theory and statistical analysis; the rise of data collection in the administrative state (initially so kings could collect taxes); wealth-generating industrialization; the creation of insurance markets, which allow us to pool and manage risks, for homes catching fire, getting sick, and many other calamities.[16] Unless you accept an unlikely historical determinism, those prerequisites for economic development, along with our now comfortable standard of living, simply might not have been. The good efforts of the many who built them came to fruition only with fortune and good timing. We naturally count on what is familiar and mostly unchanging. But stable expectation easily bleeds into a sense of entitlement, in which we act as though we had it all coming, rather than counting ourselves blessed.

The pretense of control spans political opinion. In a right-leaning version, the limits of control almost always thwart social planning (the cure being worse than the disease, with numerous unintended consequences). Yet individuals have magnificent powers to decide their fates and fortunes! We are like gods in dignity, and so must suffer accordingly. Our relative fortunes are more or less deserved: the "loser" is lazy, the "winner" is industrious, hardworking, even courageous and, yes, also "fortunate," but no less deserving of his

15. If our changing climate is not unnerving enough, consider the rich world's shock and amazement that in 2014 Malaysia Airlines MH370 seems to have vanished after taking a sharp turn over Malaysia and Indonesia, out into the vast Indian Ocean. The rich world presumptuously wondered, how could it possibly be that we are not in control of events—not even the event of finding out what happened?
16. For the grand story, see Ian Hacking, *The Emergence of Probability* (Cambridge, U.K.: Cambridge University Press, 1975).

huge share of social resources.[17] After all, we've already got equality of opportunity (because "anyone can make it, if they just work hard enough").[18]

In a left-leaning version, the individual is relatively powerless, with his or her class station and talents determined mostly by arbitrary factors, beginning in early upbringing, with willful effort at self-improvement a marginal influence upon what was settled in the lottery of birth.[19] Yet, it is believed, collective action and social planning can solve nearly every social problem, perhaps with savvy use of markets and "nudge" policies (for example, you're automatically enrolled in health insurance, and can choose to opt out, but probably won't do it).[20] Every social problem being cause for regulation, on pain of collective moral unseriousness, a society is thus responsible for almost everything that happens to anyone.[21]

The key assumption, which is often shared on both sides of the advanced-world aisle, is that, either individually or collectively, we are mainly in control of what happens. When things go south, someone or other (depending) must then be to blame. The concept of control sweeps away the workings of fate and fortune, and we live and argue in the moralistic fiction that any question of responsibility can be settled, pretty much, by deciding who was in control of what.

17. As the old joke goes, the rich man built the log cabin he was born into with his own bare hands. And if the poor weren't born with talent, well, they should have thought of that when they chose their parents.
18. That idea can legitimate unequal outcomes in principle. But the assumptions about control I'm questioning can make it seem that inequality nearly always reflects a difference in effort. The only solution is just to work harder—which guts the ideal of equal opportunity of all but rhetorical meaning.
19. John Rawls's *Theory of Justice* is sometimes read this way, though I myself think he isn't a "luck egalitarian." Justice is about socially created differences, while any further "natural" inequalities are a different matter of unfairness in cosmic fortune.
20. Cass Sunstein and Richard Thaler, *Nudge* (New Haven, Conn.: Yale University Press, 2008).
21. Even liberal philosopher John Rawls was republican enough to speak of "division of labor" between citizens and society. While the left-leaning view in question may de-emphasize personal responsibility because right-leaning types are thought to overemphasize it, its genuine role is often left unclear.

Can the concept of control bear the weight of our blaming? Is the old idea even up to the modern complexity of risk management?

In fact, what is and is not "within one's control" simply isn't well enough defined, or perhaps not even *definable,* so as to rightly mark a general difference in the deservingness of "winners" and "losers." Are we really masters of our fates and fortunes? Certainly not as individuals; we are enabled to take responsibility for ourselves only provided the cooperation of others, starting with our parents and friends. But if cooperation is necessary, is society responsible for everything? Doesn't a lot of major shit just happen?

The surfer answer is that we have less control than we usually think, so we should worry less about placing blame than about extending grace and try to "just be cool." Sure, I have "control" when I raise my arm or steer a car. Yet these are rather special instances, and nothing like a good model for deciding who is responsible and for what in the delicate matters of risk that pervade our lives. I moved my arm to turn the car wheel, but the question of my responsibility is whether or to what degree I could have reasonably expected the pedestrian to be put at risk, with a high enough probability (how high?) of severe enough consequences (how severe?). To these questions, the answers are often unclear—a matter of judgment in which mistakes are easily made.

It's true that people don't do well when they feel "out of control" of their lives and circumstances, without a sense of efficacy. We *can* do what we ought to do, if we indeed ought to do it, as Kant noted. But knowing that intellectually is not the same as the confident know-how of action, which must be seeded, cultivated, and renewed. Beyond making some good choices, a person is carried through the days and weeks by worthy self-given purposes only provided a measure of encouragement and support, which doesn't make a big deal of their obvious shortcomings. Gentle criticism or a friendly reminder can certainly alert one in a foggy or careless moment. Yet it is fair to say that no one is stoked by exacting blaming, in a scolding, interrogation, or smug tounge-lashing, especially not in the good name of "responsibility" or "accountability." (Political officials are another matter; vigorously holding them accountable, in bold protest and sharp challenge, is the raucous music of republican democracy.) People would still be imperfect and sometimes at fault, of necessity: it's only for all the mistakes, misjudgments, lapses, or confusions that grace becomes necessary; otherwise, there'd be nothing to "be cool" about.

If we could give people the benefit of any doubt in the matters of risk that pervade human existence, standing ready to believe that the human being is mainly managing, ultimately just coping and adapting to what fate or fortune just happens to bring, we might actually rise to a less exacting perspective. We'd worry less about who was "in control" and in what ways, going easier on each other. We'd be as understanding with others as we are—or ought to be— with ourselves.[22]

Efficacy Without Control

In discussing "flow," the psychologist Mihaly Csikszentmihalyi disparages what he calls "passive obliteration of the self, a 'going with the flow' Southern California–style."[23] For him, getting into the flow apparently requires one to be rather controlling of one's mental activity: "Unless a person knows how to give order to his or her thoughts, attention will be attracted to whatever is most problematic at the moment. . . . Entropy is the normal state of consciousness— a condition that is neither useful nor enjoyable."

22. The advanced countries already pay for an ambulance to pick up a fallen sky-diver, even if he stupidly didn't double-check his parachute and might have instead gotten his kicks playing chess, saving the public a huge expense. And so maybe, in a posture of extending grace, we'd be even more inclined to share liability for our different fates, to better manage misfortune. That's contrary to "luck egalitarianism," which allows the stupid to suffer if their misfortune is deserved or the result of risks they've chosen.
23. *Flow: The Psychology of Optimal Experience* (New York: Harper & Row, 1990), p. 64.

This is a rather dim view of such lovely pastimes as letting the mind wander, daydreaming, lazing around, and idle resting. Some people of course chronically struggle to get going in a productive direction, even beyond healthy procrastination. Some could really use a regime of mental discipline, with just enough "structure" for healthier habits, at a school or university, church, mosque, or synagogue, a twelve-step program, or the military. But for the fairly well comported, the SoCal style, at its best, is definitely the way to go on the road to flow.

The goal here would be to get and stay "dialed in," which is to say, to allow yourself to become ever more attuned in your activities to your environment, through faithful attention and consistent practice. You become successful as a person—"happy," or in a condition of *eudaimonia,* the ancient Greek term that roughly means "human flourishing"—by being efficacious without undue control. Not by lacking all "control," in a complete lack of composure, but by letting go of any need for it. One can have what others call good "control" in part because, in being attuned, one cares not about it.

Is there a self-help guide to surfer success? Perhaps, in these seven steps.

First, take it easy. Enjoy the fine weather. Watch the waves. Maybe go for a paddle if the waves aren't doing it today. Chillax. For those of a nonaquatic lifestyle, take ample time in leisure, and don't try to do too much. Leave time for becoming attuned to your books or your music, your garden, or the birds in your neighborhood.

Second, accept. Accept your present circumstances. Because nothing interrupts attuned adaption to this coming moment like resisting the fact that one is, for now, where one is. Seek reconciliation. Check feelings of entitlement. Cultivate grace and gratitude.

Third, persist. Get into a nice rhythm. Check the waves daily. Surf around work. In good or bad waves. Eat. Sleep. Relax with a friend or your children. Repeat. For the nonaquatic, persist in learning or in a creative project.

Fourth, focus. Do what is most worth doing. Pass on what is not.

Skip other fine and good activities in order to focus your attention on waves and surfing them.[24]

Fifth, leave time. Don't blow a lot of time in mere entertainment, let alone get yourself tied up in a time-sucking, high-maintenance house, even if you can afford it. Keep the schedule light, so you can be on it when the waves turn on. When the waves are flat, or you're in a creative lull, seize the day to get miscellaneous tasks done efficiently, so as to free up more time for the most worthy activities. Most important, in a world of long workweeks, of e-mail never leaving you alone, of "stacked" schedules and a zillion empty activities performed in the name of a supposedly "full life," the one thing to control is your time. With vigor and virtue, protect it against an out-of-control, money-hungry work culture that cares not about how much you surf, or your quality of life, and that threatens to devour it.

Sixth, with all good wishes of peace for your fellow man and woman, let your watchword be "What are the Joneses to me?" Resist comparing yourself with them, and look away when you do. If they're confused enough to blow their time and stretch their resources on an even bigger house, even pricier cars, and ever more demanding jobs to pay for all this, the proper response is not envy but sympathy. Sadly for them, they aren't fortunate enough to be surfers. If they *are* surfers, they may be confused. And if the surfer Joneses seem to have everything—including enviable regular surf trips to world-class waves, with photographs for you to see regularly on Facebook—well, gosh, I know, that's harder. But maybe just focus on the waves near home and the very good life you have (and check social media a lot less).

Seventh, mix it up. As the seasons change, switch up surf breaks and equipment. In California, when the swells come from the South

24. Csikszentmihalyi comes closer to the best of SoCal style when he recommends "gradual focusing of attention on the opportunities for action in one's environment" (ibid., p. 151). But this needn't involve imposing attitudinal self-discipline. You can check the waves daily mainly because you are super stoked to go surfing. A reminder not to forget should suffice.

Pacific, from mid-spring through mid-fall, you'll probably want to surf the south-facing breaks, and then in winter, with chillier air and water temps, the north-facing breaks. Push yourself a little, so as to keep things interesting. And maybe, so as to constantly progress rather than stagnate, try different surfboard shapes. Each one helps you see the wave slightly differently, so as to take a different, new approach and develop your surfing in a new direction. Try playing a new instrument. Do a new kind of art or craft project. Read a new genre of books.

In sum, then, the surfer wisdom for success as a person is this: Take it easier. Accept. Persist. Focus. Leave time. Don't compare. And mix things up.

The way of the surfer thus is to be a free, effective agent of sporting actions, planning his or her life according to truly worthy purposes. It is to feel efficacious in one's being, for knowing how to go with the flow and knowing that one knows. A bit of planning is needed, so that the limbs get moving in the direction of the beach, and the body paddles into the waves, regularly. That won't call for any very self-preoccupied "self-control," in some regime of mental self-discipline—unless the waves are terrible on a cold morning and you have to "force yourself" to get out there. (I tell myself I'm permitted to come in from the water after I catch any three waves— after which I rarely want to stop surfing.) Nor must the surfer body be controlled in the gym, to stay in shape. That also comes easily, as long as you persist. When you're chasing waves for hours on end, you become fit automatically as a welcome side effect. Most surfers don't need to be persuaded to get off the couch; they're already game, even desperate to get out there. Surfing is *enthralling,* and not easily forgotten, so no heavy hand is needed to "order" the surfer's psyche against supposed entropic tendencies toward "chaos," as Csikszentmihalyi suggests. The order comes naturally, with the know-how of one's pursuit. If you leave the surfer mind unattended, free to imagine and wander, it flows naturally to thoughts of *waves* and *surfing them,* which is all to the good for being ever more attuned.

Even stokedness waxes and wanes, of course. Being faithful in practice means firmly accepting the ebb and flow of effort and spontaneity. It means waiting, as one waits during a lull in the waves, trusting that another wave is coming. Faithful practice, focused on something worthy, is the surfer's way of risk management, of "hedging" against the winds of timing, changing weather, and spells of bummedness, like any good investor. Just leave ample time in one's definition of the "successful" venture and then . . . wait. Persist. Maybe you were unlucky; you got skunked in Indo one season when you showed up on the wrong weeks. Well, okay, that seriously sucks, but, you know, go back the next season and the next. Keep at it. Persist. There will be good luck and bad luck, and the thing to do, in either case, is accept what has happened and flow *through* the different moments, in each case doing the next right thing.

That is how to "create your own luck"—with no magic, no powers to control the future through "intention" in some more mystical sense. Simply persist in attuned adaptation. Focus on something worthy, and stick to a rough plan for its realization, while staying open to its gradual refinement or its deeper reconceptualization. Trust your noticing. The very fact that you have this plan or intention will lead you to notice opportunities for its advancement that otherwise wouldn't have caught your interest, or that you wouldn't have as eagerly taken up if you hadn't firmly adopted this objective as a priority. Plans or intentions by their very nature focus the mind, coordinate action, and direct the energies over time, with no further "effort," no further "trying." So until you revise your intention—for what had better be an especially good reason—you'll automatically be watching for opportunities chance might bring, adapting your means and sub-plans so as to avail yourself of them.[25] You just take each step as it comes, and an incomplete plan gradually comes together, before being completed in action. Things come together

25. This is why making a "bucket list" works: now a priority, taking a cruise to Alaska, say, isn't just a nice idea, which you might otherwise have dropped in view of the costs and complications of doing it. It's a priority, because it's on the list, and so you accept the costs and work around the complications, looking for opportunities to actually go.

as a consequence of flowing adaptation to each of many chance happenings, which are largely beyond your control. People may call you "a master of your fate." From your own perspective, success comes precisely by giving up the aim of control and staying attuned, even in wait.

Sartre warns against the "bad faith" in self-limiting beliefs, and rightly so. If I thought my abilities as a surfer were now completely settled, this would be a *decision* not to progress further, not a mere *observation* about how the world is or is going to be. "Even assertions such as 'I am ugly,' 'I am stupid,' *etc.*, are by nature anticipations [or intentions]," Sartre explains. "We are not dealing here with the pure establishment of my ugliness but with the apprehension of the coefficient of adversity which is presented by women or by society to my enterprises."[26] Whatever the societal messages, and whatever the surfer Joneses do in middle age, my view about my future can simply be "we shall see." I can hereby decide, today, to keep practicing, in hopes of further progress, and with no view at all, favorable or unfavorable, about how good a surfer I will have been on my last legs. If I accept my lack of control over the future, but stay faithful, I'm willing to be surprised by what fortune might bring.

None of this means one should be *ambitious,* despite all the cultural stress about "killing it," getting ahead, leaving the competitors in the dust. Efficacy requires no such thing. It is good to stretch oneself a bit, in order to keep things interesting, to mix things up. For that, change and steady learning can be quite sufficient, without accomplishments that would wow the Joneses.

Descartes recommends ambition and Sartre agrees (quoting him approvingly): "the will is infinite," and "it is necessary to try to conquer ourselves rather than fortune."[27] But must our relation to fortune be so adversarial? Am I not fortunate already? Am I not myself

26. *Being and Nothingness,* p. 592.
27. Ibid., p. 620.

already? Surely I'll still be so in the future, more or less, until I keel over. What of myself is there to "conquer," beyond doing what is worthy of my time and efforts, such as staying faithful in my surfing practice?

So we aren't "condemned" to choose after all, in the onerous sense of having to decide our whole being in every moment "down to the slightest detail," as Sartre says. A person can just go along with the flow of experience, directing it here and there, for worthy purposes, without *willing* and *owning* and *pushing* the world in one direction or another. A person can ease up on the striving willfulness that denies us presence and still be effectual, for being more present in steady action.

The Easy Road

The Buddhist also recommends faithful attention and consistent, trusting practice, so as to be harmoniously related to one's environment. For many Buddhists, especially in the ascetic traditions, this comes with extraordinary ambition: to abandon all desire, along with the very idea of the distinct self. Yet it's fair to say that most surfers, in all their lusty leering and quasi-pornographic attention to waves, will not be down for the hard road to Buddhist enlightenment.

The surfer is akin to neither the Zen master nor the Stoic sage. For the Stoics, the happy person adjusts his or her desires to his or her circumstances. As Epictetus explains, "Do not seek to have events happen as you want them to, but instead want them to happen as they do happen, and your life will go well."[28] Or as Siddhartha Gautama—the Buddha—advised, in a remarkable convergence of Eastern and Western wisdom, one should not desire what will not be attained.[29]

28. *The Handbook of Epictetus,* trans. N. P. White (Indianapolis: Hackett, 1983).
29. This is Gautama's basic organizing principle according to A. J. Bahm, *Philosophy of the Buddha* (New York: Harper, 1958).

That ain't easy, and Gautama, perhaps unlike the Stoics, appreciated how difficult it can be to never desire what will not be attained. For, in order to stop, one will have to desire this. But won't *that* desire, of a higher order—*the desire to stop desiring what will not be attained*—often go unsatisfied, itself bringing frustration? The reformed addict has cravings she'd rather not feel. The tragically handicapped surfer has longing daydreams of being in the water, his equanimity spoiled in disappointment. Desires come unbidden and can be hard to shake. For the Stoics, changing them is as easy as redirecting one's attention, to revise one's judgment of whether desire is appropriate, with desire following suit. Gautama offers a more accommodating solution. The thing to do when a frustrated desire persists—"the middle way"—is to simply accept that much unhappiness: to be as happy as you can be by being willing to be as unhappy as you are.[30]

For the ascetic Buddhists, this is but a temporary fix. Ultimately, one seeks the abnegation of *all* desire, especially any desire for sex. The problem is desire's very source: the idea of a persisting "you," a distinct "self," who wants this or that and is stressed about not getting it. For the Buddhist, the "self" is in fact an illusion, and the hard road to nirvana, in four or eight or however many difficult steps, strives to unmask the egoistic fiction. With no "I," the "I want" is unintelligible. With no "I," there's no "I was wronged," no "I'm not getting my due," and so no occasion for stressful anger that deadens one's compassion for others or one's appreciation of natural beauty. Then there's simply *no occasion* to try to be happy in unhappy frustration, and no longer any need for Gautama's "middle way" of moderation. There is only a state of bliss, full-on nirvana, in radical self-transcendence. But the egoistic illusion *is* very persistent. In the meantime, as Gautama says, I can graciously accept my condition as the unfortunate condition it is, as long as it lasts. All is impermanent. The wind flips directions. The tide ebbs and flows. I can simply wait. Yet for perfectionistic Buddhists, I am *waiting* for

30. Ibid., p. 19.

a radical self-transcendence in persistent meditative practice. I am waiting to fully realize that, after all, I have no self.[31]

The surfer is happier in his or her own skin. The surfer's condition isn't so full of suffering that he or she would wish to wholly transcend it. It is certainly good to transcend the usual self-preoccupation. The easy road to this begins from the surfer's very love of waves and surfing them, which attunes him or her to something beyond him- or herself. What must be abandoned is not the self who is the surfer but any reluctance about self-acceptance that would inhibit the love of waves from organizing one's life. One can happily stay oneself, and so maybe one wouldn't try for self-abandonment even if the hard road were easier than it is.[32]

If some enterprising surfer is game for diligent meditation, in a constant state of mindful self-awareness, or in intense concentration on some fixed point, okay, fine. I say try it, brother—but do count the cost. One will invariably spend less time in life absorbed in the dynamics of waves, maybe with less stoke. Perfectionistic striving may leave one less grateful for one's being such as it is. And isn't caring so much about perfecting one's virtue itself rather self-focused? If others will benefit indirectly but eventually, and they are what matters, why not pay more attention to them from the start? I should share a wave, from *fairness to others* or *respect for them*. Is this by reason of *my* own personal virtue, my *own* happiness, rather than *theirs*? Shouldn't the other guy enjoy a wave just for *his* own sake? In a human condition that is often ugly and unjust, time is short, and there are better uses of one's energies than to try to perfect one's own character. You can serve or start a charity,

31. Miri Albahari explains how coming to know this might be possible in "Insight Knowledge of No Self in Buddhism: An Epistemic Analysis," *Philosophers' Imprint* 14, no. 21 (July 2014), at http://quod.lib.umich.edu/cgi/p/pod/dod-idx/insight-knowledge-of-no-self-in-buddhism-an-epistemic.pdf?c=phimp;idno=3521354.0014.021.

32. To switch religions, could the surfer even countenance heavenly "bliss" by a quick and easy rapture from Earth, without real water and waves? In an eternal banquet, forever eating and stuffed, never surfing in real water, with a real body to be in tune with?

not in order to *be a good person,* but simply to *help out,* to *give back,* just for others' sake. In fact, giving up the control required for self-perfection might itself benefit others. When one is less exacting with oneself, it gets easier to extend grace to others as well. Easier to accept the human's mixed-up predicament, taking people as they are, more or less, relaxing any hope, even any wish, of their perfection beyond the good enough, whether in Buddhist enlightenment or Christian sanctification. Even if grace comes freely, to "be ye perfect," as Jesus said, takes a lot of work.

So in the surfer's ethic, instead of striving for a personal or spiritual best, you should just "be cool," as in "Just be cool, bro. Don't be an asshole. Enjoy. But share the waves."

Love's Risk

In giving up control, even over his or her doting love of waves, the surfer acquiesces in the whims of fortune and chance, despite risks of genuine frustration. If the surfer you are speaking to doesn't quite seem to be paying attention, or keeps losing the conversational thread, he or she may be suddenly awash in dreams of waves and surfing them, which descend upon the mind with overwhelming force and vivacity, at any time of the day. When the wind has suddenly clocked into a favorable direction, and there is building swell, and the tides are good over the next few hours, the surfer who is suddenly sixteen years old again, and for the moment without a care in the world—other than for *waves* and *surfing them*—is enthralled but not contented. With work to do, and the business of the day, and a bunch of other things in the way, the surfer may, like a teenager in a forlorn, love-struck state, become majorly bummed. The waves can go flat for weeks. Or maybe they *were* epic on the better tides, or lighter winds, which you missed. (In Bruce Brown's *Endless Summer,* the surfer world travelers were repeatedly told upon arrival, "Yeah, you should have been here yesterday.") The waves can turn on at the Worst Possible Time, and while you can try to keep your options open, by taking a flexible job and deep pay cut, you invariably live in anxious suspension upon the whims of the gods of wind, swell, and tide, who *may* deem you worthy of being blessed with waves when your time is free. Or not, in which case you'll certainly hear all about how freaking good the waves were on the best tides, which you missed, in order to sit in a meeting with an overbearing boss, or under a dentist's drill. With all the bizarro global weather patterns we've been having lately, with nature becoming ever less predictable, you can see why the surfer might get a bit edgy, and why, instead of virtue, the surfer would try yoga or, more often, drink beer.

Having long ago staked his or her whole fortune on nature's caprice, the surfer mainly gets used to frustration. Here the Stoic might press: Should you then be so dependent upon nature for happiness? Beyond the euphoric rush when it all comes together, staking one's whole self on the ocean's caprices may bring frustration as often as contentment. Is not surfing an "addiction" one might be wise to let go of?

Drug addicts often do come to this sort of realization. Almost no surfers do. And why should a person who is fortunate enough to love surfing stand ready to give up that very love? Why be so circumspect? Why not double down on good fortune, raising one's stake, even on what fate might finally take away?

Before the Stoics, Plato and Aristotle worried that the flourishing life is subject to fortune. Our very moral character, a constituent of happiness, is subject to luck, in events beyond our control. Poor, poor Oedipus, thwarted at every turn. Surely he fared worse as a person for having killed his father and married his mother, however inadvertently. Wouldn't his life have gone better, even in virtue, if such awful things hadn't happened, because the gods were kinder to him, even if he'd never have known the difference? If so, then happiness has *objective* conditions, which are beyond one's knowledge and one's control.

The Stoics for the first time rejected that thought: a person can be immune even to fortune. By my simple act of will, I can pay attention to one thing rather than another, which changes what I judge to be true or worthy of doing or feeling or wanting. But the surfer really is fortunate to love surfing. The addict is unfortunate for being controlled by a desire that is *unworthy* of a person's time in life. The surfer is genuinely happy, precisely for being attached to things of real beauty and importance. And if that means being unable to adapt with equanimity to anything that might happen, such is the burden of loving devotion. Love is surely part of a good life. Loving attachment to something beyond oneself is inherently risky. But detachment is also costly, for what one gives up in loving less.

Plato and Aristotle agreed that relationships were risky for happiness; they differed only over what risks to take.[33] Running for office can bring personal ruin. Even friendships are betrayed occasionally. For Plato, the risks are too great; one should play it safe by retreating into solitary contemplation. A few surfers do bail on society for a cheap tropical place with reliable waves. Yet most side with Aristotle, who thought that the risks of friendship and even political engagement could be taken and managed well enough, even if things occasionally go south. Aristotle never knew the hurried confusion of "advanced" society, where people have supposedly become so smart. While the modern surfer might *try* to take it easy, if society is ever more hurried and confused, ever less sane, it is a fair question whether one would be wise to be more cautious, as Plato suggested. But surfers just aren't *that* worried. Aristotle celebrated the joys of friendship as well worth the slight risks of betrayal. Likewise, surfing a wave is so wonderful as to be well worth trying to manage the mild risks of loving it, wholeheartedly, irrevocably— even with no happy way back to invulnerability.

Yet if the surfer must suffer in attachment, the human condition is not so terrible for those who persist in wave chase. Depending on the year, the waves can get good a lot. Often enough, mundane imperfection relaxes, and on the good days or waves the surfer

---

33. On this theme, see Martha Nussbaum, *The Fragility of Goodness: Luck and Ethics in Greek Tragedy and Philosophy* (Cambridge, U.K.: Cambridge University Press, 1986).

reaches a state of steady attunement, a state of having found the flow and, for a perfect stretch of moments, stayed there. And if days of earthly rapture come only occasionally, the dreaming memories, of waves and surfing them, do tend to last.

It would be an exaggeration to say that the whole meaning of human existence could be contained in one moment, in a single act of riding a wave. Yet it is *as though* the whole meaning of human existence can be contained in one moment, in a single act of riding a wave.

In surfing's best moments, things really can feel that profound, that intense, that wonderful, that complete. Those moments really might just be the whole meaning of life if they would last. The main trouble with the human condition is that they don't. As so often, joy is complete, but also fleeting. Surfer self-transcendence can come relatively easily, by hitting the waves after work. But even the stoked surfer will have to paddle out again, hoping for flow, and catch another wave.

Part Two

Metaphysics

4

Flow

The loss of the sense of a self separate from
the world is sometimes accompanied by a
feeling of union with the environment.

—Mihaly Csikszentmihalyi, *Flow*

A SURFER GOES ALONG with a flow, finding a sublimely beautiful
relationship with a wave. So talk of "going with the flow" is not just
a soggy metaphor. Surfers quite literally do it, many of them regularly, day after day, year after year, from youth through retirement.
For the most fortunate, it's the main way they've spent their limited
time under the sun.

Going with the flow is said to be good for anyone. We'd take
things a little easier. Blow off petty frustrations. Let go of anxious
striving. Focus on what's most worthy of doing. On the best days,
we'd find ourselves living like a surfer surfs a wave—absorbed in
our activities with skillful good timing and fluent ease, succeeding
gracefully. Ideally, we'd come into this blessed state naturally and
often, arriving at the Greek's state of *eudaimonia,* a condition of
happy, human flourishing.

So "being in the flow" seems to have something to do with a person's life going well. But what is it for a person's life to go well? And
what then is "being in the flow" such that a person's life goes better
than it otherwise would?

Psychologists often treat "flow" as simply a kind of enjoyment. It
contributes to our happiness as a particularly good state of experi-

ence, a way things go well in one's inner life. The influential psychologist Mihaly Csikszentmihalyi calls it "optimal experience," meaning the occasions on which "we . . . feel in control of our actions, masters of our own fate . . . a sense of exhilaration, a deep sense of enjoyment that is long cherished and that becomes a landmark in memory for what life should be like."[1]

Here psychologists seem to have forgotten the ancient wisdom of Plato and Aristotle. Being happy, doing well as a person, can go beyond one's felt experience. Surfing is of course enjoyable, but "being in the flow" for the surfer is a way of transcending the self, in a virtuous exercise of skill that relates one to what lies beyond.

The Elusive Flow

How to live? This is a question of know-how. So we might answer by looking to the expert at the peak of his or her performance—the top surfer, world-class heart surgeon, pro athlete, or chess master. On a good day, the chess master in a "lightning match" (of super-quick play) just *sees* the next right move and does it, straightaway. He has no need of any very self-conscious self-regulation according to the game's rules or the novice's strategies. He'd do worse if he thought very much about why this or that move is appropriate, turning his eyes on himself and his performance, except in correcting for a mishap. He's all in, engaged and *present,* intuitively sensing the space of possible moves, sliding the rook or bishop in a flash of insight, with a snap judgment, which he may or may not be able to articulate. He's *full on* attuned to the game.[2]

If one can be an expert in games, sports, or special tasks, is there such a thing as being expert in life? It sure can seem so. Behold the

---

1. *Flow,* p. 3.
2. Hubert L. Dreyfus, "Overcoming the Myth of the Mental: How Philosophers Can Profit from the Phenomenology of Everyday Expertise," *Proceedings and Addresses of the American Philosophical Association* 79 (2005), pp. 47–63; and "The Return of the Myth of the Mental," *Inquiry* 50, no. 4 (2007), pp. 352–65.

fortunate souls who live by their own purposes, who seem almost *constantly* enthralled, switched on, going from strength to strength, living in zesty fascination with one thing after the next. (Think, for example, of the space and energy and auto entrepreneur Elon Musk.)

And then of course there are the rest of us, which is to say, most people, most of the time, who are mainly trying to get by. This is not for lack of tips in living. If you haven't already tried thinking kinder thoughts about your boss, and practicing something you're good at for only ten thousand hours, with regular prayer or meditation or deep breathing, then you could also make sure you eat mostly plants, that you stay hydrated (note: in and out of vigorous exercise, because hydration is really important), and that you shift around in your work chair rather than sitting still, which actually burns a surprising amount of calories (in which case there's yet another reason for you to be thinner).

Much of the advice is well taken, especially the encouragement to "mindfulness." So if you find yourself longing for the Joneses' gorgeous new car, their huge ocean-view house, and their amazing, twice-yearly vacations, simply be aware of your current feelings, without judging yourself for *comparing yourself to the Joneses yet again,* for *being so distracted,* and for *judging yourself yet again.* Just be aware of your present state of experience and affirm yourself anyway, with kindness, as your mother did, or should have. There are other good ways of training one's attention as well. It's good to stay in the moment, dwell on something of beauty, perform a kind act, or focus on a worthy cause. Yet all the thought regulation is a lot of work, and there's now even more you can do that you aren't doing to find the flow. Which can all begin to feel effortful—rather like the striving you thought you'd somehow avoid.

Once one is in the flow, one is assured, things will come easily. And if easy happiness would last, it certainly would justify the efforts at attaining such a blessed condition. But while you may possibly get there sooner or later, with enough discipline and striving, it may be *much* later, and then only temporarily. The unfortunate fact of life is that the state of flow is hard to come by and, once attained, fleeting.

This is both frustrating and philosophically interesting. What is "flow" such that it is the sort of thing that would be fleeting, rather than steady like a strong stream? And how can we manage the ebbs so as to find flow, for once or yet again?

Controlling Consciousness

As noted in the last chapter, Csikszentmihalyi sees the mind as prone to "chaos." Yet for him achieving an orderly state of flow is possible with enough mental self-discipline.[3] Our modern discontentment, he explains, lies in our vacillation between mindless boredom on the one hand and anxious alienation on the other—between the passive pleasures of TV watching and feeling anxious, strained, stretched in yet another day of powerless toil at the office. When we find a stable middle between these twin evils, life feels meaningful. This eludes us, Csikszentmihalyi claims, only because we fail to "control consciousness." If we did just take control of our thoughts in self-directed activities, we'd find the flow state of "optimal experience" and stay there. Whether in playing chess, skiing, painting, getting a degree, or starting a business, we'd become focused on interesting challenges, for our own purposes, without external pressure or distraction, with time flying, in deep enjoyment.

As suggested in the last chapter, the Stoics broke from Plato and Aristotle and for the first time put our happiness under a person's control.[4] But they didn't assume psychic virtue would necessarily bring enjoyment, or that just anyone could attain *eudaimonia;* many

3. In *Flow,* taking "control" over one's "consciousness" is a major theme that appears on pp. 3, 5, 8, 9, 16, 28, 124, 127, 170, and 213.
4. Kant broke from the ancients by divorcing morality from happiness. He still followed the Stoics by putting our "moral worth" under our control, as a matter of our motives, rather than the outcomes of our actions, which may or may not be under our control. For Kant, this is part of our freedom. Sartre was a Kantian in that regard.

of us are not born capable of the sage's virtue, or not well enough raised. In Csikszentmihalyi's neo-Stoic perspective, happiness is available to everyone, because happy "flow" is nothing more than a heightened *experiential* state, which is internally induced.[5] The happy aren't simply fortunate for their mental constitution, for their blessed genetic endowment; they demonstrate what almost anyone can attain in choosing to discipline one's attention. So when you aren't quite flourishingly happy—because you're all flowed out, in a bummed spell or a funk—well, that is in a way your own fault, or at least your responsibility. You have no one to blame but yourself. If you happen to be lacking in the virtue department, you'd do well to shape up.

Csikszentmihalyi goes so far as to say that "being in control of the mind means that literally anything that happens can be a source of joy." Surely he can't mean *literally anything*. Including counting blades of carpet nap on one's bedroom floor? Or pushing Sisyphus's weighty boulder up the hill, yet *again*—in a state not of willful defiance but of joyful delirium? I guess one could find a pencil sharpener fascinating while on LSD. Flow states make you feel good, and the "flow junkie" can get more of that particular feeling by juicing up the brain with feel-good neurochemicals. But if "flow" is just an induced experiential state, the question is how it differs from a mere trip. How does the flow experience differ from drug use or erogenous zone stimulation? Is it simply a question of a neurococktail delivery system?

It's true that "flow" comes *from within*, by controlling one's thoughts, instead of from an external bodily intervention. Csikszentmihalyi adds that flow comes along with "meeting challenges and developing skills," which lead to growth and add "complexity" to

5. Csikszentmihalyi mentions "a feeling of union with the environment" but still puts this as a *feeling* rather than a real relationship (ibid., p. 63). He also says the flow experience is good, not in "an absolute sense," but only because it makes "life more rich, intense, and meaningful," increasing "the strength and complexity of the self," albeit subject to "more inclusive social criteria" (ibid., p. 70). Perhaps this isn't strict "experientialism," but it also doesn't clearly cite the need for a real, attuned connection between the self and reality.

the self.[6] But still, why would it matter how an experiential state is produced? Maybe flow that comes from within is healthier, more sustainable, and even better for your productivity than cocaine or caffeine or Adderall. But then the question is still one of drug choice. LSD in micro-doses evidently works creative wonders for programmers in Silicon Valley.[7] Are we to conclude that *judicious* drug use, along with work, could equally bring success and lasting happiness?

When Csikszentmihalyi attempts to clarify, he tells us that the internal complexity produced by work and virtue is an "escape *forward* from current reality, whereas stimulants like drugs lead backward." But why the need for escape? Healthy psychic order surely depends on complexifying activity, forward-looking planning, and the like, in some measure. But, apparently, staying in a flow state to him requires escaping the present. But why again can't one just contentedly *be*? Isn't being in the flow partly a matter of *being*, of being present with something beyond oneself?

Happiness in Attunement

So being in the flow state is supposed to make a person's life go better by optimizing the quality of his or her felt consciousness. This poses the ancient question of happiness: When, in general, does a person's life go better rather than worse? What does a good life consist of?

According to "experientialism," the quality of a person's life depends *simply* on the quality of his or her experience. The quality of a person's experience—even when illusory—is *all that matters* for how well or badly his or her life goes. That's the theory. So if a

6. *Good Business: Leadership, Flow, and the Making of Meaning* (New York: Penguin Press, 2004), chap. 3, sec. 5.

7. "For best results," one expert explains, you micro-dose "every fourth day, taking the drug in the morning and then sticking to your usual daily routine." See Andrew Leonard, "How LSD Microdosing Became the Hot New Business Trip," *Rolling Stone*, Nov. 20, 2015, http://www.rollingstone.com/culture/features/how-lsd-microdosing-became-the-hot-new-business-trip-20151120#ixzz3unLY6Koq.

virtual reality machine is completely convincing, you shouldn't care, in respect to your own happiness, whether the experiences are real or machine generated.

Surfers do know something about flow, and it isn't simply how to give themselves pleasure, by means of riding a wave. They certainly wouldn't be indifferent to the distinction between actual surfing and virtual surfing. For it's not as though the surfing act would be of exactly the same value, in exactly the same way, if you *merely* experienced it on a super-convincing experience machine, in which you'd be having these amazing wave-riding, going-with-the-flow experiences, exactly like the ones you'd be having if you were actually surfing, except that you're really sitting in a La-Z-Boy, in dry clothes, with electrodes taped to the skull, while surfer-scientists work the brain controls so as to ensure top-quality waves and radical maneuvering. You wouldn't tell the difference, but there would *be* a difference in how well your life is going. Likewise, surely a super-convincing orgasm machine would not be just as good as real sex if the two were experientially indistinguishable. Surely someone who *only* had convincing virtual sex would be missing out on something, because it makes at least *some* difference, and often a profound one, if a real person is included, such that a relationship is being expressed or deepened.[8]

Surfing has superb experiential flow qualities. You often surf better if you think less and let the surfing come, maybe coaching yourself with "Okay, don't get bogged down in technicalities; just go with the flow." When things are really coming together in a session or over a week, the flow experience comes on in full force. You surf your best without trying, doing fluid, radical turns, which start feeling automatic, as though you are watching them just happen. Time seems to slow. You feel open, connected, empathetic, and yet effectual, in riding along with the physical liquid flow that is a breaking

---

8. And so wouldn't such a person still be a virgin? A mere virtual surfer would not be a surfer. Like real sex, surfing is an exercise of skill, which requires contact with an external reality, as I explain below.

wave. Those times of peak attunement are also fleeting. No less important are the ordinary days, in ordinary waves, with all the mellow and harmonious feelings, the sheer fun and beauty of the deed, the pleasantness of being immersed in salty air, a wispy breeze, and glassy, gently shifting, luminously reflecting seas. "It's good just to get wet" is what surfers say. You need it, often if not daily, to feel sane and stay stoked.

Such enjoyments aren't bare, raw sensations, like a dull pain or melancholy mood, except of nice experiential quality. They are *of* or *about* something real beyond the surfer's mental states. Surfers don't surf *just* for the fun of it, for the sake of pleasing mental states; they surf as an end in itself, "for surfing's sake," which is to say for the sake of what is intrinsically wonderful about it, for the sake of what all of its pleasures are ultimately of or about. What's really wonderful about surfing, beyond the elation, ease in physical exhaustion, and good existential vibes, is that a person is actually *in the relationship of adaptive attunement,* a relation of harmony in change, which all this subjective consciousness takes as its object. The enjoyment, in a word, is good because it is *true.* It matters that you are *really* surfing in flowing water and not just thinking or dreaming about surfing and enjoying the wet fantasy. You're attunedly related to an objective liquid physical reality that is beyond you, beyond your control.

Which isn't to dismiss the virtual as unimportant. If virtual surfing ever gets awesome, I'll of course want to try it. The virtual experiences would have their own value, and maybe their own reality as virtual.[9] If one were forced to choose between a miserable life of surfing crappy waves in physical reality and spending time on a seriously epic experience machine, I suspect many surfers would differ on the reality/quality trade-off. The relative purists would opt

9. The eminent philosopher David Chalmers, who has become quite good at Pokémon, takes this view of the virtual: "Virtual reality is a sort of genuine reality, and what goes on in virtual reality is truly real." See "The Virtual and the Real," MS, or this excerpt at http://www.abc.net.au/radionational/programs/philosopherszone /the-value-of-virtual-worlds-david-chalmers/7677304.

for real surfing, the relative hedonists virtual surfing. Or suppose you found out that your whole life had been lived on an experience machine, and you couldn't be very confident that life would be tolerable if you unplugged. (In *The Matrix,* a movie that poses the trade-off between reality and quality, Neo, our hero, chooses the virtual and gains in code mastery and control over the virtual reality, in comparison to life in non-virtual reality that completely sucks.) Then you might be wise to be conservative: maybe don't mess with the good gig you've got already, and so stick with virtual surfing, even if surfing in real water would be good as well.

The problem is not entirely hypothetical, and it has only become more pressing since the philosopher Robert Nozick first posed the question in the 1970s, as one of whether one would rationally hook up to an "experience machine."[10] Now with all the temptations online, where we spend inordinate hours absorbed in Things Awesome elsewhere, our surge of remote consciousness makes it harder than ever to be present in one's body, in one's physical environment, in this room, or in this café, or with this person. Unsurprisingly, we're all having a bit of trouble staying attuned to non-virtual reality, in life and in our politics.

The value of surfing, in real water, means only that these are genuine conflicts of value. There is a real balance to strike between quality and reality, and a pretty good reason to put down the smart phone and go surfing, in order to be *wet* in liquid reality.

But if the virtual can be real as virtual, isn't that real enough? How would it differ from real real, non-virtual reality, and what turns on the difference? The answer, in part, is that virtual surfing on a machine just isn't *surfing,* the skilled activity, which requires a bodily engagement with liquid reality.

Suppose you're on a flow machine and the experiences are pre-programmed. Then you aren't really *in* the flow; you're merely a passive viewer, as though watching a startling movie. But now suppose the machine allows you to be actively engaged, interacting with and

10. *Anarchy, State, and Utopia* (New York: Basic Books, 1974), pp. 42–45.

changing your flow of experiences, like working a joystick. Then you might be exercising a skill, as though playing a video game, and maybe you are flowing through the routines and climbing the levels. But the skilled activity in question still won't be that of wave surfing. The game play may be real as virtual, but you ain't surfing—not the skilled activity, which is essentially a bodily interaction with the non-virtual world in its liquid physicality.

Doing well in a skillful activity—in speaking a language fluently, in having a fascinating conversation, in flowing between oncoming pedestrians on a crowded street, in surfing with clean lines and turns—is *by its very nature* a way of being related to the world beyond one's head.

Why so? Because you wouldn't count as "doing well" in surfing, or in weight lifting, or in bike riding, if this was merely your experience on some dream machine. The skill of surfing has to be *exercised* to be *exercised well*. And it just isn't exercised, well or badly, when you aren't getting wet in water, attunedly moving the body, based on your ongoing perception of your changing wave environment. So if flow is just a way of doing a skilled activity well, being in the flow must be a relation to something beyond oneself. And so experientialism about flow must be mistaken: flow just isn't all in the head.

I suspect psychologists focus on the experiential quality of flow due to the lingering influence of late-eighteenth-century utilitarianism. As first proposed by Jeremy Bentham, the English jurist, philosopher, and social reformer, happiness is a matter of having pleasure and avoiding pain, and nothing more. Any pleasure will do. The "lower" pleasures (of warmth, play, food, sex, and so on) count as much as any other. "Quantity of pleasure being equal, pushpin [a game of darts] is as good as poetry," Bentham famously said. This flatters the surfer who is not fond of books. Yet the higher/lower dichotomy also just doesn't fit the pleasures of surfing. They aren't the "higher," intellectualized pleasures of reading a novel or a poem or a philosophical treatise. They also aren't akin to the "low" pleasures of scarfing a cheeseburger, either. The pleasures of surfing are somewhere in the middle, like the pleasures of jazz improvisation or fine cooking.

After a strict upbringing under Bentham's teachings, John Stuart Mill hoped to show that a hedonic utilitarianism is not so beneath human dignity as to be "worthy only of swine" as it can seem. To Mill, Bentham's mistake was to discount the "higher" pleasures: "There is no known Epicurean theory of life which does not assign to the pleasures of the intellect, of the feelings and imagination, and of the moral sentiments, a much higher value as pleasures than to those of mere sensation."[11] So Mill placed the pleasures of poetry and intellectual contemplation categorically above such mere "lower" pleasures as warmth, play, food, and sex. Better, as he put it, to be a human dissatisfied than a pig satisfied, to be Socrates dissatisfied than a fool satisfied, and, I presume, to be an angst-ridden existentialist philosopher than a contented non-reflective surfer.

Is this just elitism? Mill thinks not. Any "competent judge," he says, would have a "decided preference" for the higher over the lower. The people who "addict themselves to inferior pleasures," such as the pleasures of surfing, simply don't know what they are missing. They aren't "susceptible to both classes of pleasure," so, you see, they don't "ever knowingly and calmly" prefer the lower. It's simply a matter of surfers not learning the pleasures of reading books, that is, the unwashed's lack of exposure to the finer things.

To which the surfer will respond, yeah, actually no; that's definitely wrong. To take myself as a counterexample, I enjoy both surfing and philosophy immensely, and I wouldn't necessarily give up surfing if I were forced to choose between them. I firmly prefer a lot of both, intermingled, with a flexible schedule. The thought of giving up either one for the other feels less like a "deliberate preference" expressive of happiness than an existential crisis. I'm glad to have philosophy in case I become injured or aged and incapable of surfing. I'm also banking on surfing if a head injury leaves me unable

11. "Utilitarianism" (1863), in *Utilitarianism and Other Essays* (New York: Penguin Classics, 1987), p. 279.

to do philosophy. I have no plan if or when I become unable to do either. (I hope fate will spare me that terrible situation.)

It's odd that Mill defended hedonism at all. If a "decided preference" has authority in the matter, why not just say that happiness is a matter of getting what one prefers? This became the standard view in economics (on which Mill had great influence). Happiness, called "utility," is just a matter of getting what you want, of having your preferences satisfied. Even today this view is often confused with hedonism (see a lot of social science), but the two are very different.[12] Although having a desire fulfilled might be the cause of pleasure, this view implies that happiness is not generally a matter of good experience. Suppose you have a nice conversation with a stranger on a train, and as she exits for her stop, you find yourself wanting her to do well in her life. Even if you never heard from her again, if she does in fact prosper, you will have got what you wanted. Your preference would be logically "satisfied" (the preferred state of affairs obtains), but without knowing "satisfaction" in experience.

But this means that a bare "preference" can be for *anything*, much of which may have little to do with the person whose happiness is in question. Say I prefer that the number of stars in the galaxy be even. If it turned out without my knowledge that the number *is* even, it doesn't seem that *my* life goes better for the world's being as I preferred. Or had the stranger from the train instead suffered a horrible accident, your desire for her prosperity would not have been met, but *your* life wouldn't have gone any worse had you never received the news.

Even when a preference concerns a person's own life, it may not seem entirely relevant. If a previously dedicated surfer only wanted to stay home and count blades of carpet nap in his bedroom, the satisfaction of *that* desire wouldn't necessarily count as good for him. If he refused to leave the house, the poor guy's surfer breth-

---

12. My discussion that follows closely tracks Derek Parfit's famous appendix, "What Makes Someone's Life Go Best," in *Reasons and Persons* (Oxford: Oxford University Press, 1984).

ren would be more apt to worry about sudden mental illness than view him as flourishingly happy for doing exactly what he wanted. A surfer, of all people, should know what he's missing.

So one can see why Plato and Aristotle took happiness to be an objective condition. The good life is made up of *goods,* things like a person's character, health, longevity, success in her projects, quality of relationships, and quality of experience. These elements are objectively valuable for the person who has them, quite aside from his or her beliefs or desires. Even felt pleasure is not of unqualified value. If I take secret satisfaction in the news that a hated colleague has fallen into a terrible illness, the "improper" pleasure of schadenfreude wouldn't make my life go better (even if I seem "way too happy").

The ancients never asked why one should strive to be happy in the first place. It is a question worth asking: Why not forget about yourself and your "happiness"? Just seek the goods that bring happiness, and so do what's most worth doing, with happiness coming along as a by-product. Aristotle did say that human flourishing "supervenes" upon, or "comes along top" of, the pursuit of something else. As Joseph Butler, the eighteenth-century bishop, theologian, and philosopher, developed the point, if I start the day *trying to be happy in general,* I won't know what to do. I'll have to find more particular things to do, like checking the waves and maybe trying a new surfboard. Yet those particular activities may have little to do with myself, and instead concern ways I'm related to others or what lies beyond. Thus surfers say they surf not for fun, not for their own sakes, but for *surfing's* sake. They find their happiness without seeking it, convinced that this independently wonderful activity is ever so worthy of one's limited time in life. If they even know or care what the elusive "happiness" is, it is surfing.

All of this is a natural consequence of the idea that doing well as a person is an exercise of skill, a matter of "virtue." Skillful activity is a way of being related to what lies beyond one's subjective experience. But then doing well as a person, *eudaimonia,* will also be a matter of how one is related to the world beyond one's head. And that is finally why "surfing" on a convincing experience machine, though fun for the moment, won't ground a flourishing life, while actually being wet, in the water, surfing, might. As much or more than almost anything else, surfing expresses, clearly and purely, the value in being objectively related in an attuned harmonious dependence to what lies beyond oneself.

Chasing Flow

Because flow can't be induced, not at will and by popping a pill, it is the sort of thing one can wait for or one can chase. For those who give chase, there is something of a discipline to bringing it on often and forcefully. In a recent book that celebrates flow seeking, Steven Kotler praises big-wave surfers for having "mastered" flow, by organizing life around triggers for optimal experiences.[13] Certain external conditions or "flow triggers"—such as risk, creativity, and altruism—bring the flow state along, at least eventually. And if one can optimize for flow, shouldn't one capitalize, striving to get as much as possible?

Of my adrenaline junkie big-wave surfer brethren, I would like to submit that it is possible to spoil surfing for oneself, sowing the seeds of one's own discontentment. Even in surfing, but *especially* in big-wave surfing, the blessed "flow state" of peak performance is difficult to attain and mostly short-lived. For each month of the year, there's a different surf break in a different part of the world that's likely to produce huge but readable waves. Despite all the advantages of advanced surf forecasting and global transportation, scoring optimal conditions requires elaborate planning, last-minute travel, and expenses that preclude ordinary living. It's easy to miss out on the best days, just by a day, having flown from the other side of the planet. And even when one is scoring often, this brings only a cycle of highs and recoveries, which may leave one ruined for

13. *The Rise of Superman: Decoding the Science of Ultimate Human Performance* (New York: Houghton Mifflin Harcourt, 2014).

readjustment to normality. Chris Malloy, a world-traveling surfer turned filmmaker and cattle rancher, describes his comedown to a more ordinary existence this way: "Not all of us experience a happy life after doing this shit for a couple of decades. I bet there are some PTSD similarities. . . . [I]t can be hard to get excited again. Ever. And that feeling sucks."[14]

In Plato's *Gorgias*, Socrates compares two jars, one sound and full, one leaky. The man with a full jar can rest content that his costly milk, honey, and sugar are secure and that he won't have to work just to keep them. "He can relax over them." The leaky jar, a metaphor for the pleasure-chasing hedonist, must be refilled constantly, bringing anxiety to its owner, who can never rest in happy contentment, for fear of seepage and insufficiency. "He's forced to keep on filling [the jar], day and night, or else he suffers extreme pain."

Socrates's interlocutor, the wily Callicles, argues to the contrary that a leaky jar is the way of happiness, for pleasure comes instead from "having as much as possible flow in." The admirable, worthy person will "allow his appetites to get as large as possible and not restrain them. And when they are as large as possible, he ought to be competent to devote himself to them by virtue of his bravery and intelligence, and to fill them with whatever he may have an appetite for at the time."[15] Happiness comes in the chase.

The fortunate surfer is akin to the man with a full jar. Being able to transcend the mundane on a regular basis by hitting the waves, the surfer can make peace with the ordinary, finding joy in abun-

14. Ibid., p. 161. Jamie Wheal, executive director of the Flow Genome Project, suggests that this "dark night of the flow" is a hazard for "bliss junkies" "who think the magical ease of the flow state is the goal," and so could equally well take drugs. But if the "bliss junkie" is somehow different from healthy flow seekers, the unanswered question is what explains the difference (ibid., pp. 160–61). Kotler himself says flow is a "morally neutral" technology, which can be used for good or ill, and so could be abused. He suggests many of those drawn to "the flow path" are moved not only by "hedonic instincts" but also by ends such as "autonomy," "mastery," and "purpose" (pp. 164–65).
15. Plato, *Gorgias*, trans. Donald J. Zeyl (Indianapolis: Hackett, 1987), pp. 64–67, at 492a and 494a.

dance in ordinary being. As for losing oneself completely in ecstatic self-transcendence, it's super when it happens, when the waves get epic. On most days, though, in life's normal course of events, it is good enough to be harmoniously related to what lies beyond in average waves, while one is waiting for the next set, with a swell passing beneath, pulled by the slight current, under a vast sky, in reflections that quicksilver around the dark of the deep. There is still the gentler joy in connection, in flowing attunement, that allows one to slide through the more mundane tasks of life with no worries, being efficacious without control, even in unexcited tedium.

Ecstatic bliss—whether in big-wave riding, getting a glimpse of nirvana, or being flush with the Holy Spirit in church—is presumably worth chasing, if you've got some time away from work. Even for those who manage to behold the beatific vision, the peaks will come only occasionally and then quickly pass. The chase is exciting, but not a durable basis for daily peace. If one's happiness *must* be peak happiness, or even a steady averaged increase—because ordinary life, in ordinary waves, could only be mundane, dull, and drab, never quite sweet enough—well, one could often be left discontented despite all the mountaintop or big-wave experiences. And that is, frankly, rather unappreciative of the colossal fortune in having wound up a surfer. It is in flow as it is in love: you just have to wait. You faithfully persist, for better and for worse, in sickness and in health, accepting the ebb and flow of ordinary life.

The flow "triggers" make experiential flow more likely, but *only* more likely. They work to any real degree only for the person who remains faithful in practice. There's no "hack" whereby flow can be engineered, not in the way one can indeed juice the brain chemicals by taking drugs or improving one's diet and getting more sunshine. One must persist, faithfully, in disengagement and rest, through the ebbs and troughs of normal human existence. We can be nudged along by mood management. The architects, of buildings and of societies, can help flow experience come a bit more readily at work, at the museum, and on the street, steadily reducing the average level of the lows, while steadily raising the average quality of experience overall, over enough time. And we could work less, with more time and flexibility for leisure and creative endeavor of the sort that might bring flow more regularly. A few people can afford to pay a good architect to build a dream home, so maybe *they* have the luxury of maxing out on flow states. Even so, as Plato or Aristotle might say, the home in question is a person's "soul," the overall organization of his or her personality, virtues of character, and place in the world, all of which are subject to fortune's caprice. The happiness of a person can only be a steady, ongoing achievement. As Aristotle says, "As it is not one swallow or one fine day that makes a spring, so it is not one day or a short time that makes a man blessed and happy."

The artist and the surfer both know something about waiting. Success in creative endeavor does not necessarily come to the hardworking or to those greatest in natural ability, spatial-conceptual intelligence, sense of music, or fine wit. It comes to those who weather the ebbs and the angst, the anxieties and insecurities of the creative process, those who know how to stay open and attuned long enough for a roughly imagined vision to be gradually brought into being, in a material, public realization, as artwork on the wall, the film, the novel, the ballet. The faithful in creative practice learn to wait for the flash of insight, the moments of spontaneity, the spells of effortless productivity. They wait trusting, hoping, the blessed creative flow will return to them, at some point, before too long, so as to be ready when the fever strikes. When the jazz saxophonist Sonny Rollins was asked why he practices all the time, despite being so accomplished, he said he wanted to be there when the spirit comes.[16] No rituals or routines suffice. What once worked goes stale; an inspired social movement becomes wooden or cultish; new wine is not put in old wineskins. And while one can improve one's odds, trying different things that help, trusting that flow will return in fortune's due course, one can only place one's bets in a

---

16. The interviewer was Jack McCray, who reported his conversation at http://jazzartistsofcharleston.org/sonny-the-times-and-pbs/.

faithful practice. The *expectation* that flow can be controlled, that it's a mere matter of mastering oneself or one's circumstances, is a recipe for boring unoriginality, not to mention frustration and discontentment.

Whether new or old, the Stoic pretense of self-mastery pays too little heed to fortune, to what is beyond our grasp and control even in our very selves. Happiness is not within one's control, if only one could virtuously discipline one's attitudes. The blessed "flow state" is too occasional and fleeting to by itself offer a sturdy contentment in one's being. True joy, true happiness, come with favorable circumstances beyond our control, which, in faithful practice, must themselves be surfed.

The Importance of the Ordinary

Aristotle noted that we are what we repeatedly do. Skilled excellence is not an act but a habit of action. Centuries later, William James, the philosopher who founded modern psychology, explained how we acquire excellence through habit:

> The more of the details of our daily life we can hand over to the effortless custody of automatism, the more our higher powers of mind will be set free for their own proper work. There is no more miserable human being than one in whom nothing is habitual but indecision, and for whom the lighting of every cigar, the drinking of every cup, the time of rising and going to bed every day, and the beginning of every bit of work, are subjects of express volitional deliberation.[17]

Practice conserves attention. A resource in limited supply, our ability to attend to something is thus freed for other uses. I had to think about sinking my weight into a long carve in my early years of surfing. The habit formed, after a thousand acts of carving; I now

17. *The Principles of Psychology* (1890; New York: Cosimo, 2007), vol. 1, p. 122.

do it automatically. This frees my mind for whipping the turn into a tighter rotation, or for noting the next wave moment coming, so as to speed my transition. With each new habit that I "hand over to the effortless custody of automatism" by practicing often, my thoughts are further freed for the next level of attainment. I can now pay ever more exquisite attention. The more I practice, the freer I am to take in new facets of my wave situation, and I become ever more attuned.

This is the ordinary basis of self-transcendence. The loss of myself in my consciousness can be fluid and a matter of degree.[18] My trained reflexes are open adaptive patterns, a whole repertoire of skills that stand ready for action. I know how to use them when I can engage them at different times in different directions, without having to pay much attention to them. Having been practiced, they now run automatically, which allows my thoughts to range over changing situations, noticing myself or my movement, and then not, depending on what I'm doing. Occasionally, I'm *utterly* absorbed in the wave's moment. I see only the wave wall that I'm rushing along. I've practiced enough to let myself fade into the background of my awareness, and I may not know what exactly my body is doing, or have time to check where exactly my leg is. Other times I do know, because I'm mindfully present to where my weight is held and where I'm headed over an extended wave section, with only passing moments of complete self-effacement.

Though especially important in sports, the fluidity of attention's focus also enables the most ordinary of doings. We are nearly always more or less absorbed in one task or another. I know how to walk through a doorway, opening the door as I see who might be in the room. I turn the doorknob, and, as Heidegger noted, I won't usually be thinking of my hand on the knob. The knob turning is still something *I* actively did, even without thinking, because I've got that much mastery of doorways and the world around me. I've done it

18. On this dynamic shift of attention among elite athletes, see John Sutton et al., "Applying Intelligence to the Reflexes: Embodied Skills and Habits Between Dreyfus and Descartes," *Journal of the British Society for Phenomenology* 42, no. 1 (2011), pp. 78–103.

plenty. But that action of mine can simply fade out of my consciousness as I enter the room and think only of whether I'll see a certain friend at the party, who said she might attend.

So surfing brings self-transcendence of an everyday sort. I really am related in my flowing exercise of skill to what lies beyond, to the wave on which I'm sliding along. I may lose myself entirely in the rushing moment. But this has no need of ecstatic or mystical experience, whether religious or natural, let alone a metaphysical merger with the world and loss of self. Surfer self-transcendence has a mundane foundation, in showing up to surf, day after day, in the routine of everyday practice. The extraordinary thus depends on the ordinary, and if one loves the ecstatic, one also must honor its sturdier basis.

Cosmic Flow

When Leo Tolstoy, the great novelist of *War and Peace,* anxiously considered the possible meanings of life, he rejected a hollow Epicureanism that seeks happiness in nothing beyond the pleasures of the moment. The surfer agrees: if surfing were just about the pleasures of the moment, it wouldn't offer enough by way of meaning. Surfers aren't exactly after pleasure, leisurely good times, or even momentary happiness. If life really had no larger meaning, I guess one could just seek pleasure—eat, drink, surf, and be merry, for tomorrow we die. But surfing is not only worthy of life's final act; it is also worthy of a life's whole narrative arc. Its simple pleasures are ultimately of or about something beyond our experiential states, and its meaning is a sturdier basis for contented peace in one's being over a whole life's course.

Being at peace in one's life means not the mere absence of struggle or stress but having enough meaning to be secure in one's being, in the world where one is, by accepting the world in full awareness of the mess that it is.

This can vex the naturist, the religionist, and the partygoer alike, who each must confront the day *after* a spell of natural or religious or social ecstasy. Once the absorbing chase is over, and the buzz passes, what comes after the party—when one is hanging, wondering, needing something further, some understanding of how all the heightened experience makes some kind of sense?

The problem is only more pronounced in the wake of the bloodiest century in human history. Csikszentmihalyi arrived at his ideas about "flow" by asking how survivors of the Holocaust found meaning. Yet if flow is just "optimal experience," as he says, it is hard to see how it would supply a basis for peace and contentment beyond the flow chase. Is the question of meaning just *avoided,* in the distractions of work or pleasure? Maybe experiential flow is better than momentary pleasure, because it's longer lasting, or forward-looking, or complexifying, and thus *feels* meaningful. Maybe in a productivity-obsessed society we for the moment experience endless work as meaningful, because there's experiential flow in "pushing ourselves" in doing the relatively unimportant, with money or status as our reward. Surely this could all be a frenzied delusion. Most slog through on willpower, on self-determination, in anguish, choosing another day of work, because it's the responsible thing to do (given the kids, bills to be paid, and so on), much as Sartre suggests. The nineteenth-century French poet Charles Baudelaire said, "One must work, if not from taste then at least from despair. For to reduce everything to a single truth, work is less boring than pleasure."[19] Okay, the guy plainly wasn't a surfer (unless he'd count the exercise of skill in surfing as "work" and call it less boring than such self-amusements as solitaire or pleasuring oneself). But might not the "amusements" of work for money or "productivity" be just more distraction, just a way of coping with a meaningless existence?

The "go with the flow" metaphor promises something bigger, something that could give the anxious soul rest. For you see, there's such a thing as *the flow,* beyond the subjective flow of one's own consciousness. It's perhaps like basking in a warm washing wave, or in a gentle cosmic stream, treading along but at ease, being swept

19. *Journaux intimes* (Paris: Mercure de France, 1938), p. 16.

along to wherever, which will assuredly be a nice place to go and have been. Or whatever the image, the point would be that one can escape the mundane even in the ordinary, living graciously in one's daily routines, being fully present in the morass of task, tedium, and toil, and yet at peace with it.

In the Stoic version of this picture, the universe is rationally ordered. We can simply trust that events beyond our control will work out according to the world's natural laws or purposes. Or as people still say, "Everything happens for a reason," perhaps in view of a divine master plan, or cosmic karmic scheme. For the Stoics, nothing could have been different than it was without changing almost everything else, with alternative possible worlds far off into the metaphysical distance. It is pointless to hold out for what is barely possible but will invariably not be, so one should simply go along with events as they are already determined to happen, however unfortunate they may seem, like a dog leashed to a cart happily trotting along at the cart's speed. If this seems quaint, G. W. Leibniz, the eighteenth-century German philosopher and mathematician, defended an even bolder version of this picture: our world is not only rational and trustworthy but the very *best* of all possible worlds. There's no need to take control of events, because no one's life could have gone better or worse than it already has and will. For both Leibniz and the Stoics, our anxieties are simply failures to accept the world for exactly what it is and will be. If one could manage to just accept it, one could find the cosmic flow and stay there, at peace in one's being.

Yet the "go with the flow" metaphor could also be a metaphor, and only a metaphor, for a simple reason: there is no such cosmic stream. The metaphor has no literally true cosmic meaning; it simply calls up a quixotic philosophical dream. As Voltaire asked of Leibniz in *Candide,* would the best of all possible worlds have produced the Lisbon earthquake? Let alone, we might add today, *the Nazis?* Is there not a better possible world in which Stalin or Pol Pot never rises to power, because forces for moderation hold off the psychopaths? The bloodbaths of the early to mid-twentieth century help explain why Sartre would speak up for the absurd, the arbitrary, and the limits of abstract morality. Should one join the Free French resistance against Nazi Germany, abandoning one's needy mother at home? Or must one stay home, betraying one's countrymen and countrywomen? These were urgent questions that confronted the French in Sartre's lifetime, not an abstract exercise. As Sartre notes, Kant's famous "categorical imperative"—to act only as everyone can also act in one's situation—offers no determinate answer. To fill in the abstraction, we have to ourselves make a further judgment about which action could be practiced as a universal law. (For instance, if everyone cut in line at the post office, there'd be no line to cut in; so one must wait, instead of "making an exception of oneself." But few examples are so clear-cut.) As for joining the resistance, which is it? Do you stay home or fight?[20]

If science finds one sort of rational order, in mathematically regular laws of physics, the cosmos isn't so rational as to leave us without a genuine problem of evil and suffering. Not to mention the problem of colossal blunders. In the best of all possible worlds, would we have gotten rich in delusions of ecological abundance while spoiling the global climate, with civilization itself disrupted and vast numbers of present and future people at mortal risk? How could God allow this? How could we be so foolish? (How could God allow us to be so foolish? How could so many be so foolish as to assume God would never allow our foolishness?) In the portending ecological doomsday, where is the "rational order" in what could be a slow-motion, world-historical train wreck? And if answers are not forthcoming, then what? Resignation? Should we resign in disappointment, or commit suicide in protest, or bitterly withdraw to such islands of relative sanity and safety as gated communities and billionaire condos? Can we be reconciled to our condition, to be at peace with it?

Sartre tells us we are abandoned to absurdity. Yet from the lack of plain, determinate cosmic meanings, we may also come to a more

20. *Existentialism Is a Humanism*, p. 30.

surfer-friendly conclusion: that we face *too much* meaning. There are *too many things worth doing*, too many reasonable ways to proceed, too many reasons for action in a rich plenum of values that saturates nearly every decision with meaning. In our modern age of self-determination, we've rightly given up on the ancient project of deciding the one best life by comparing overall ways of living. Even the life of a surfer/philosopher probably can't be called the single best life for anyone, and that's not easy for me to admit. There's no single best life to have lived. (Surfers themselves most certainly don't want everyone surfing, which would only add to the crowds.) Could we still have a general ethic? Sure: Don't make things even worse; try to leave them a bit better; and find something good and wonderful to do in the sublime mess—something like surfing. But any ethic would have to be general enough for each of us to have an ample liberty in creatively shaping a life in any number of worthy directions. We'd each color in the details according to our situation and fancy, in the anguish of having too many good options, or of being unjustly not afforded quite enough of them.[21]

Still, the world might seem so absurdly ugly, unjust, and untrue that one just can't bring oneself to fully embrace one's existence, feeling not quite at home, not quite at peace in one's being. The Stoic answer to this dis-ease is that everything happens for a reason: with any awful event, things would have gone even worse had it not happened just as it did. This seems a firm basis for making peace with how things happen to be, but may be also a bit too convenient, and more than a little pat. And if such thoughts fail to bring cosmic reassurance, the question is still whether we can at least find good enough reason to reconcile ourselves to the human condition, foul as it can be.

They say there is always hope. We accept what is for what it might be or eventually become. Maybe the arc of the moral uni-

---

21. Does this leave too much room for too many right answers, because God or religion isn't setting some definite path? Possibly, but then we should ask, why must there be a meticulous script for how to live, down to the slightest detail? Why would a loving God write one? Might a creative God prefer co-authorship?

verse is long but bent toward justice, as Martin Luther King Jr. said. It's only if people are so incurably amoral and cynical as to dash all reasonable hopes of progress that you throw in the towel.[22] If we can at least reasonably hope that progress will continue apace, perhaps despite great setbacks, it would now be completely sensible to labor in the long cause of nudging things a little further along. Having labored in good faith, one could look back and say that the life of at least one mortal was well enough spent, at peace in one's death, even if our world remained, for now, a pretty unsavory place.

On the other hand, labor for justice is a lot of work. Maybe it is necessary for peace. Is it also sufficient, by itself—even without something like surfing? The good souls who dedicate their lives in charitable service to others need to find service joyous in something like the way surfing is joyous, if only to keep the sails full, to keep on keeping faith. They can find joy in the very people being helped, taking succor in a sweet and easy personal connection, and maybe going surfing or playing soccer/*fútbol* together on a fine afternoon. A few surfers do "give back" in charity. They appreciate water and seem especially keen to help people's water be clean.[23]

Along with the previous chapters, we now have something of a surfer view of meaning. Value is, at bottom, simple. The balance of values is complex, and how to trade them, to choose the worthiest course, is the problem of how to live. Life has its absurdities, which we might expect and find humor in. As for the meaning of life itself,

22. Kant writes darkly, "If justice goes, there is no longer any value in human beings living on the earth." Writing with World War II in mind, Rawls suggests that if a "reasonably just" social order is "not possible, and human beings are largely amoral, if not incurably cynical and self-centered, one might ask, with Kant, whether it is worthwhile for human beings to live on the earth." See Immanuel Kant, *The Metaphysics of Morals,* in *Practical Philosophy,* ed. and trans. Mary J. Gregor (Cambridge, U.K.: Cambridge University Press, 1996), p. 473; and John Rawls, *The Law of Peoples* (Cambridge, Mass.: Harvard University Press, 1999), p. 128.
23. Here see www.surfaid.org. My own effort with Damien Wao from Nias Island is at www.helpavillagewith.us.

in human history, we have yet to formulate an answer. But we have found good enough reasons to potentially find meaning in our own situation, enough so as to find personal peace. We needn't resign from life or withdraw, but can instead ready ourselves for being ever more attuned, in faithful practice. For the basic joy in the surfer's kind of relational connection, even in an ordinary surf, is a real basis for peace in the sublime mix of the beautiful and the grotesque, of the fortunate and the unfortunate, of the just and the unjust. One can relax the perfectionist scruples, ease up on the angst, and be less anxious. One can get stoked and simply *engage* in worthy activities that give one the grace needed to call the present good enough within a life that's being well enough spent.

So flow is a kind of relationship to the world beyond oneself. But how is such self-transcendence possible? What about the human's being would explain its possibility?

5

Being

When the voice was heard in the silence, I felt my
body harden and the Nausea vanish. . . . [T]he music
was drawn out, dilated, swelled like a waterspout. . . .
I am *in* the music. . . . This movement of my arm has
developed like a majestic theme, it has glided along
the song of the Negress; I seemed to be dancing.

—Sartre, *Nausea*

THE SURFER IS BLESSED, yet not so special. To knowingly surf, for
one's chosen purposes, is to express human nature, the human's
nature as an adaptive being.

Being Oriented

Sitting on a park bench, on an otherwise ordinary day, the hero
of Sartre's novel *Nausea*, Antoine Roquentin, suddenly encounters
Being itself, in the twisted black roots of an ancient chestnut tree.
Roquentin explains,

> I was sitting, stooping forward, head bowed, alone in front of
> this black, knotty mass, entirely beastly, which frightened me.
> Then I had this vision. It left me breathless. Never, until these
> last few days, had I understood the meaning of "existence." I
> was like the others, like the ones walking along the seashore,
> all dressed in their spring finery. I said, like them, "The ocean

is green; that white speck up there *is* a seagull," but I didn't feel that it existed or that the seagull was an "existing seagull"; usually existence hides itself. It is there, around us, in us, it is *us,* you can't say two words without mentioning it, but you can never touch it. When I believed I was thinking about it, I must believe that I was thinking nothing, my head was empty, or there was just one word in my head, the word "to be." Or else I was thinking . . . how can I explain it? I was thinking of *belonging,* I was telling myself that the sea belonged to the class of green objects, or that the green was a part of the quality of the sea. Even when I looked at things, I was miles from dreaming that they existed: they looked like scenery to me. I picked them up in my hands, they served me as tools, I foresaw their resistance. But that all happened on the surface. If anyone had asked me what existence was, I would have answered, in good faith, that it was nothing, simply an empty form which was added to external things without changing anything in their nature. And then all of a sudden, there it was, clear as day: existence had suddenly unveiled itself. It had lost the harmless look of an abstract category: it was the very paste of things, this root was kneaded into existence. Or rather the root, the park gates, the bench, the sparse grass, all that had vanished: the diversity of things, their individuality, were only an appearance, a veneer. This veneer had melted, leaving soft, monstrous masses, all in disorder—naked, in a frightful, obscene nakedness.

Roquentin had been feeling nauseated. The mood came upon him "cunningly, little by little," and then "never moved," after he'd taken up journaling. He wanted to bring presence to his mundane doings, by describing the day's events in every nuance, however trivial. He'd classify them and "see clearly." Suddenly he sees the emptiness of his ambition, and the source of his disorientation, in the radical limits of descriptive language. The words, try as he might to find them, can never capture what can only Be, and be encountered directly, right over there, in the knotty, beastly roots, next to which he is but another lump in reality, merely *in the way*. The words fail even to capture their very failure, atop the great chasm between language and reality. As Wittgenstein put the idea, we lack the concepts needed to articulate how words "picture" reality, aside from all the ways of speaking metaphorically (for example, as though words "picture" reality). Once we see this, we can kick away the philosophical ladder that carried us up to this high vantage and behold the ineffable, the "mystical" that escapes all words.

This is to upend Modern Western Man's sense of control. Before the world can be measured, predicted, organized, and manipulated, through science and wise policy choice, it must first be *described* in words. Yet if the world is simply unruly, bumptious, finally beyond our control because beyond description, how can we keep our bearings, staying oriented through constant change? Modern Western Man confidently posits that, yes, the natural world is rationally ordered. Science can transcend our varying personal perspectives and trace its objective laws. We can know the world as it is from an impersonal view from nowhere or—in the religious version that birthed the scientific revolution—from a God's-eye vantage that traces God's organizing thoughts in creation. But then everything depends on whether this detached perspective can be kept up. And if we can't reliably view ourselves as though looking from nowhere, *sub specie aeternitatis,* from the perspective of eternity, we seem abandoned to Roquentin's nausea. In disappointment founded upon high expectations, the postmodernist embraces a sense of dread and distrust, while the fundamentalist cleaves to authority, whether religious or scientific, in need of a surer foundation. Better that than being ungrounded, disoriented, adrift, at sea.

To which the natural surfer question is, "What were you expecting?" Surfers never put much trust in words, including the words of theories, worldviews, or texts. Even science is much as the logical positivist Otto Neurath imagined, akin to a distressed boat at sea: "We are like sailors who have to rebuild their ship on the open sea, without ever being able to dismantle it in dry-dock and reconstruct it from its best components." Good theories require constant revision; we adapt our beliefs as new evidence flows in, in science as in all rational belief.[1] For the surfer, this needn't be disorienting; a person can remain oriented *in* the changing seas, if you know what you're doing. Not in the artifice of words, or in theory, theology, or any authoritative truth, but in knowing how to be in the waves. Not exactly in thought, certainty, and propositional knowledge, but in knowing how to attunedly adapt, in the world right under and in front of you.

If you happened to stroll or skate by the park in the afternoon sun, where some gnarly chestnut tree roots happen to be unveiling their very Being, you might then feel stoked, instead of Roquentin's dread. Why not find joy and wonderment in being ever closer to realities that lie beyond words, beyond so many scientific or philosophical truths, in the reality you can only be in and sense? Isn't it, in the end, just a tree? Roquentin repeatedly finds relief from his nausea in the sound of music—in becoming attuned. "So strong is the necessity of this music." And yet he is troubled that "it would take so little to make the record stop," perhaps a mere "broken spring."[2] How, if at all, could attunement become a steady, normal way of being? Yet for the surfer, it is. The tree, the music, the waves, it's all good, in just another day of feeling connected, another afternoon waiting for a wave in one's daily surf, buoyed in an undulating sea. Until the right wave mounts and crests and one is carried along.

Heidegger called the "being" of the human situation "being-in-the-world," by which he meant being *engaged* in a particular setting, knowing how to do things defined by one's "life world." We live out the everyday meaning found in our material culture, getting

---

1. In *Surfing Uncertainty*, Andy Clark uses Thomas Bayes's analysis of how we rationally update for new evidence as a full-blown theory of animal and human perception and action. The "predictive brain" is in this way inherently adaptive, and so the surfer's brain is the human's. We will return to the brain later.
2. *Nausea*, trans. Lloyd Alexander (New York: New Directions, 2013), p. 22.

absorbed in its skills and tasks, keeping our bearings in absorbed skillful coping.[3] But for Sartre, freedom means being free *from* the cultural matrix, which one can choose not to plug into. If both perspectives have certain attractions, the surfer suggests that both Heidegger and Sartre overlooked a possibility: one can have freedom *and* flow, together, being free to move in or beyond one's social world, for being naturally attuned, to the ocean and its waves.

Surfing Like a Girl

Is there such a thing as throwing a ball like a girl? The 1960s psychologist Erwin Straus maintained that there is:

> The girl of five . . . does not stretch her arm sideward; she does not twist her trunk; she does not move her legs, which remain side by side. All she does in preparation for throwing is to lift her right arm forward to the horizontal and to bend the forearm backward in a pronate position. . . . A boy of the same age, when preparing to throw, stretches his right arm sideward and backward; supinates the forearm; twists, turns and bends his trunk; and moves his right foot backward. From this stance, he can support his throwing almost with the full strength of his total motorium.[4]

Because girls throw like a girl at such a tender age, Straus finds the apparent difference from boys hard to explain. In which case, he concludes, it must be part of a girl's "feminine essence."

To this, Simone de Beauvoir, the feminist pioneer (and Sartre's lover), answered that, yes, girls and women can feel weighed down and heavy, as though carrying a fearful and mysterious burden, in puberty, menstruation, and pregnancy, their individuality

---

3. This is Hubert Dreyfus's reading of Heidegger in *Being-in-the-World*.
4. Erwin W. Straus, "The Upright Posture," in *Phenomenological Psychology* (New York: Basic Books, 1966), pp. 157–60.

and efficacy confined in bodily necessity. But, no, there is no fixed "feminine essence." There's no fact about being breasted or hormonally disrupted that isn't socially constructed.[5] So if some girls or women have a "girly" way of throwing a ball in sports (but perhaps not a girly way of throwing keys), this, too, is a fluid cultural product, created in tender early upbringing.

Why do women often sit on a bus bench with compressed composure, legs closed and arms folded in, while men recline, legs spread-eagle? Perhaps the risk of being seen as "loose," while being peppered with unwanted attention, is reason enough just to avoid the unpleasant leering. That sounds rather sensible under the circumstances, quite aside from any "feminine essence" that inhibits public relaxation. And why do many men "manspread" on a crowded bus or a subway? Is this part of the guy's "manly essence"? Or is he just airing out his crotch area (as according to one woman's theory)? Most likely he's being insensitive, pushing the burden onto others of asking for a seat put there for general use, because his mother never taught him better, while his father and culture taught him to own all available space, to, you know, Be a Man.[6]

If people don't have an essence beyond the roles they own and perform, whether feminine or manly, could it be that gender culture keeps people from getting into the flow, from being fully attuned? Could it limit both flow and freedom?

Gender and surfing are both part of culture. So you'd expect them to interact and change together with the times.[7] The Hawaiian sport of kings (as well as its even earlier Peruvian development) was always equal in opportunity. The queen herself surfed. More

5. *The Second Sex* (New York: Vintage Books, 1974).
6. In particular, the guy is giving an almost theatrical performance, according to the feminist Judith Butler. Drawing from Merleau-Ponty, she argues that our gender roles are nothing but a performance in "Performative Acts and Gender Constitution: An Essay in Phenomenology and Feminist Theory," *Theatre Journal* 40, no. 4 (Dec. 1988).
7. Indeed they did according to the history offered in Westwick and Neushul, *World in the Curl,* chaps. 3 and 13.

recently, after surfing was male dominated for much of the postwar era, girls and women have returned to the waves. In the United States, 1970s Title IX policies encouraged girls in sports, and these days surfer girl marketing and women's professional surfing have arrived commercially. Keala Kennelly has been charging heavy, heavy waves at Teahupoo (the ones men were once said to need "balls" for, in a now dated way of putting it). Most important, more and more women and girls are feeling empowered to get out there to enjoy the waves.[8]

Men and women do seem to surf differently on average. During the years I was growing up, the difference was explained by center of gravity: with women centered in their hips, and men centered in their torso, women sort of somehow, you know, don't get as easily into a fluid and directed motion . . . or something. Then the world champion Lisa Andersen came along and refuted the idea that women can't surf better than nearly all men. At the same time, she was also said to "surf like a guy"—this being meant as a compliment.[9] Unlike fashion generally, and despite all the female-targeted brands, men still set the style trends and standards of quality in surfing.

Now that many women surf better than most men, the average male surfer should not feel emasculated in the comparison.[10] He doesn't have to feel "weak" or "lame," not even by the standards of manly "power surfing," with its big moves, thick carves, and explo-

8. The cultural theorist Krista Comer explains that for many women, being a "girl" in surfing, despite all the labors of second-wave feminism to explain that women are not girls, has come to represent empowerment through development of skill and permission to have fun. In the name of "girl power," women are becoming a force for "from below" globalization. This after Bruce Brown's 1966 *Endless Summer* mainly inspired men to travel and images of domesticated Gidget persisted. See her *Surfer Girls in the New World Order* (Durham, N.C.: Duke University Press, 2010).

9. Lisa Andersen's rise as a role model was even connected with her having shed conventional ideas of femininity. According to Comer, "For younger Generation Y girls, what it meant to 'be Lisa' is to be the kind of female who will not settle, who will pursue, in and out of sport, a no-matter-what philosophy of life" (ibid., p. 91).

10. One *Surfer* magazine cover shot of the superb woman surfer Carissa Moore had the caption "She surfs better than you do." This was meant to be emasculating. Much surf media is still pitched mainly to men, enacting a male culture.

sions. Surfing is becoming ever more inclusive. The new rotational aerials are often gentle and technical, with moments of passivity, lying back and recovering. It is a lot like ballet, although ballet is actually more "masculine" than the stereotypical ballerina for its own display of control, speed, and power. Flow, balance, elegance, and style have preeminent importance in surfing, even in powerful carving. And aren't those qualities generally seen as rather "feminine"?[11]

So could it be that the very best of surfing is some optimal mix of gendered features, or somehow gender-neutral, or even beyond gender?

The former world champion Joel Parkinson is widely touted as an ideal surfer despite being underscored in competition for making his extraordinarily radical repertoire look too easy. (Lately he's been conspicuously forcing his turns in competition to suggest difficulty and overcoming.) In life generally, men and women gradually age out of their stereotypical gendered features. Newer generations might seem to merge the best of "male" and "female" qualities (for example, younger men learn to listen, ask questions, give rather than take credit). Might surfers get enough sex and be secure enough in their sexuality to own surfing's gender transcendence? Might surfing be a sport that is truly for all of humanity?

It's a nice idea, but also incomplete without the acceptance of a surf-as-you-please tolerance of deep stylistic difference. Surfing is freedom, which partly means the liberty to surf however you want. So maybe some women have a feminine style of surfing, even or especially because of gender constructs. Why not celebrate the difference, as some feminists celebrate having breasts?[12] Style, after all, flows from the very nature of human consciousness, along with the constructs that shape our very being. For all the profound influ-

11. As Carissa Moore once noted in *Tracks* magazine.
12. Iris Marion Young, "Breasted Experience: The Look and the Feeling," in *On Female Body Experience: "Throwing Like a Girl" and Other Essays* (New York: Oxford University Press, 2005).

ence of culture, men and women might differ in styles of bodily comportment for rather deep reasons of our very bodily sense of space.

The philosopher Iris Marion Young developed this point powerfully, drawing on Merleau-Ponty's views of embodiment.[13] If the body is sexed and gendered, men and women might have a very different sense of the space available to them for movement, which then shapes sporting actions. A girl can throw like a girl, walk like a girl, sit like a girl, tilt her head like a girl, carry a book like a girl, and surf like a girl. Not because of her socially unconstructed "feminine essence," but because of the way her upbringing and society shape her basic, intuitive experience of her body, its space, and what motions she at once can and cannot make.[14]

Young explains, speaking from her own sense of the problem,

> For many women as they move in sport, a space surrounds us in imagination that we are not free to move beyond; the space available to our movement is a constricted space. Thus, for example, in softball or volleyball women tend to remain in one place more often than men do, neither jumping to reach nor running to approach the ball.[15]

The girl who throws like a girl doesn't quite bring her whole body into the motion. She's partly immobile, throwing with just the arm or only the forearm. Perhaps she sees herself as incapable of carrying a heavy object, underestimating what she can lift. After a halfhearted effort, in which she "fail[s] to plant [herself] firmly and make [her] thighs carry the major portion of the weight,"

13. "Throwing Like a Girl," in ibid.
14. That doesn't mean girls or women aren't good at math. The inhibitions wouldn't necessarily permeate the whole of experience. Yet the stereotype of women's being overwhelmed by their bodily experience might create the false impression of mathematical inability. If teachers then fail to encourage them, and girls sensibly choose greener pastures, this then may confirm the prejudice.
15. Ibid., pp. 33–36 (for all of the quotations below).

maybe she gives up in frustration, in what became a self-fulfilling prophecy. As Young puts it, "We frequently fail to summon the full possibilities of our muscular coordination, position, poise, and bearing." It's an "inhibited intentionality," which "simultaneously reaches toward a projected end with an 'I can' and withholds its full bodily commitment to that end in a self-imposed 'I cannot.'" Or as the lyric in Carly Rae Jepsen's pop song puts it, "Call me maybe."

Sartre tells us that consciousness is freedom, so one might wonder why a free person wouldn't just throw off cultural expectations and choose to put herself completely into open, unbroken movement, which fluidly calls forth capacities to follow all the way through. Why all the timidity, uncertainty, and hesitancy? "Typically, we [women] lack an entire trust in our bodies to carry us to our aims," Young explains. Many women do gain confidence through practice, in the schools or families that help them practice. Yet the woman who throws like a girl often began in an "ambiguous transcendence": she constitutes her bodily space but also sees herself as an object to be dealt with, managed, or maintained. Her body is experienced as both a capacity for action, as "transcendent" in consciousness and aspiration, and a mere object. It is at once for touching and being touched, grasping and being grasped, to be respected, but also shaped and decorated, showed off, and used for sex.

A coach would tell you that this sort of duality can lead a person to take her eye off the ball. Being constrained in her very being, a girl or woman might not find herself fully attuned to her bodily action. Young calls this "discontinuous unity": "Our attention is often divided between the aim to be realized in motion and the body that must accomplish it, while at the same time saving itself from harm." She continues,

> We often experience our bodies as a fragile encumbrance, rather than the medium for the enactment of our aims. We feel as though we must have our attention directed upon our bodies to make sure they are doing what we wish them to do,

rather than paying attention to what we want to do *through* our bodies.[16]

So if we experience a natural sense of harmony when we're fully dialed in, as Merleau-Ponty says, a person can also be only partway there. A man can be overcontrolling, throwing his weight around without being tuned in. And a woman's "feminine spatiality" can keep her body from being all in. For different reasons, neither might find a fluent flow in surfing.

Attunement

Before the big 2004 Indian Ocean tsunami, a poor Sri Lankan boy with little education had been reading discarded issues of *National Geographic*. There he learned about the sea rushing out when an enormous, long-period wave is approaching, because of an under-water earthquake. One day, down at the boat dock, he saw it happening. He had time to persuade his village to head for the hills and saved everyone, because of his new attunement to ocean dynamics.

Being in a state of *basic attunement* to something means at least being "in tune" or "in sync" with a pattern that emerges over time. I hear the sound waves emitted from a violin as musical, rather than as noise. I'm attuned by my recognition of sound wave patterns through my brain, auditory system, and innate feel for music.[17] I'm attuned on a steady basis, as time elapses, as I follow the tune and get taken up in its crescendo, with rising expectations of an approaching release.

This usually comes by the usual five sensory modalities as sight, sound, taste, touch, and smell combine to present a unified experi-

16. This is a deep kind of "unity" in view of Kant's idea that all of our thoughts and experiences are united by an "I think." The body can also bring unity to thoughts in action, as argued in Samuel Todes's *Body and World* (Cambridge, Mass.: MIT Press, 2001). This sort of disunity is thus especially deep.

17. Daniel J. Levitin, *This Is Your Brain on Music: The Science of a Human Obsession* (New York: Plume, 2006).

ence of the world around us. It can also come "intuitively," without conscious attention or deliberation, or even knowing one's reasons for one's sense of a situation, as when the fire chief "just knew" the building would blow and managed to get everyone out safely.[18]

Of a sailor who reliably navigates dangerous rocks and currents, without being able to say how he does this, Aristotle at one point concludes that he is simply "fortunate by nature." Some people are just such that "things work out for the most part." The sailor's success can't be explained by reason, because he can't articulate a science that could guide other navigators. And the gods would never unjustly intervene and save him from his bad choices. So his fortune comes "by nature." But Aristotle might have just said that the sailor was *attuned*. He's not like the guy in a dice game who keeps on winning, rolling sixes over and over. He's like the fire chief whose intuitive reactions have been tutored by his accumulated past experience, in fire after fire over the years. He's fortunate for what has become second nature to him.

We are rarely *fully* attuned, not for very long anyway. Even when I've caught on to a pattern, I can gradually become *more attuned* in small increments of increasing sensitivity. I can tell the ambient sound is music rather than noise but haven't yet caught a melody. I listen more carefully and then get the tune. When I step back from a pointillist painting and the scene of a pleasant picnic comes into perspective, I start to understand it, and maybe even recall trends in the philosophy of perception around the time this artist was working, with sense-datum theory beautifully captured right there in the hanging art object.

Being attuned in these ways may not require much by way of adaptation. One can be attuned without necessarily acting on that attunement. Someone who rarely listens to music could have perfect pitch and correctly judge a sound vibration as middle C. But maybe she can't sing or play an instrument, let alone blow a good

18. Daniel Kahneman, *Thinking, Fast and Slow* (New York: Farrar, Straus and Giroux, 2011).

note on the trumpet, with even the faintest sense of the skill in a jazz artist's improvisational riffing. In tracking the stellar constellations from one's window, watching and waiting, the eyeballs would move. By comparison, standing there at the window requires nothing like the adaptive demands of sailing a boat by the stars across the Pacific. (A surfer I met in Java explained to me how he did this: using his fingers at arm's length as a sextant, he takes measurements at dawn and dusk, while geo-positioning himself given his knowledge of Earth's rotation and stellar positions that season.)[19]

The surfer, by comparison, is *adaptively attuned,* which is to say at once attuned *and* adaptively acting, at once sensing and doing. Perception and bodily action are linked, inextricably.

In surfing a wave, my different bodily acts—rotating the torso, jutting my arm forward, shifting my weight—coordinate together efficiently, because of my larger purposes and my present sense of what's coming. This awareness only comes from my bodily practice. I won't sense where I am and what's coming unless I'm already in an engaged position. I'm in a crouch, flying down the wave line, and as the new section forms, I already *roughly* know how to surf these situations. I now adapt to the fresh moment, seeing it as for-turning, for-pumping, for-snapping, and I let my body engage its new particularity spontaneously, in fresh action. I keep doing this in light of what seems, as I go, to be working.

If this is adaptive attunement, what then explains its possibility? Let us consider the matter carefully.

---

19. "Slomo," the man who chucked his materialistic life as a hardworking neurologist/psychiatrist to spend the day skating in Pacific Beach, California, says that he tunes in to gravity-induced "lateral momentum" in order to glide continuously, if slowly, along the boardwalk. He does this with a minimal adaptation: skating on one leg and leaning over with a stable, fixed "flying" posture. He goes slow but is steadily carried along. He reports great happiness in this. For a mini-documentary, see https://www.nytimes.com/2014/04/01/opinion/slomo.html?_r=0.

Embodied Awareness

For starters, there is a way of sensing with one's body. When I experience a hammer, it shows up for me not as a mere thing but as *grabbable*, as "ready to hand," as Heidegger put it. It shows up for me as an opportunity for action, along with other practical possibilities. As Sartre explained the idea, when a hammer counts as "alongside" certain nails, over there on a table, "the expression 'alongside' loses all meaning if it does not outline a path which goes from the hammer to the nail," which is to say they are experienced together in a single possible construction project.

Sartre muddled the point with his dualism about mind and body. He *claimed* the two can't be wholly separate but then obscured their basic unity, suggesting that I know my body as mine as though by the gaze of others. It was Sartre's colleague Merleau-Ponty who shook off Descartes's dualistic influence fully. Our very awareness of the world and ourselves is all about our *bodily* sense of space.

As Merleau-Ponty put it, "Consciousness is originally not an 'I think that,' but rather an 'I can.'"[20] I am not originally a subject of thought, as Descartes and Sartre claimed. I do think, and I am, but as one who acts and intends surfing actions, as a minded, embodied being, in a particular setting. I'm not a *bare* subject of thought, a bare thinking something. I am always defined by my possibilities of action—of rising from bed, of walking along, of grabbing my board and paddling out into the waves. My bodily experience of space shapes nearly all of my experience in the very first instance. I am a surfer, constantly adapting my body to my next moment for action. And so are we all, in a very general sense, in our most basic way of being.

How does a hammer show up for me as grabbable when it's off to the right of my body? I have a bodily sense of how to extend my arm to grab it, how to hold it in my hand, how to raise my arm and

20. *Phenomenology of Perception*, p. 139.

hammer down forcefully, so as to bang a nail. The reach of my arm has its own kind of "intentionality," or "aboutness," which is to say, its own way of being *about* something else. This is different from simply *thinking* of a hammer, perhaps as lying on a table in a certain part of the house. I could equally think of Paris or Nias, and my thought would be about each place. The intentionality is of a different, bodily sort, a "bodily intentionality" or awareness, in the "aboutness" of my reach.

Where is my arm? I know the answer. Somehow I know the answer without seeing it or touching it with my other arm or hand. I know by "proprioceptive" awareness of a sort that doesn't come by the five senses. But my awareness also extends beyond my skin. If I'm reaching with my right arm, and I touch it with my left, I'll feel flesh and bone. But with my reaching arm itself, I am reaching beyond my body, *toward* the hammer, which I may or may not quite grasp. I'll then have a very different experience, which I can have while touching nothing, because the object is just beyond my reach.

When I grab my surfboard, I can feel how it might "go" on a wave, when it will feel like an extension of my body, once I'm flowing along the open wave face. I sense this in the way a blind man "sees" beyond the end of his walking stick. What he's sensing is not the stick but his environment *through* what has become an extension of his arm and organs of perception. Through the stick, he knows how to "see" his surroundings, much as I know how to surf.

Just so, we human beings orient ourselves in space. The hammer or the surfboard shows up in my basic consciousness of the world as from here, where I am. But where am I? *Here,* of course. "I am here" is always true, as true as any truth. But "here" when I say or think it is itself defined by my possibilities of bodily action. As Merleau-Ponty puts the idea,

> My body appears to me as a posture toward a certain task, actual or possible. . . . When the word "here" is applied to my body, it does not designate a determinate position in relation

to other positions or in relation to external coordinates . . . [but rather] the anchoring of the active body in an object, and the situation of the body confronted with its tasks.[21]

So physics may well tell us the truth about space and time in its impersonal coordinates, from a view from nowhere, from a God's-eye perspective. Yet my own experience of space is of my bodily space, in my own possibilities of bodily movement in this or that task, from a view from *somewhere,* my body's somewhere, in my skin, in my shoes, embedded in a certain situation, in relation to certain possible tasks. This is a real kind of space. It is no less real, in the ordinary, perfectly good sense of "reality," than the impersonal space of physics. As Merleau-Ponty provocatively puts the idea, "There would be for me no such thing as space if I did not have a body."[22]

David Foster Wallace wrote of the tennis spectacle that is Roger Federer and the kinetic human beauty we find in great athletes. He explained the universal appeal this way: "What it seems to have to do with, really, is human beings' reconciliation with the fact of having a body."[23] But the fact of having a body, as opposed to what? Not having a body, and therefore not being a surfer, yet somehow still oneself? Am I supposed to be thinking something like this: Had I been luckier, I *could* have been a disembodied soul or spirit, but now that I'm stuck here in *this* fleshy mess, I have to sort out my feelings about my predicament?[24] Wallace concluded that being embodied is after all pretty great; the superathletes "seem to cata-

---

21. Ibid., p. 103.
22. Ibid., p. 105.
23. "Federer Both Flesh and Not," in *Both Flesh and Not* (New York: Little, Brown, 2012), p. 8.
24. Wallace doesn't clearly answer. On the "great deal that's bad about having a body," he cites "pain, sores, odors, nausea, aging, gravity, sepsis, clumsiness, illness, limits—every last chasm between our physical wills and our actual capacities." But for these events there is a real alternative, in a healthy body and virtuous disposi-

lyze our awareness of how glorious it is to touch and perceive, move through space, interact with matter." It is indeed pretty great, but a problem of *reconciliation* suggests that there was some alternative to having a body that I could at least intelligibly wish for and still be myself. And if there's no possibility of surfing or of tennis without a body, then there's nothing to be reconciled to in the first place.[25] You just count yourself fortunate for being, and that's it.

Why do we find the demigod genius of Federer's tennis or Kelly Slater's surfing glorious? It's not that we long to escape our bodies, but how very far *ahead* the phenoms are beyond normal expert capability. It's an extreme refinement of the very abilities of bodily adaptation that have cumulatively, over epochs, made up human nature.

Perception

If we wished to build a human, we could begin with a fleshy body in space and build up the being's faculties. We'd want to add basic sensory perception. What is it to sense one's surroundings, with the usual five senses, or in a more "intuitive" awareness?

The surfer's answer would be this: All sensing, all perceptual awareness, is a matter of being embodied in a particular situation and knowing how to attunedly adapt one's body to one's environment. That is, seeing wouldn't always come first, with action following. Action would also shape seeing, or rather seeing would *be* action.

When I surf, I see features of the wave—the *lip pitching,* the *section bowling*—and these guide my glide along the wave's face. These features only show up in experience from a certain perspective; it isn't that anyone would see them if they were just positioned

tion. He adds that "it's your body that dies, after all." But then we've merely circled back to the different question of how to accept death.

25. This is true even for souls that eventually get immortality but must begin in a body, as many of the big religions now believe. Plato by contrast held that our souls were somehow present in the eternal world of Forms even before our bodily birth.

in the right angles. When I'm adaptively engaged with the wave in question, I already know something of how to turn, or to bear down in a crouch, at the right time. Those prior abilities are necessary for me to even *see* the lip pitching or the section bowling, in the sense that guides my next attunement.

Surfer seeing is like color vision (on some theories of color): the redness of an apple depends on our color sensibility, for instance, given the way an apple normally looks to people in daylight with normal vision. The qualities that guide the surfer along the wave—the pitchingness of the lip, the bowlingness of the face—can depend for their very presence on the surfer's cultivated perceptual sensibility (as "response-dependent features," as philosophers call them). A color-blind person lacks the necessary sensibility, and so won't see the apple as red. And without knowing how to surf already, you won't see what surfers mean when they say to each other, "You know those ones, the ones that roll and then pop, or the ones that wedge up and lunge. Yup, those ones are sick." But perhaps you'll take my word for it that some waves really do roll and then pop, wedge up and lunge. And yes indeed, those waves really can bowl and tube and be good for surfing.

In this way, we are not so different from other animals. They too get along in the world by gradually gaining a more and more refined sense of the world according to their opportunities for action—what the psychologist J. J. Gibson called its "affordances." Certain plants or berries are seen as *edible,* as affording opportunities for eating in a certain ecological niche. Having been birthed by a species that's adapted for that very situation, the animal knows how to eat already, reading its situation accordingly, updating as the familiar niche changes, or dying off.

This is roughly how we higher animals learn to feel corduroy or silk. To take one of Merleau-Ponty's examples, we learn to move our hand at a slow, steady speed, with expectations of a new brushing sensation that we'd otherwise miss. To perceive silkiness is to know how to engage a silky blouse with this adaptive sensitivity. Likewise in seeing such sturdy objects as a dining room table. As we move around the room, we learn, at an early age, how to understand and engage the gradual changes in its apparent angles. What could appear as a jumble of cubistic shapes and angles, as in some Picasso-inspired painting mishap, or in a bad LSD trip, instead shows up for us as a single table in multiple dimensions, its changing apparent angles being smoothly integrated as experiences of one object. (Perhaps that was Picasso's point, in showing that a jumble of angular shapes could still present themselves as an intelligible guitarist. Our experience of ordinary objects is in this way constructed.)

What psychologists call "perceptual constancy" is thus infused by bodily action. As the psychologist Jean Piaget explained, "Perceptual 'constancy,' seems to be the product of genuine actions, which consist of actual or potential movements of the glance or of the organs concerned."[26] Of such "sensory-motor" movements— the moving of the eyes, turning of the head, walking forward to reach and touch—we can then ask a philosophical question, about perceptual awareness: Is understanding those movements not just the way we perceive but the *very nature* of perceptual awareness, including our seeing a sturdy table or feeling a silky blouse? The answer is yes according to philosophers such as Alva Noë (who took up surfing while he taught at UC Santa Cruz). To see, to sense one's environment, is just to understand it by use of such sensory-motor know-how—the know-how of making sense of the shifting · angle of the table as of the same object, seen only from a different perspective.[27]

If this is human sensing, it fits surfer experience nicely. Sensing one's surroundings is a matter of bodily adaptive attunement.

26. *The Psychology of Intelligence* (1950), trans. Malcolm Piercy and D. E. Berlyne (London: Routledge, 2001), p. 91.
27. Alva Noë, *Action in Perception* (Cambridge, Mass.: MIT Press, 2004); and *Out of Our Heads* (New York: Hill and Wang, 2009).

How to Go On

This would explain why surfing cannot be learned by reading. Learning to surf comes from both sensing and bodily doing. I have to learn both, each in light of the other, gradually refining both abilities. I learn to move my body, to unweight, set the rail, ease into a crouch. At the very same time, I learn to "read" the wave face, by coming to see the different wave moments, which afford different opportunities for action. The two come together. For no one will learn to do a bottom turn on a wave without learning to conceptualize the trough area of the wave as a turnable contour, and no one will come to conceptualize the wave in just that way without being oriented to it in action, in leaning in and shifting one's weight so as to turn. You don't learn the "sensing" without the "action," and vice versa. In faithful practice, you learn both sides of the perception-skill pairing, simultaneously.

The surfer is constantly learning, in taking each new wave moment afresh. This can seem magical. How can one "go on" in a *completely* fresh moment? If the situation is novel, one couldn't have *already* learned how to respond to it, having never been in it before. And if a situation is completely novel, why isn't any adaptation completely arbitrary, at best a guess? How could a new reaction be "learning" or "understanding" or "progress," as opposed to a blind stab in the dark?

The founder of phenomenology, early-twentieth-century German philosopher Edmund Husserl, suggested an answer. Before I encounter the new moment, I begin with a sense of my whole experiential situation. I also have my rough surfing purposes, which I project forward and then gradually fill in. I can then draw from my developed sensibility as I go. I draw from what Merleau-Ponty calls the "intentional arc" of my past experience and skilled bodily dispositions, which already incline me to respond in one way rather than another. Not as with Pavlov's dogs, in some stimulus-response, knee-jerk kick. My history of practice will have given me flexible general *capacities* of movement. These aren't fixed, so I can spontaneously refine them in response to my new situation, if I just stay present with it, sensing how it is similar, but also different, from what has come before.

Then, from my rough expectations of what I might encounter in a new moment, I can update as I go, checking my work, getting feedback from an ongoing sense of what seems to be working. What does "working" mean here? Nothing too fancy. I can move closer or farther from a painting and gradually bring its meaning into focus. In the same way, I'll need nothing more than my natural tendency to sense what adjustments in my positioning are at least *not not-working,* which I can sense as I go.

So I can forget about what is "best" or "optimal" according to an ideal of flowing in the abstract. I can simply go by what feels "off," or causes me to "bobble." When surfers advise me to "stay in the pocket," they mean that I should sense moment by moment when I'm *out* of the pocket, when I'm no longer in or near the wave's moving propulsive source, because I'm slowing or stalling. Without speed, I'm no longer afforded possibilities of a creative adaptive moment, in a snap, fade, or cutback. I won't feel free. So I can dispense with a positive ideal of "optimal" surfer flowing, with ambitions of perfection, toward which I'm striving. I can let go of all such aspiration. The flow comes as long as I stay present with each new moment, and therein lies its beauty. I draw from my ongoing sense of what movements are taking me out of the wave's flow, and doing this moment after moment, I trust that I'll stay with it, whereupon a larger flowing pattern emerges, supervening upon my various adaptive actions. That's what I'm celebrating when all goes well, at the end of the wave. When I'm hooting, "Yoooo! Whoah!" I mean, roughly, "Everything totally came together! I am fortunate."

I might also want to say, "*This* is surfing. I'm dialed in." My achievement is a sort of practical understanding, a harmony between my action and my situation. In going along with the wave's upsurge according to my surfing intentions, I'm united with the world beyond me in action. I glide through to the next section, and I feel this as harmonious, as *making sense,* as *working,* as *right* or even *correct,* which propels me through to the next fresh moment. Or as Merleau-Ponty puts the idea, "To understand is to experience the accord between what we aim at and what is given, between the intention and the realization."[28] This understanding, this harmonious accord, is the sound basis for my stoke. I'm stoked, because, for the moment, things are right.

Surfer Reason

What then of human reason, the one thing that sets us apart from the beasts? Our capacity to reason self-consciously, to consider a practical question and reach a conclusion about what one ought to do, is often said to distinguish us from the mere adaptive animal.

David Hume denied this: In his view, people and animals are both ruled by passion. Reason is only calculative or instrumental, the slave of desire. Awoken by Hume from his dogmatic slumber, Kant constructed a theory of what he thought Hume was missing: we self-consciously deliberate about what to desire in the first place, this being the touchstone of moral action and human dignity. (Here Sartre largely followed suit.)

The affective revolution in psychology revived Hume's perspective with its own reply to Kant. Yeah, but putting aside the question of dignity and all the heavy moralizing, that's just not how we get around in the world. In fact, reason is "slow thinking," a slower process than the affective system's "fast thinking," which orients us to the world via intuition, feeling, or emotion.[29] So the surfer's "intuitive" sensing is *just affect,* just emotion. "Reason" comes along after, often as rationalization or confabulation, the emotional dog wagging the rational tail.

To which the surfer will reply, isn't this whole research program trading in a false dichotomy? If I may speak up for the surfer's and the human's dignity, the dog-food distinction between quick emo-

28. *Phenomenology of Perception,* p. 146.
29. Kahneman, *Thinking, Fast and Slow.*

tion, on the one hand, and slow, calculative reason, on the other, is unfit for service at the table of fine philosophy. Reason can also be quick. Being quick doesn't make it emotion.[30]

The surfer's reason is part and parcel of his or her bodily *perception,* of the wave, and what it calls for. What are the surfer's reasons in action? They are found in those situational perceptions, in the moments of adaptation. These go beyond the surfer's passing affectations. Sure, you might feel fear, or excitement, and this will help focus your attention. The action of attunement brings plenty of emotion, and, as Aristotle suggested, the pleasure and good vibes swell with greater expertise. But much of this is itself the work of embodied surfer reason, honed over a life of surfing practice.

So I shifted my weight, in a well-timed reaction. I didn't have time for deliberation or calculation. If I'm later asked for a justification— "Why that exact reaction, at that exact moment?"—I might say that I'm really not sure, not exactly. It just seemed appropriate. Here people do often make up stories. Yet our unreliability at *explicating* our know-how into propositional language doesn't mean we didn't know what we were doing, or that we didn't do it for reasons. Often I can say enough, quite correctly, to show that the reaction was *my* action, as opposed to something that just happened to me. I was headed into a steep wave section, I saw the section coming, and went for the snapping turn. Maybe the mounting lip of the wave was speaking to me, almost calling out, "Hit me, hit me." That can be my reason: the wave section, in that particular cresting formation, at least when you're approaching off the bottom with a head of speed, called out; "it was asking for it," as one might put it. So I answered. I geared down and shellacked the lip. Because this was only appropriate. And if you don't understand how that is possible, well, then we're going to have to review a few things about the top turn, which I might propound with hand motions and something of an articulation.

That's why my approach and turn made sense, why it isn't some-

---

30. See also Peter Railton, "The Affective Dog and Its Rational Tale: Intuition and Attunement," *Ethics* 124, no. 4 (2014), pp. 813–59.

thing that just happened to me. It was my action, my virtuous reaction. It is my body and my practice and so my deed. The act is well reasoned. It came from my ongoing uptake of what was continually being given, my sense of which has been refined in a thousand moments of reflection and correction. It's originally born of surfer reason, given all the reasons I started and continued surfing, rising every morning. After countless hours of thought and deliberation, on waves and in visualized daydreams, I've internalized my cumulative practice, and my surfing actions express my cumulative knowledge. This is reason, baked into muscle memory, the know-how of reason in practice.

Brains Don't Surf

Descartes thought the mind has certain internal representations, or pictures, that may or may not match the world beyond one's skin, where causal forces impinge upon one's body. So one could be in thought and cut off from external reality completely, for instance, in a massive dreaming delusion. Descartes shut himself in an egocentric cage, and like Sartre he struggled to escape.[31] But the door was always open, if one puts the body first.

In the surfer optic, seeing or sensing is not simply a matter of having certain pictures in one's head. To perceive is to know how to engage what lies beyond one's head, in the first instance. It's already to understand how to adapt one's body to one's environment in action. So there's no deep difference between "in here, in my head," and "out there, out in the world."

Here the "body" is the body of the whole person and not just the electrified meat sitting in the skull, between the ears. Perceptual experience can't be in the brain, not as a "picture" or "representation"

---

31. Descartes claimed the bare possibility of being in a massive dreaming delusion meant that he couldn't be certain he had any real contact with the world or his body. Finally only God could explain why he could trust his senses. *Meditations on First Philosophy* (1641), trans. Elizabeth S. Haldane, in *The Philosophical Works of Descartes* (Cambridge, U.K.: Cambridge University Press, 1911).

somehow configured in the brain's synapses, as cognitive science often imagines.

For the brain is located in one's head. But to perceive is to know how to engage what lies beyond one's head. Hence perception is not simply located in the brain.

Yes, the "mind" includes perceptual seeing. But all that follows from this is that the mind isn't simply the brain, or even contained wholly within one's head.[32]

Nowadays people will say odd things such as "My brain made me eat the chocolate" or "My brain was telling me that we were lost." Taken literally, and applied to the surfer, it is as though the brain somehow surfs the surfer's body, which surfs the surfboard, which surfs the wave. This seems absurd. Brains don't surf. For brains do not have legs, or arms, or a body. And a body is needed to surf a wave. Hence the surfer is not his or her brain.[33]

The world champion surfer Kelly Slater says he surfs so well because he "surfs with his whole body." To a lesser degree, this is true of all surfers. Surfers see or "read" what next moment of the wave is approaching by understanding possibilities of bodily movement, through a kind of bodily sensing. Their brains adapt to wave types and wave environments as a result of a history of these body-world interactions, through adaptive learning.

The surfer can't be completely brainless; you do need a brain to surf. Somehow—science can't yet say just how—one's brain "maps" a familiar surf break, along with the various "affordances" of differ-

32. See Noë, *Out of Our Heads;* for this "externalist" view of cognition, see Andy Clark, *Supersizing the Mind: Embodiment, Action, and Cognitive Extension* (Oxford: Oxford University Press, 2008); for representation, see Mark Rowlands, *Body Language: Representation in Action* (Cambridge, Mass.: MIT Press, 2006); and for knowledge, see Timothy Williamson, *Knowledge and Its Limits* (Oxford: Oxford University Press, 2000).

33. To put the point another way, someone must be surfing when surfing happens. The brain is not itself a someone. But surely there's no homunculus surfer inside the surfer brain that surfs the brain, which surfs the body, which surfs the surfboard, which surfs the wave. So we should admit from the start that the brain does not surf. The surfer is the man or woman who surfs, the whole human being, him- or herself. The brain merely helps the person surf.

ent waves. The surfer can then just see, spontaneously, certain wave motions. A mounting wave is about to shift off in a certain direction as it draws off the rock or sandbar bottom in a distinctive way. This wave, now approaching, will be one of the few that bowls up and tubes, in which case one had better hustle over to get in position for a steep take-off and quick "scoop" under the wave's lip as it throws. As this somehow became "mapped" into the surfer's brain, the surfer was that much more attuned to his or her larger environment. But the surfer's attunement to a wave, by know-how and "intuition," *also* depends on the way his or her body really is objectively situated in and before the waves. Attunement comes only within an embodied perceptual relationship with his or her wave surroundings, formed in a certain close history. With enough practice, enough time in the waves, the surfer and the waves become synced.

This is rather wonderful, and neuroscience knows very little about how it happens. Much is known about particular neurons. There is hopeful talk about "neural networks." At the moment, this is either (1) a point about computer modeling and the amazing strides in "deep" machine learning, none of which has a clear relationship with the electrified brain meat within the skull of an animal, or else (2) grand speculation about how what's known about particular neurons could *eventually* connect up with the cognitive science of vision.

I'm not saying this moon-shot-like project isn't exciting enough to have gotten lavish funding, with the many billions of dollars and euros promised toward brain science in America and Europe. And yes, functional magnetic resonance imaging creates some really pretty pictures, even if they only mark out very general regions of activity and say little or *nothing* about the nature of consciousness.[34] What you wouldn't realize from all the media hoopla is that brain science is now resting its hopes on the falling cost of supercomputers, which are needed to model neural "networks" of any sophistica-

34. On why consciousness is hard to explain, see Thomas Nagel, "What Is It Like to Be a Bat?," in *Mortal Questions*; and David J. Chalmers, *The Conscious Mind: In Search of a Fundamental Theory* (New York: Oxford University Press, 1996).

tion. Some sort of networking, it is hoped, will *eventually* put us in a position to say something useful about how the study of particular neurons or small neural areas could add up to more than what some neuroscientists call mere "stamp collecting." At an interdisciplinary conference of neuroscientists and philosophers at NYU in 2013, which was attended by many luminaries, the scientists admitted this frankly. They asked, even begged, the *philosophers* for a concept of "emergence" that would relate the neuron to the eyeball. There's nothing at all wrong with this situation; such is simply the current state of an immature science. It does make it rather foolish to doubt the practical relevance of philosophy.

In point of fact, some of the big recent advances in robotics and artificial intelligence—the ones that justify fears of robots taking over the world—came because scientists started listening to Heidegger and Merleau-Ponty as philosophers explored the idea of embodiment in human experience.[35] So if sociopathic robots do destroy the human race, one could argue that the surfer's philosopher, Merleau-Ponty, is partly responsible. Perhaps we should wish that philosophy mattered less than it does.

So we have something of a surfer theory of human nature. The human is related to the world beyond, in adaptive relationship, in his or her very being.

How we see ourselves as self-conscious beings is quite another matter. We can spoil our own attunement in self-preoccupation, taking ourselves out of the flow. So we should now turn to the human's higher functions and ask how far we can in our own eyes transcend ourselves.

35. Hubert L. Dreyfus, "Why Heideggerian AI Failed and How Fixing It Would Require Making It More Heideggerian," MS, http://leidlmair.at/doc /whyheideggerianaifailed.pdf; *What Computers Still Can't Do* (Cambridge, Mass.: MIT Press, 1992); as well as Hubert L. Dreyfus and Stuart E. Dreyfus, *Mind over Machine: The Power of Human Intuition and Expertise in the Era of the Computer* (New York: Free Press, 1986).

6

Transcendence

I can imagine that the oceanic feeling could
become connected with religion later on.

—Sigmund Freud, *Civilization and Its Discontents*

"Look at that wave! Shit, I gotta get out there." I'm putting on
my wet suit and sunscreen in an excited rush. Shall I now "mindfully" ask how I am feeling, right this moment, without passing
judgment?

Let's see: I'm definitely excited to see that last wave peeling off
and eager to get out there. Okay, fine; that's the honest truth, which
might have helped me if I weren't now just *standing around* not
going surfing, less focused on the waves. Shall I keep asking how
I'm feeling in the next new moment, or *just get out there* and not
judge myself if I can't hang with all this meta-reflection? They say
you can be "mindful" while you do anything else. Self-observation
is certainly helpful as an occasional resource, but one must know
when to start and stop.

I see a wave breaking, peeling off. I'm conscious of it, just in
the seeing. Usually I'm not thinking about *myself,* standing here on
the cobblestone, let alone noticing my foot resting on the smooth
rocks. I'm seeing *the wave,* peeling off, forgetting about *my seeing it.*
Because waves are wonderful enough for thoughts of myself not to
be my focus. As Sartre suggests, "When I run after a streetcar . . .
there is no I. . . . I am plunged into the world of objects . . . which

present themselves . . . with attractive and repellant qualities—but me, I have disappeared."[1]

But do I ever disappear to myself completely? Are you always in some sense aware of the bottom of your feet? Of the back of your head? Or of the hum of the nearby refrigerator—at least faintly? The refrigerator hum stops suddenly, and I don't recognize the new silence. I realize that the hum colored my experience of the room. I noted it occasionally, but it remained all along in the background of my consciousness, on its periphery. And so might my very sense of self. I "disappear" from myself in fleeting moments, but maybe never *entirely*. My self is always in the periphery of my consciousness, with at least a faint presence.

This poses the question: How, or how far, can we transcend ourselves?

Consciousness as Work

Sartre points to moments of complete absorption—in chasing a streetcar or in counting cigarettes. The larger question is whether they come readily or often. Sartre's deeply self-conscious philosophy begins with Descartes. "I think, therefore I am," *Cogito, ergo sum*. This is great news if you happen to be in doubt about your existence. (You are somebody!) The matter is less pressing if you happen to be surfing, and you know you are said surfer already, because you know your moving body immediately, and therefore must be. Sartre rejected any "transcendental ego" that necessarily stands outside all experience, so as to own it. "The ego is not the owner of consciousness, it is the object of consciousness."[2] The ego is constructed in the flow of experience, along with a person's identity, his or her choice of who to be. But such labors of existence can bring self-

1. *The Transcendence of the Ego,* trans. Forrest Williams and Robert Kirkpatrick (New York: Farrar, Straus and Giroux, 1957), p. 48.
2. Ibid., p. 97.

preoccupation, limiting one's ability to steadily turn one's gaze away from oneself.

I once saw the depth of Sartre's insight while searching for yoga classes with a friend, which landed us in an incredibly long Buddhist service. After a couple of hours of yoga and meditation, along with coaching about breathing, self-discipline, and so on, I still hadn't lost myself in mere being, thinking of nothing. All I could think of was the anti-Buddhist idea that Sartre got from Kant, upon which much of Western civilization is premised. Try as you might to get free from it, the "I will" just kicks in, like it or not, for good reason or not. Are we going to a movie after this? How long can this "doing nothing" really last? Is yoga in fact good cross-training for surfing, or is this whole yoga thing another BS SoCal trend? Can't we at least *do* something, whatever, anything, however arbitrarily chosen?! They say you can learn to settle in completely with practice, being ushered into an ever-present meditative state of egoless, timeless consciousness. Which sounds terrific, except that all the practice before you reach nirvana sounds exhausting—too much like the work you thought you were getting away from.

Maybe the problem is human consciousness itself. Sartre agreed that consciousness is always consciousness *of* or *about* something else. I am aware of the apple, right there on the table. But in being aware of it, as an object of my consciousness, I know something about myself. I am equally aware that I am *not* the apple. For I am my consciousness, and I know that my consciousness is never identical to its object (it can't be if it is of or about that object). I must know this, pre-reflectively, because whatever is true of my consciousness is something I am automatically conscious of as true.[3] But then it seems I can never just see an apple. I'm always aware, at least faintly, that *I am now aware* of the apple as well. I never just see the wave, peeling off. I am aware of *myself now seeing* the wave, peeling off. And in doing the bottom turn on the wave,

3. This is Arthur Danto's reconstruction of Sartre's own tortured reasoning in *Being and Nothingness*. *Jean-Paul Sartre* (New York: Viking, 1975), p. 67.

I'm aware that *I'm now doing a bottom turn*. There is no escaping the sense of oneself, not even in surfing.

Perhaps Sartre only means that I'm *accountable* for my experiences, upon reflection. Do I see the apple? Do I see the wave? "Yes, I see it," I say in response to someone's questioning. I had truly lost myself in the seeing, perhaps completely. But of course now that you ask, yes, the one doing the seeing is me.[4] I own my experiences if I'm asked. That's all it means for me to own them, when my gaze is turned away from the world and back upon myself. We might be constantly turned back to ourselves, by vanity or status anxiety or social media. But then the problem is our vices or culture of self-preoccupation rather than bare consciousness itself.

Even so, the demands of *authenticity* in action are another matter. They alone might hobble any easy or sustained escape from self-consciousness. For Sartre, I am free and radically unbounded from culture and history—which sounds terrific, until I consider that I'll have to constantly think of myself, asking who I will be and what I will do next. I am responsible for myself "down to the slightest detail," and to acquiesce in my past, treating myself as passively determined in the course of larger events, would be "bad faith." Acting authentically means owning my freedom, and so I must always stand ready to choose myself again. I wake up, but shall I keep being a surfer on this new morning? The next day, I can ask again, to surf, or not to surf? The next day after, the same question. Shall I reaffirm the surfer identity I chose yesterday? Maybe I say yes. But I have to answer yes again, deciding afresh, yet again. Which sounds a lot harder than just getting into a groove of hitting the waves day after day in a regular practice, without thinking much of it.[5]

4. I figure in to such "positional" consciousness, as Sartre calls it, because I'm aware of my relation to the apple ("I see the apple"). I can also just see the apple without being aware of my position in respect to it ("non-positional consciousness"). On the present reading, the latter is easier to come by.
5. But must I constantly ask myself who to be? I cannot refuse to own my choice if I ask, but perhaps the question often won't come up. The philosopher Bill Bracken tells me he reads Sartre's discussion of one's "original project" as allowing one not to deliberately, explicitly choose a plan of life (see *Being and Nothingness*, pp. 581 and

So being is freedom, which is work. To be is to be at work, the work of constantly constructing a self. I am a constant project of making and remaking myself in my projected image. As Sartre says, "Freedom is precisely the nothingness which is *made-to-be* at the heart of man and which forces human reality *to make itself* instead of *to be*."[6]

But why the "instead"? Can't a person be, while doing and being, simultaneously? It is possible.

Doing surfing. Being in the flow of the wave.

In the flow of the wave, the surfer finds an easy self-transcendence. Bathed in the sublime and the beautiful, even on an ordinary day, the gliding surfer escapes the mundane for a lighter, more stoked persistence through the flows and the ebbs of life's rhythms. By surfing day after day, in the hum of regular practice, the surfer becomes ever more attuned, for being absorbed in what lies beyond the self.

Drawing the Bow Spiritually

In traditional Japanese archery, a Zen monastery is organized around an archery range. Eugen Herrigel, a European philosopher who traveled to Japan to learn Zen archery, charts the great difficulty in learning how to draw the bow spiritually.[7]

There are of course the rudiments of aiming to hit the target, steadying one's grip, training one's attention, timing action around

---

596). Sartre is also clear, he adds, that the will is not the privileged manifestation of freedom; passion counts as well (ibid., pp. 571 and 573). So while I could conform to a chosen plan, I could also authentically let passion rule and allow my life to take whatever shape it takes as a result. Willing a life plan even carries additional risks of bad faith, in not fully acknowledging one's embodied, situated "facticity." This brings Sartre closer to Merleau-Ponty and the surfer position, though perhaps still without a clearly stated theory of adaptive attunement.

6. Ibid., p. 568.

7. *Zen in the Art of Archery* (New York: Vintage, 1989) (for the other passages quoted in the text, see pp. 29–32, 39, 48, 53–55).

one's breathing, and managing hunger or fatigue. Yet even a "trick archer who likes to show off" might mostly land the arrow in "sheer devilry" or vain trickery. True mastery goes further, toward a more enlightened way of release.

At one major step, the challenge is to release the string from one's fingers at just the right time, so as to avoid a "powerful jerk" that causes the shot to "wobble." Yet you can't get the timing just right if you do it purposefully. As the master explains, if you yourself "call it forth, your hand will not open in the right way"; "the shot will only go smoothly when it takes the archer himself by surprise."

Worse still, trying is counterproductive; the more you "try to learn how to shoot the arrow for the sake of hitting the goal, the less you will succeed." The right timing comes along only as one falls passively into an attuned moment of release. "Everything depends on the archer's becoming purposeless and effacing himself in the event." The shot must be released "automatically, with no further need of the controlling or reflecting intelligence," like a ripe fruit falling in its ready moment.

Aristotle assumed this wasn't possible. Acting with a purpose is the very hallmark of action, and so any part of archery action is done with the purpose of hitting the target. But might "acting with a purpose" permit certain passive happenings? You certainly need working digestion and brain activity at a sub-personal level. On the other hand, these aren't things *you* do, at the person level, and it can be hard to see how a state of *not acting* could be your doing, for the sake of your ends. You can't choose to *sleep*. What you can do is choose to put yourself in conditions where sleep is likely to come over you—by *letting yourself fall* into a sleep state. As for that last passive moment, the falling, the puzzle is how it could still be your own action, rather than a condition that simply comes over you. How could you purposefully choose a completely purposeless state, as distinct from merely leading yourself up to it, before it then just happens?

Anyway, the Zen answer is that "letting go of yourself" is indeed something you do, or are at least told to do. Which means "leaving yourself and everything yours behind you so decisively that nothing more is left of you but a purposeless tension."

In surfing and in life, it's true that one can't have a "too willful will," as the Zen master says. One won't be very well attuned to things beyond oneself without paying careful attention to them, and it is difficult to pay close attention to other things if one is preoccupied with oneself. Perhaps one need only withdraw certain "attachments" consistent with one's aim of hitting the target, such an attachment to performing well, or to winning, or to pleasing one's parents or oneself.[8] But Zen seems to require more, and indeed nothing less than "withdrawing from all attachments whatsoever, by becoming utterly egoless: so that the soul, sunk within itself, stands in the plentitude of its namely origin."

Surfing simply *can't* be so exactly ego-free. No aquatic moment is so fixed to permit falling into a fully passive state; there's no time for not actively adapting. If you had to find a trance state or wakeful dream sleep, and the wave's next moment was coming quickly, you'd eat it, or quickly become out of sync. The bodily dynamism and moment-by-moment demands on one's attention naturally draw one's consciousness out into the waves, away from oneself. But this ego transcendence serves the surfer's active purposes, of being adaptively attuned. If that isn't Zen, it's a blessedly easy way of being while doing.

When not attending an incredibly long Buddhist service, but just chilling down at the beach, the "I" is not always so near. Sure, almost at will, I can, if I wanted to, direct my attention to the feeling of the rocks pressing against my heel and make myself aware of the bottom of my feet. I could take my eye off the world and reflect upon myself, my body, my relation to my surroundings, in "reflective" self-consciousness, if I wanted to. But this is simply a matter of what I attend to, of what's of most interest to me. And surely surfing

8. The psychiatrist Roger Walsh offered that sympathetic suggestion for squaring Zen with Aristotle in conversation. His suggestion is in the spirit of his edited volume *The World's Great Wisdom: Timeless Teachings from Religions and Philosophies* (Albany: State University of New York Press, 2014).

is more interesting than the bottom of my feet. Buddhist practice sharply disciplines one's habits of attending. But the surfer can be guided by his or her attachment to waves and surfing them, a love that keeps him or her ever more absorbed, ever more attuned to the waves and the surfing.

Even while up and riding, *I'm* definitely the one acting; no one else is doing the surfing. But my experience of myself can pass in and entirely out of my flow of consciousness, and then back to my bodily technique, as the wave moment asks of me. I'm flowing because I'm fully engaged in the speeding moments, with my actions drawn up into the blurring wind rush and my sense of myself fading into the background of my attention, often fading away completely, even from the periphery of my consciousness.

Maybe on some golden afternoon, I'm just present in the ocean, drawn into its sublimity, feeling absorbed in its gentle undulations as I paddle along. Maybe I'm aware of myself and the bathy warm water on my skin. Or maybe not. One can just settle into presence. Not with one's current state of consciousness, but with what one's consciousness is *of* or *about* beyond oneself. One can be free in easy self-transcendence, free from any thought of oneself whatsoever.

So there is under the sun a way of being fully present in this moment, and the next, and then the next, in watching a peeling wave, or in gliding along a wave face. Anguish does not arise from our very conscious existence, as Sartre says. The source of our discontentment is our continued *subsistence,* in a stressful work environment, with a tyrant boss, a rival colleague angling for advantage, and crap hours. Being lost in a moment, ideally with no thought of ourselves, is anguish's medicine. And so regular surfing, with time to do it, makes for health in life.

"Be Like Water"

As a plant turns toward sunlight, as the bees buzz in teeming fields, as the seasons progress, along with the times, change is said to be the only constant. Adaptation is the centerpiece of modern science's theory of living being, the theory of evolution by natural selection. And beyond science, a go-with-the-flow ethic seems only appropriate if change is the way of things. We adapt so as to grow and evolve, or rise to the struggles that the Lord hath placed before us, by *embracing* change, being ready for it, without lashing out in anxious indignation about the loss of what was and was supposed to always be.

Bruce Lee, the martial arts superstar, advised us to "be like water, my friend," by which he meant both in self-defense and as a way of being. The rub is that people are only *like* water, even as they're 90 percent composed of the stuff. Consciousness flows like a fluid, but Sartre's idea of freedom can sound as if our selves were entirely up to us, to be reconstituted as our will's instrument. Yet no one can change all at once, all at the same time, in nearly every area of life, not without losing his or her bearings completely. Any virtue of adaptability, as a general trait of good character, can ask only so much change from a person, who is by nature a fleshy, structured, and relatively fixed sort of thing. A person, after all, isn't an object designed for a purpose that can be ever further "adapted" for any old end, as when a hammer is used as an art display or doorstop. When a person adapts to a new situation, the change must follow from his or her minded state of being. No matter how much flow shapes one's personal growth journey, we're all conservatives in some measure: we agree there's such a thing as being asked to change too much, too quickly. To stay open, to learn and keep learning, so as to adapt to the unfamiliar, a person must be in a relatively assured position, banking on much that is sweetly normal, regular, consistent, and rather comfortable in ordinary living, at least for the time being.

When we must change, to "be like water" is to adapt well or skillfully, with fluency. Yet how far this brings self-transcendence depends on what sort of "adaptation" is called for and whether it can be done for its own sake.

Coping

To cope is to adapt to an unwelcome situation of necessity. It is to adapt, not for its own sake, but for the extrinsic reasons of making one's situation less bad than it would otherwise be. A tree falls across one's path, and one climbs over it. A tsunami is approaching quickly in the close distance, and one runs like hell. One loses one's job, and one tries to figure out what to do next. Or as the ancient historian of the Peloponnesian War, Thucydides, said, while the strong do what they can, the weak suffer as they must. They cope, with the warlords, with the daily machinations of bloviating, grandstanding power politics, while rarely getting a pay increase, on yet another day under the thumb of an overbearing boss. One "makes the best of a bad situation," leaving things less bad than they would otherwise be in a situation one would prefer not to be in.

Even coping can be well or badly done. When ungracious scolds hector the underemployed about taking some responsibility for their poverty, by working *even harder,* the slight element of truth is that one can make the best of things skillfully or unskillfully. You can "be like water" when a knife man is charging, redirecting his moving forces for your own ends as in aikido. A spell of unemployment *could* become an exciting new life direction—of surfing more often, of spending more time with the kids. Or not, because one can be mediocre even in coping, and maybe it takes all you've got to scrape by, to *barely* cope, to just hang on and not feel downed, beaten, done.

It won't then be especially helpful to be told that now is the time to learn patience, that you can always learn something from this, and that, you know, one should always look on the bright side of life. Whatever truth such clichés may sometimes hold, one will be forgiven for finding self-pity easy and "self-transcendence" not quite at the top of one's to-do list. Camus's Sisyphus found a shred of self-respect in pushing the boulder from defiant self-assertion, coping as well as one could in his absurd predicament. But this is a tale of heroism, and it shouldn't diminish our appreciation of the normal "strains of commitment" that hobble faithful cooperation, which

John Rawls thought any political philosophy must address.[9] Some withdraw and resign in personal dejection. Others are inflamed with passions of rebellion in self-assertion, for instance, in wanting to break a dysfunctional political order perceived as displaying contempt (for example, by voting for Brexit or Trump).

If coping is making the best of a bad situation, one might still find sport in overcoming, by adopting a certain manner of coping for its own sake. You'd rather not have to defend yourself, but you're going to when attacked, and in that case why not see if you can rebuff the pip-squeak attacker after your wallet with one hand behind your back, whereupon you finally, finally get to unleash your practiced jujitsu kick, while staging a protest in that selfsame act, Sticking It to the Man! (I'm sure the poor kid won't know what hit him.)[10] To "couch surf" is to sleep on the various couches of friends or family members, usually as a result of being homeless or underemployed. "I'm couch surfing" in response to the question "So where do you live?" is often offered as a playful joke, perhaps so as to suggest a free and fun spell of life, valued for its own sake. If the person's larger predicament is still regrettable, this manner of coping would contrast with surfing proper, which is done for intrinsic reasons in the most welcome of circumstances, as when one's time is free. Perhaps someone could surf in order to cope with what is felt to be an otherwise meaningless existence—"life is absurd, so why not go surfing?" Still, the sporting activity itself would be done for its own sake. (Later we return to what such a person might be overlooking.)

---

9. His own answer is *A Theory of Justice* or *Justice as Fairness: A Restatement,* ed. Erin Kelly (Cambridge, Mass.: Harvard University Press, 2001).
10. Oddly, surfers seem to take to jujitsu, much in the way they seem prone to take up golf. Perhaps it's that each activity is individualistic, focused on bodily technique, and requires focused progression to get very far.

Games and Sports

When work is done and the time is free, people often voluntarily choose to play a game or sport. Both kinds of play are an adaptive activity done not of necessity but for its own sake.

In the philosopher Bernard Suits's excellent definition, to "play a game" is to voluntarily attempt to overcome unnecessary obstacles. His full formulation highlights why the player would do such a thing. To play a game is

> to attempt to achieve a specific state of affairs, using only means permitted by rules, where the rules prohibit use of more efficient in favor of less efficient means, and where *the rules are accepted just because they make possible such activity.*[11]

So, for instance, to play soccer/*fútbol* is to attempt to achieve the specific state of affairs of scoring goals, in accord with a rule against using one's hands (unless one designated player is defending the goal), where such rules are accepted just because this creates the possibility of playing a beautiful game. The rules prohibit a more efficient means of achieving the assumed goal, for instance, grabbing and running with the ball as in rugby or American football.

When a game player seeks to put a ball into a hole, he or she needn't assume this specific state of affairs has any value in itself. Does anyone find getting a very small dimpled ball into a very small hole, at the center of a well-mowed grassy area, an intrinsically good thing? And if one did for some reason wish for small balls to go into small holes, or to put small balls into small holes for oneself (perhaps for the intrinsic appeal of the ball drop or swirl or plunk), surely there's no *less efficient* way of accomplishing this end than by clubbing, whacking, and scooting said ball toward the hole with a long metal stick, weighted by an oblong end, at first from a great

---

11. *The Grasshopper: Games, Life, and Utopia,* 3rd ed. (Peterborough, Ont.: Broadview Press, 2014), p. 43 (my italics).

distance, over and over on varied terrain. If you cared *at all* about efficiency, like in business, you'd just walk over and place the damn ball in the hole by hand. But in fact even (or especially) business types use the golf club. No one is so resolute about efficiency as to refuse to play on principle. There are extrinsic reasons for golf play, of networking, reputation, or getting fresh air. Yet playing golf also means seeing intrinsic value in trying to adapt to its challenges, which, as Suits emphasizes, are arbitrary and indeed *patently inefficient,* because they block the easiest means to a stipulated end. What's valued in game play is the very activity of adapting, for the sake of its intrinsic benefits rather than extrinsic ends.

Sports generally don't limit the possibilities of action as rules of a game do. Any sport has "constitutive rules" that define what it would be to perform the basic sporting activity at all, as opposed to doing something else, such as swimming, or boating, or hang gliding. You just aren't *surfing* if you're not in one way or another carried along by a wave's propulsive forces. But beyond rules that define our very concept of the activity, sports seem more open, except when they are being played as a game.

Surfing doesn't require the acceptance of rules that pose unnecessary obstacles to hydro-locomotion which are then to be overcome. It therefore isn't a game. Indeed, in what competitive surfers call "free surfing," surfers will say that freedom is the liberty to surf *however the hell they want,* on whatever sort of surfboard, with whatever sort of approach. Long boarding, short boarding, even body surfing—what matters, as surfers put it, is that you "just get out there."[12] Once the basics of staying afloat and being carried along by the natural force of a wave are behind you, you really are free to go for your preferred means of adaptation, in style or board technology or wave approach. Surfing custom is constantly evolving,

---

12. Body boarding, however, is persistently devalued by stand-up surfers, except insofar as radical wave conditions make stand-up surfing impossible or plainly inferior. Surfing is in this regard marred by prejudice and elitism.

but it's mainly a source of advice or inspiration. Even the usual contest criteria—speed, power, flow, and of course style—are very general virtues, and under constant refashioning in the fashion show of photographs and video clips that stream through surf media daily. In your own surfing, you're still free to get out there and offer your own take, doing your own thing, whatever the hell you want. Surfing is freedom. So do what you want. Express yourself.

Even surfing can be played as a game, by adopting rules that define obstacles and set new ends. Two surfers in the water could start scoring their rides by the usual judging criteria, making their session into an impromptu surf contest, the game now being to surf in order to score and win. If the hallmark of a competitive sport is the acceptance of rules that define scoring and winning a contest of skill, the purist will refuse such acceptance on principle. Surfing is to be done *only* for the intrinsic reasons that make it wonderful. Which is perhaps understandable given the risks of surfing's steady corruption. Surfing is increasingly being made into a competitive game for extrinsic rewards of making a living, winning, and such prizes as rank, travel, fame, and gold medals (surfing is now slated for the 2020 Tokyo Olympics). Competition is supposed to bring out the best in the competitors, which it certainly does. But it can also draw forth less savory motives, much as Rousseau explained. Competition is, after all, a way of comparing ourselves with others, and thus a source of strife, vice, and unhappiness, and indeed much if not all of civilization's discontents. (We return to this in the next chapter.)

Yet the most strident of purists probably underestimate the gains in performance due to competitive surfing, not to mention the spectatorial excitement in watching a good contest. And the risks perhaps aren't so terribly grave. Pro surfers themselves seem at no risk of not riding waves at least *in part* for intrinsic reasons. It is a cliché in contest interviews that, yeah, you know, win or lose, you're just stoked to be surfing the world's best waves with only a few people out there. The pros really mean it, every time they say it. True surfing must be done at least partly for intrinsic motivations, but they come easily, especially in the world's best waves.[13]

Playing

If all sports are played for their own sakes, at least partly, they differ from each other in calling upon different adaptive attunements, under very different conditions. They also differ in spontaneity or playfulness.

In golf, the awkward bodily twist must be adapted with fine-grained adjustments, for each new fairway, green, and stroke, in a relatively fixed environment. Unlike with surfing, there's no expectation of constant bodily adaptation in an ever-changing medium, without even terra firma to stand on.[14] The changing wind may call for fine-tuning, but like archery the adaptive challenges beyond a certain skill level are therefore mainly psychological. An attuned performance requires a sound "mental game," which according to one guide includes "clarity, commitment, and composure" in preparation and "feeling confident, focused, and in the flow, with body and mind synchronized in the present moment" in action.[15]

13. Could a benighted soul find himself just going through the wave-riding motions, competing only for wins and money? This is an interesting theoretical possibility. "Professional surfing" would have become a performative contradiction—just work, and not true surfing. I doubt such a surfer could remain competitive for long; staying attuned depends on the sheer love of surfing.

14. In this connection, the French philosopher Gilles Deleuze compares sports such as golf with a newer class of sports that includes surfing. In golf or running, "there's a point of contact" and "we are the source of movement" as we make an effort to overcome the resistance created at a "point of leverage" (for example, the green, the golf club). By contrast, "All the new sports—surfing, windsurfing, hang-gliding—take the form of entering into an existing wave." I take it he means skillful adaptation is required in order to be moved by an independent propulsive flow. As he elaborates, "The key thing is how to get taken up in the motion of a big wave, a column of rising air, to 'get into something' instead of being the origin of an effort." "There's no longer an origin as starting point, but a sort of putting-into-orbit." The passage appears in "Mediators," in *Negotiations, 1972–1990,* trans. Martin Joughin (New York: Columbia University Press, 1977), p. 121.

15. Joseph Parent, *Zen Golf: Mastering the Mental Game* (New York: Doubleday, 2002), pp. xvii–xviii.

Ballet is also performed on a fixed field of play, the stage. The dancers don't adapt to a changing dance space, but attune to each other in each new moment of the music, movement, or ensemble. If we can talk of "flow" generally in degrees of perfection, the "social flow" achieved in the amazing spectacle rivals and often surpasses the natural flow in surfing. Yet surfing and ballet are very different in ambition. Surfing permits a rawer, natural spontaneity. Ballet's coordination is ultimately an orchestrated *appearance* of natural flow, for the sake of a wonderful performance. The inspired performances stand at the zenith of human athletic attunement, but not because a flow state of effortless action is being achieved. The routines are born of incredible rigor, in each disciplined move of each body, in each dancer's streak through the choreography, after inordinate hours of sweat, in constant muscle pain, with exquisite attention to detail. Even at the peak of performance, the seemingly effortless dance is in fact immensely effortful. The art lies in creating a flow spectacle from what in fact involves a hell of a lot of work.[16]

Surfing also takes work; you paddle a lot, maybe constantly if there's a strong current. Yet you rest often, and the constantly shifting wave environment precludes any very meticulous orchestration. There can't be a routine, which is freeing for those with control fatigue. You can relax and let loose, taking each wave as it comes with a natural authenticity that has its own human kind of beauty.

16. The philosopher Barbara Montero explains why seemingly effortless dancing is in fact effortful, drawing on her own experience as a ballerina: "Often I would be thinking about how to capture, accentuate, or play with the music in my movement, thinking, perhaps, 'let me extend that note beyond the end' or some such loosely formulated idea. . . . [T]his . . . involved deliberation (should I do this here, or wait) . . . and concerted concentration. Sometimes my thoughts would be . . . [about] aspects of my performance quality, presenting a movement with more attack, or making some other movement flow." "A Dancer Reflects," in *Mind, Reason, and Being-in-the-World: The McDowell-Dreyfus Debate,* ed. Joseph K. Schear (New York: Routledge, 2013) (draft at https://barbaramontero.wordpress.com /category/publications/page/2/). For her general account of why focusing on what you are doing does not interfere with performance, and often enhances it, see her *Thought in Action: Expertise and the Conscious Mind* (Oxford: Oxford University Press, 2016).

For its playful, improvisational nature, surfing is perhaps more similar to basketball and especially jazz improvisation. Each activity demands moment-by-moment adaptation, often with little time for planning and forethought. Yet the improvisation is attunedly guided. Each next move is understood in light of the one prior, and the ones coming up. There's the memory of how things have so far unfolded; an expectation of what will follow; ideas about where things might be taken; a sense of what to go for generally, and the different ways to go for it.

The basketball player's "no-look pass" comes in expectation of his or her teammate's approaching for the dunk, perhaps at a time in the game that permits the risky gambit. The jazz drummer "lays in the pocket," waiting in anticipation of where the soloist is headed, starting a phrase to help express his or her idea of the moment's music. The surfer "coasts" through a mounting section, taking the high line while the wave face is building, before down weighting in a crouch and then doing a snap on the other side of the quickly steepening section.

Neither the player nor the surfer is "doing nothing," not with the complete passivity of the Zen archer's bow release. For *being and staying present,* especially while waiting, is improvisation's active motion, the very action of attunement. In surfing and in music making, by giving ourselves to the moment we can transcend ourselves in attunement to the larger movement.

Meaning in Life

So I can flow out of myself by imagination in what Kant calls a "free play" of my faculties, in a "free harmony" of thought and feeling that is something like the bodily harmony of the surfer in riding a wave. Call it mind surfing or daydreaming or whatever, but it seems rather good as a way to live and be.

Of course, even if we play games and sports for intrinsic reasons, the appearance of intrinsic value could be a delusion brought on by an electrolyte imbalance or too much sun. For Camus, our plight is simply to cope, and coping is easier when one acts *as if* something were intrinsically worth doing, when in fact nothing has any extrinsic or intrinsic value. We gave an answer in chapter 4: our existential predicament is that of having to define ourselves with too many worthy choices in a rich plenum of values. Yet this does not quite answer Camus's question of suicide as he himself understood it. His own test of a question's urgency is the "actions it entails," and, he notes, "I see many people die because they judge that life is not worth living" in acts of suicide "prepared within the silence of the heart, as is a great work of art."[17] What can philosophy say to them?

Perhaps not much. If the philosopher must "preach by example," as Camus says, I would recommend surfing and sunshine, along with a good therapist, and maybe travel. On the other hand, if we are to judge the importance of a question by real action, as Camus suggests, then it is relevant to consider our natural motivations, including among non-depressives. And while the human spirit can be defiant in self-assertion, it is also fundamentally playful. Animals of course play—romping puppies pretend not to bite, and dolphins in their own way surf.[18] As animals ourselves, we can transcend what is routine or oppressive in human culture, by living playfully.[19] As the cultural theorist Johan Huizinga explains, play for *Homo ludens* is prior to all human ritual and culture, but therefore a means of transforming serious adult business. "In play we may move below the level of the serious, as the child does; but we can also move above it, in the realm of the beautiful and the sacred."[20]

A child is acting like an elephant, hunched over, lumbering forward with a heavy gait, arm outstretched, dangling in sway like a

17. *Myth of Sisyphus*, p. 4.
18. They glide along just beneath the surface of a wave, with occasional breaks or jumps. They are carried along by the wave's natural momentum, but under rather than in the tube, or on the wave face, in the sporting human surfer way.
19. As for how, see Ian Bogost, *Play Anything: The Pleasure of Limits, the Uses of Boredom, and the Secret of Games* (New York: Basic Books, 2016).
20. *Homo Ludens: A Study of the Play-Element in Culture* (London: Routledge and Kegan Paul, 1949), p. 19.

trunk. Only a spoilsport won't play along with the imaginative pretense. It is merely a pretense, of course. It would be *true,* albeit rather obtuse, to say to the child, "You aren't really an elephant. You're a human." The child is not confused. What she really believes in is the *value* of play, and nearly all of us agree. Whether in make-believe, a game of Parcheesi, or a day in the waves, play is worth doing for its own sake. That claim of value is *not* mere pretense, and if the spoilsport attempts to deny it, it is he who would seem to be missing something. What could be more human than getting caught up in a game, sport, or creative project with little thought of anything else, finding this a very good thing?

A few kids play soccer/*fútbol*, passing a lovely afternoon, finding it really satisfying to kick a ball, booting the thing squarely from underneath. Because, why not? It's the sort of thing one really should try at some point before one's death, along with dragging paint across a large canvas, reading many great books, and being taken along by a wave (even on a boogie board in tiny waves, if you can't swing the long process of learning to surf). There's a lot to do, a lot that really is worth doing with one's limited time under the sun. Doing it can have no pretense of greater meaning, no risk of the absurd's gap between pretense and reality, no risk of cosmic mistake. With a few friends going surfing and the forecast portending an epic session, none of them will pause to consider Camus's question of whether life is worthy of being continued before the swell hits. Suicide, if someone did think of it, would definitely have to wait until later, maybe much later. Even a depressingly long flat spell will be over by the time you've caught up on the work you neglected during the last swell. The swells vary with the seasons, but the lapping waves and crashing breakers keep coming in the ocean's steady rhythm. For the surfer, this is meaning in life, and all the meaning needed to keep on living from week to week, year to year, in a fortunate life.

Surfing is sport, but not that alone. It can be as totalizing as a religion, by organizing one's whole existence. It is not just absorbing in the engaged moments, as with a novelty item or hobby; once you lose yourself in the pursuit, you can lose your life to it, and count yourself fortunate. Surfing is so intrinsically wonderful that I want to *be*, rather than not, just to be present when it happens. How fortunate I am—for the confluence of circumstances when I started surfing, for the lucky breaks that let me keep going, and now for the years behind me. My good fortunes have vested, my wealth banked, my time under the sun blessed, whatever happens next. The past being past, not even God can change it. And while death will happen, maybe sooner than expected, maybe in some gnarly accident, it's all good for the already fortunate. The days or years or decades remaining are gravy.[21]

I could of course dwell on the fact that I will die eventually, asking myself whether I'm living worthily with time so short. I could contentedly answer that, yes, indeed, this, this day, this nice week, was well spent surfing, if I did ask. Heidegger thought being "authentic" meant living in that question, constantly asking whether one's actions are worthy in the shadow of one's demise (what he called "being-toward-death"). This for him is to live without denial, without needing distraction or dreams of eternal life to get the week to make sense. But in all the surfer tales of death and other gnarliness, and despite having a ready answer to the personal question of meaning, surfers don't constantly ask themselves whether a week or year or decade of surfing could make sense given the shortness of life. Maybe it's that the answer is too obvious for the question. "Of course!" is the answer, of course, so why ask? More likely, such self-preoccupation is untrue to the moment, to the fine swells marching in, or to the upcoming week's waves. When the waves are pumping, day after day, and surfers begin to comment on their special fortune, the sense of the extraordinary beauty of life, enjoyed in such abundance, isn't about oneself. You're stoked just to be there and partake of it, and if someone mentioned it, you could just shrug

---

21. Thus the benefits of being older. The young risk having stumbled into surfing and then losing it after only a few years. The middle-aged and aged surfers are the especially fortunate ones.

death off. "Yup, of course. But no worries. Check this insane next wave! I guess I will surf again."

So we can and do find self-transcendent presence in ordinary hobbies, games, sports, and music. We can lose ourselves by engaging them for the sake of those activities themselves. And when or if one can square them with work, pursuits like surfing, ballet, and jazz play really can transcend mere "leisurely" preoccupations and organize a whole life. Could they even organize the whole, or at least the better part, of social life?

Defining "play" to include any intrinsically valued activity, including games and sports, Suits argues that play is the *only* activity that allows us to imagine a utopia after the end of all labor and striving for merely instrumental purpose.[22] Suppose that machines have brought the end of work; that material abundance is achieved; that psychology has treated all psychic disturbances; and that all strife and competition is removed from love and admiration, science and philosophy, and art and sex. Just suppose, for the sake of argument. What then would we do with ourselves? Is this post-striving "utopia" even morally attractive? Or as Arthur Schopenhauer put the question,

> Certain it is that work, worry, labor and trouble, form the lot
> of almost all men their whole life long. But if all wishes were
> fulfilled as soon as they arose, how would men occupy their
> lives? What would they do with their time?[23]

Suits's answer is that we would play games and sports! We could still play for its own sake. And if some people intrinsically valued doing things now regarded as trades, such as house building, they

22. *Grasshopper,* pp. 182–95.
23. "On the Suffering of the World," in *Studies in Pessimism,* trans. T. Bailey Saunders (New York: Cosimo Classics, 2007), p. 6.

could do that too, but done as sport, for intrinsic reasons of the building craft. "In addition to hockey, baseball, tennis, and so on, there would also be sports of business administration, jurisprudence, philosophy, production management, motor mechanics, *ad*, for all practical purposes, *infinitum*."

For Suits, the fact that we can approvingly imagine this form of society shows that the idea of utopia is intelligible to us. And while it won't happen anytime soon, the thought experiment in the "metaphysics of leisure time" shows the deep meaning of what we often trivialize as "pastimes." The games and sports we now play may in fact be "intimations of things to come," "cues to the future" whose "serious cultivation now is perhaps our only salvation."[24]

Yet this is unnecessarily utopian. "Pastimes" such as surfing aren't intimations of things to come. They are, world historically speaking, a consequence of the leisure revolution already begun. Now over seven decades under way, pure capitalism has been long since abandoned. We no longer allocate labor and time simply by the market, as in a pure laissez-faire economy, which before the early twentieth century left most people scarce time beyond work. With the institution of the forty-hour workweek, and then an accumulation of wealth unprecedented in human history, instrumental activities have long ceased to be the whole of life. Most people in the advanced world now have at least a modicum of time for play in games or sports. Many still mainly cope, working to make the best of their unwelcome situation, rather than working as sport, for its own sake. But the possibility of self-transcendence in both play and work is a present reality rather than a utopian dream. The long revolution is not away from capitalism as such, to a postcapitalist "utopia" of the sort Karl Marx thought would invariably come about with the rise of the proletariat. The revolution is *within* capitalism, and the question is whether and how our social contract might be

---

24. In the film *Traffic*, the Benicio Del Toro character, a Tijuana police officer, hopes to convince U.S. drug enforcement officers of their common cause in the "war on drugs." Drawing them into a swimming pool, he asks, "Do you like baseball?" and the scene flashes to a pleasant Little League game.

further adapted in the present century. We return to this in the following chapters.

For the moment, note a major result of our inquiry up to this point. The surfer's preferred society, of working less with more time for surfing or hiking or stamp collecting, would not be an unrealistic utopia, at odds with human nature. For Sartre, the difficulty of relaxation is existential, unavoidable. Being is inseparable from active doing in self-creation, seen as a kind of work. Our natures limit the realistic possibilities for culture and society and may well limit the relaxation of work culture. But in the surfer view of human nature, which we've now developed, the causes of angst and heavy living are not fixed in our natures. They follow from what we together make of ourselves, in the kind of culture and society we choose. Culture steers our attention, and it can spoil our attunement by encouraging preoccupation with ourselves, our identity, status, and appearance in the eyes of others. Self-escape thus *becomes* a kind of work. But this is not inevitable; we can transcend ourselves readily, at least in favorable circumstances. The leisure revolution began in the postwar era by calling forth our natural powers of play, in surfing and other self-transcending leisure pursuits. Nothing in our very nature prevented it, and nothing in our natures would keep it from continuing as the present century unfolds.

Is the Sublime About Us?

Kant committed surfer blasphemy when he said that "the broad ocean agitated by storms cannot be called sublime." The stormy ocean, he says, is merely "horrible."[25] The sublime is simply the *feeling* we have in the face of the horrible when we are drawn out of our experience of the ocean itself to thoughts of *ourselves*. For when we "abandon sensibility" and have "higher" ideas, they turn out to be rather self-involved thoughts of our "superiority over nature." Kant writes,

25. *Critique of Judgment*, p. 246.

For although we found our own limitation when we considered the immensity of nature . . . we also found, in our power of reason, a different and nonsensible standard that has [a grasp of] infinity itself . . . ; and since in contrast with this standard everything in nature is small, we found in our mind a superiority over nature itself in its immensity.[26]

Under Kant's influence, the poet William Wordsworth picked up the theme of superiority and praised the sublime's egoistically ennobling effect. He alludes to Kant's comment that the "starry skies above" are one of two things that awe us most (the other being "the moral law within"). He then writes,

Of a majestic intellect, its acts
And its possessions, what it has and craves,
What in itself it is, and would become.
There I beheld the emblem of a mind
That feeds upon infinity, that broods
Over the dark abyss, intent to hear
Its voices issuing forth to silent light
In one continuous stream; a mind sustained
By recognitions of transcendent power,
In sense conducting to ideal form,
In soul of more than mortal privilege.[27]

So the sublime is ultimately all about *us*. The awesome wonder is not the stormy ocean but the observer on the cliff; not the tsunami, but the moral beings swept up in the surge; not the hurricane, but the people watching it in safe horror on TV from their couches.

Mill reports that he was drawn out of a deep depression by read-

26. Ibid., p. 120.
27. *The Prelude,* in *The Complete Poetical Works of William Wordsworth, Late Poet Laureate,* ed. Henry Reed (Philadelphia: Porter and Coates, 1851), p. 545, or at http://www.bartleby.com/145/ww300.html.

ing Wordsworth's poems. They allowed him to be excited again about natural beauty and the human love of it:

> What made Wordsworth's poems a medicine for my state of mind, was that they expressed, not mere outward beauty, but states of feeling, and of thought coloured by feeling, under the excitement of beauty. They seemed to be the very culture of the feelings, which I was in quest of. In them I seemed to draw from a Source of inward joy, of sympathetic and imaginative pleasure, which could be shared in by all human beings; which had no connexion with struggle or imperfection, but would be made richer by every improvement in the physical or social condition of mankind.[28]

Mill thus found an answer to Schopenhauer's question about life after the end of work. "When all the greater evils of life shall have been removed," Mill concluded, we could find a perennial source of happiness with "no connexion with struggle or imperfection." We could discover it in the beauty of nature.

Now we are talking! This rings true to surfer experience, yet it rings with no hint of what Kant calls "our superiority over nature." Surfing is lofty and ennobling precisely for its power to draw us out of ourselves. Kant had it right when he said elsewhere that the "mental attunement" befitting a sublime object is "*not* a feeling of the sublimity of our own nature" (my italics). What is it like to see the stormy ocean as sublime? A wave peels off, cresting, cracking, powerfully tubing. To surf such a wave is to have a sense of the ocean's sublimity and the beauty in going along with the flow of its waves. The ocean agitated by storms is part of the raft of material conditions that make waves at our shores. All of which is completely sublime, *just in and of itself,* really and truly, even when we aren't actively appreciating it. To sense this is to experience the *ocean* as sublime, as an apt object of awe and wonder, not just have a feeling

28. *Autobiography* (New York: Penguin Classics, 1990), chap. 5.

about it. Our feelings on a given day, which might be excessive, flat, or out of place, are another matter entirely. But feeling wonderment when it is apt brings a sense of harmony. One's feelings and the world are aligned, attuned.

Is the great philosopher confused? The problem is partly that Kant isn't really after the felt quality of an experience. I see a cup on the table, resting there at a distance, in the ordinary way. What makes this experience possible? What must be true of our minds such that we could experience an object in space and time in that ordinary cup-there-on-the-table way? Kant's answer was to lay out the "transcendental" conditions that lie *beneath* my ordinary experience, which must hold for it to be possible. He thus posited deep super-sensuous "categories" of human understanding (time, space, causality), which we all operate with innately. We all more or less see the cup there on the table in the same way, because the basic categories of our minds construct our experience in the same way. But the sublime is different. It can't be "contained in any sensuous form"—can't be experienced like a cup on a table or its properties—because it is a different part of the background structure of any sensory experience, what he called an "idea of reason."

So I'm guessing Kant thought our experience of the sublime would lead back to us because his transcendental philosophy bled into his description of our experience. That philosophy (which is sublime in itself) was hugely influential in Western thought. Yet I think Kant would have to agree that none of it is plain *in* ordinary experience. It isn't part and parcel of a surfer's experience of *what it's like* to be in, and palpably sense, the ocean and its roaring waves, when you're right in front of them. It took philosophers like Edmund Husserl, the early phenomenologist whom Sartre followed, to get us to *just look* at the surface, at the *intrinsic character* of our experience *as it comes to us*. So if we're sticking to what it's like to be a surfer, we can leave the sublime *in the waves*.

On the other hand, Kant would call waves "beautiful," straight up. So the sublime is more like the beautiful in Kant's own account, which does nicely fit surfer experience. The sight of a wave can bring disinterested pleasure, the sort of enjoyment that comes from the free play or free harmony of one's imagination and understanding. That spontaneous enjoyment is potentially *apt,* or appropriate to its object, because it lays claim to being "universally valid," or at least "communicable." There's no *proof* to be given among those who disagree about beauty, of course. Yet there are reasons to be exchanged, which one could bring up in a discussion. Maybe I say Jackson Pollock's paintings are beautiful, while you say he's just some guy slinging paint (to prove it is possible to sling paint in just that way). We then discuss whether the various features of this painting make an organic unity (in a phrase used by G. E. Moore, the early-twentieth-century analytical theorist of the good). If you weren't seeing the beauty in surfing already, I could point to its various features—the crystalline tube, the surfer's flowing attunement, the manifest harmony between person and nature. I could aptly say that for those reasons you really *ought* to enjoy it, disinterestedly, whether or not you care to do anything else about it. It'd be nothing like a proof, but also nothing like arguing about the relative merits of one flavor of ice cream over another, which really is a matter of taste.

The surfer watching a grinding tube, which is peeling off without a drop of water out of place, is always an aesthetic objectivist. Certain waves *are* sublimely beautiful. Their value is in that respect objective, though not in the otherworldly sense of Plato's eternal Forms. The crucial thing is that aesthetic judgment is not a simple matter of opinion, feeling, or taste, being true only "in the eye of the beholder," with no greater authority. The "beautiful" and the "sublime" are not just names for certain pleasurable feelings, which waves just happen to induce. Waves *are* sublimely beautiful, themselves, quite aside from the fact that surfers like to surf them, or find them agreeable for surfing purposes. Which is to say the pleasures of waves and surfing are *appropriately* enjoyed, attended to, and engaged with imaginatively, even when we aren't in fact paying attention to them. That, right there, is all the objectivity a surfer needs. The aesthetic truth of the matter need only be invariant with respect to ways our particular thoughts or feelings might have been different.[29] Even if I didn't find the peeling wave agreeable, it would still be sublimely beautiful. Someone who disagreed, who just couldn't quite catch it, would be making a kind of mistake. The error might be corrected, by his paying closer, steadier attention. But the error would be one of *perception*, of not quite sensing what waves and surfing are manifestly like in their sumptuous, sensuous reality.[30]

Is the Surfing Experience Religious?

Sigmund Freud, the philosopher and early psychologist, writes of "oceanic feeling," or a "feeling of oneness with the universe."[31] Though he says he can't quite discover this feeling in himself, a colleague told him about it and said it was a defining part of religious experience, which he and millions of others feel daily, as "a sensation of *eternity*, a feeling of something limitless, unbounded, something 'oceanic.'" Freud presumes this is the same feeling another writer described as "out of this world we cannot fall," a sense of "belonging inseparably to the world as a whole."

Freud, being Freud, notes this to debunk the human impetus for self-transcendence, especially in religion. He writes,

I can imagine that the oceanic feeling could become connected with religion later on. That feeling of oneness with the

29. Your various "relativisms," "subjectivisms," truth-in-the-eye-of-the-beholder-isms, and so forth, all deny objectivity by letting the truth about beauty vary with our subjective reactions. Objectivity is thus "invariance." I argue for this in my "Objectivity of Values: Invariance Without Explanation," *Southern Journal of Philosophy* 44, no. 4 (2006).

30. The seminal paper here is John McDowell, "Values and Secondary Qualities," in *Morality and Objectivity,* ed. Ted Honderich (London: Routledge and Kegan Paul, 1985). The approach I prefer is "constructivism," for reasons I explain in "Constructivism About Practical Reasons," *Philosophy and Phenomenological Research* 74, no. 2 (2007); and "Constructing Protagorean Objectivity," in *Constructivism in Practical Philosophy,* ed. James Lenman and Yonatan Shemmer (Oxford: Oxford University Press, 2012).

31. *Civilization and Its Discontents* (1930; New York: Norton, 2005), p. 47.

universe which is its ideational content sounds very like a first attempt at the consolations of religion, like another way taken by the ego of denying the dangers it sees threatening it in the external world.[32]

Freud never gave any actual *argument* against the existence of God. He simply assumed God's unreality and proposed to explain how religion could have emerged anyway (in threats to the ego). But of course God might also exist. In which case Freud's story wouldn't be necessary: the ocean could then be a revelatory medium, with surfing as a form of religious experience.

Some Christian surfers do report a sense of God in surfing. Yet it is fair to say this is not quite the general surfer experience, heathen and rebel alike. Surfers seem no more or less religious than their cultures or subcultures of origin, sociologically speaking. Many of them—especially in Australia—aren't especially disposed to mystical or spiritual awareness, but certainly do appreciate what is distinctively wonderful about riding waves.

Are they simply missing something? Rudolf Otto, the German Lutheran theologian, called our sense of the divine a sense of the "numinous," a feeling of awe in the presence of the wholly Other. That also goes beyond the surfer feeling, which is limited to a sense of dependence upon what is *immanent* in nature, often with a sense of close, harmonious connection to bigger things. The relational intimacy to God of the mystic Saint Teresa of Ávila might be a closer fit; God is not *wholly* Other but *close* in one's immediate experience, even in routine business. Yet this still seems too transcendent for the general surfer experience. The relational connection in surfing feels grand, or wonderful, not because it takes us *beyond* the universe. What you feel is connected to more of that universe in its local and liquid manifestation. There's the water's undulating restlessness. Its wetness. The blend of sky and sea, which merge into something larger, something grander than any single percep-

32. Ibid.

tion of this or that, over here or over there; one senses something like the whole space, in which the kelp brushes one's leg, the clouds shift in the wind, the next wave rolls in, all at once. Yet the sense of dependence upon something bigger doesn't plainly reach beyond the sky, into the heavens, into a supersensible, supernatural realm. The ocean feels plenty big enough.

For Baruch Spinoza, one of the first modern Jewish philosophers, the surfer draws nearer to God, or rather a divinized nature, or naturalized God, which comes to the same thing. Which is it? Being a pantheist, Spinoza is deliberately ambiguous, speaking of "God, or Nature."[33] He writes, "That eternal and infinite being we call God, or Nature, acts from the same necessity from which he exists."[34] In which case one should surf a pleasing "sport":

> It is a feature of a wise man that he makes use of things and delights in them as much as he can (though not to the point of disgust, for that is not to feel delight). . . . [H]e renews and refreshes himself with moderate and pleasant food and drink, and also with scents, the beauty of plants in bloom, dress, music, sports, the theatre, and other things of this sort.[35]

This is not simple hedonism; the delightful pleasures bring genuine self-transcendence. Although he identifies God with Nature, Spinoza still tries to do justice to the traditional idea that God is the most perfect being. He defines pleasure in terms of a transition to a state of greater perfection. ("The more we are affected by pleasure, the greater the perfection to which we pass; that is, the more it is necessary that we participate in the divine nature.") So when we experience pleasures of surfing, we become more perfect and hence more like God.

33. Or "Deus, sive Natura," as in the Latin version of his *Ethics,* which Spinoza omitted from the Dutch version in order to avoid appearing less heterodox than he was.
34. *Ethics* (1677; New York: Penguin Classics, 2005), pt. 4, preface.
35. Ibid., pt. 4, proposition 45, scholium.

So surfing is at once natural and spiritual. If a surfer already subscribed to Spinoza's pantheism, I suppose he or she could so experience God, or Nature, in riding a wave. But again nothing so totalizingly metaphysical seems to come along with the general surfer experience, which needn't spiritualize oceanic feeling at all. Surfing seems *open* to spiritualization but doesn't supply it by itself. The surfer would also have to accept a philosophy or theology or world picture that brings a spiritual gestalt.

Freud overstated his own point when he called oceanic feeling a "feeling of oneness with the universe," or of "belonging inseparably to the world as a whole." The surfer feeling isn't even so totalizing over the natural order. When surfers get really dialed in on a good day or wave, and cosmic matters are being contemplated over a beer or a spliff, it can indeed seem arbitrary to draw sharp lines around that to which you were or were not attuned. The ocean is vast, and when the wave you just surfed at a California beach was whipped up thousands of miles away by a storm two weeks before, you can feel grateful to be so fortunately placed that the elements did coalesce, just so, just as they had to, for the wave you just surfed to have been surfed as it was. But you wouldn't feel any special connection to the Andromeda Galaxy, or to inland China, or to the wild shores of West Africa, not without pondering a map of the globe or our neighborhood in outer space. What one feels connected to is more diffuse, neither localized nor so well defined as the world "as a whole."

The moments of connection do bring feelings of belonging, of being at home, though not of "belonging inseparably" to the world. You can still know the surfer feeling of being out of place, in pushing against heavy, unforgiving surf, or of being separated, for being in a funk, never quite getting attuned to the waves that day. The surfer sense of "oneness" is felt as a definite achievement in being, as success in a kind of good relationship, which easily might not have come. The surfer feeling of connection is better described as a relation of *harmony,* the harmony in adaptive attunement, between a person and a wave and its sea.

Ordinary Reality

This isn't quite *oneness*, strictly speaking, not if one means "numerical identity," literally being one and the same thing. The relation of harmony is between *different things*, the person and the wave, which leaves you still feeling *yourself*.

That is to accept the very image of "self" that many Buddhists wish to dispel. Bhikkhu Bodhi, a leading scholar monk, writes of "the delusion of self, the idea that at the core of our being there exists a truly established 'I' with which we are essentially identified."[36] This, he says, is "an error, a mere presupposition lacking a real referent." Trapped in the "dualities of 'I' and 'not I,' what is 'mine' and what is 'not mine,'" he explains, "we fall victim to the defilements they breed, the urges to grasp and destroy, and finally to the suffering that inevitably follows." In order to overcome this, "the illusion of selfhood that sustains them has to be dispelled, exploded by the realization of selflessness."

The idea is that our most ordinary thoughts of self—that "I am thinking," that "I feel upset," that "I would be happier if such and such were to happen"—are all radically false. They come to us readily but carry a heavy factual presupposition: that the pronoun "I" actually refers to something, a uniquely personal center of experience and agency that persists over time, from birth to death, as metaphysically distinct from both other "selves" and impersonal events. But, Bodhi suggests, there is no such fact. Our sense of self is simply an illusion, and nirvana comes when we clearly see this for the illusion it is. Beginning from "one's" experience, with enough meditation and learning, one can undo the myth from within.

This view can be hard to completely grasp. Who is supposed to understand it? You, I—meaning the you and the I who *aren't real*? Should I believe it? If *I* accept the picture, don't I then *exist*, in

36. *The Noble Eightfold Path: The Way to the End of Suffering* (Kandy, Sri Lanka: Buddhist Publication Society, 1994), p. 56, which is cited in Albahari, "Insight Knowledge of No Self in Buddhism."

which case the picture is false, or somehow self-refuting? Can we ever completely escape Descartes's *cogito,* which after all has an element of truth?

David Hume, the early modern empiricist, suggested how we might escape this dilemma. Only seeing is believing, and there is no directly observing the self. "When I enter most intimately into what I call *myself,*" he writes, "I always stumble on some particular perception or other, of heat or cold, light or shade, love or hatred, pain or pleasure. I never can catch *myself* at any time without a perception, and never can observe any thing but the perception."[37] Similarly, am I not the "same person" as the child borne by the woman I call my mother? Well, if we look to the most sophisticated treatment of the metaphysics of personal identity of all time, Derek Parfit's *Reasons and Persons,* we wind up at roughly the Buddhist position: there is no metaphysically robust self, no fact of the matter that makes people numerically separable in the way we ordinarily speak of them. All our talk of "me" and "you," "mine" and "thine," is simply a useful convention.[38]

I'm sure advanced monks do attain a radically altered state of consciousness, a state of "no mind," in which they lose all *awareness* of themselves as distinct from anything else.[39] But surely that is still *someone's* awareness (the monk on the mat, who got into this business hoping for self-transcendence, maybe to please his parents, or to disappoint them). Aside from altered states of consciousness, could we obliterate our very concept of self, completely and consistently, and still lead anything like an ordinary existence, which includes ordinary surfing?

The surfer is full-on, all-out engaged in the world right before her senses, in the salty water she can taste and touch. In the surfer's

---

37. *A Treatise of Human Nature* (1739), ed. L. A. Selby-Bigge and P. H. Nidditch, 2nd ed. (Oxford: Clarendon Press, 1896), bk. 1, chap. 4, sec. 7.
38. Parfit was surprised to learn of the convergence between his views and Buddhist metaphysics but welcomed the accident. This view offers certain comforts: if you don't exist as a distinct individual, you won't ever die, and so needn't worry at all about death.
39. D. T. Suzuki, *The Zen Doctrine of No-Mind* (London: Rider, 1949).

easy self-transcendence, she remains herself, desires and all, but becomes attuned to things beyond herself—to each moment of the wave she surfed, and to a whole raft of material conditions that made the act both possible and happen as it did. In this *relational* sort of self-transcendence, you *have* to remain your distinct self. The surfer in the flow isn't absorbed like a drop into a cosmic sea of being, even if she paddled out in profound Zen-like awareness of the gently shifting water and the water droplets of each rolling line of white water. The person is one thing. The wave is a different thing. The two are not identical. The surfer's ordinary post-work nirvana is achieved in a *relationship* between the surfer and the wave surfed, which leaves the two dynamically related but distinct.

Or so we'd ordinarily say. We ordinarily experience the world in our shoes, our particular personal perspective. I see you, and you seem friendly enough. If we had a friendly chat, I must be a separate person, because it takes two to really communicate. Could that really be a dreamlike illusion from which we can detach? Hume denied our ordinary idea of the self, but then disarmingly admitted that he couldn't keep up his skepticism outside his study. Our sense of self can't be completely shaken in anything recognizable as an ordinary human life. But in that case, why not say our talk of being different selves is as real as anything else? What odd idea of "reality" would say that it isn't? Why not go by our ordinary standards for ordinary "reality"?

I lay my hand on a table. Physics tells me that the "touch" of my hand on the table is a repulsion of forces in which my skin never quite lies flat against the smooth surface, in the ordinary sense. It's tempting to say ordinary life makes some kind of error. Physics shows that my hand and the table never *really* touch! Here Sartre seems right: this is a bad use of the word "really." Of course my hand can touch a table! It *really* can, in the perfectly good and ordinary sense, which physics just isn't characterizing, and perhaps can't. The physicist's talk of repulsive forces sounds in a different register.

Like a hand touching a table, a self comes along with the deep structure of human experience. Our concepts of touch and reality are after all human concepts; they are for us ordinary humans, made from and for our ordinary experience. We of course *shape* them by convention and culture, which varies from age to age, from East and West, in ways that surprise us. And yet, I can be myself, and you yourself, really and truly, in a perfectly good and ordinary sense.

If the Buddhist has found some new dimension of reality, that would be impressive. It wouldn't, however, be the discovery of the *one true* (and different) reality, about which ordinary life is completely mistaken. The concept of reality is itself rather fluid, with different meanings for different domains of discourse. The relevant standard of "reality," for selfhood and surfing, is not whatever paradoxical thing physics is saying at the moment. It's the warm sunlight of ordinary sense.

The Surfer Metaphysic

What is real? What is the nature of reality? What is there and what is it like very generally speaking, especially as discerned by means other than the empirical sciences, such as physics? These, roughly, are the questions of metaphysics. In these last chapters, we've arrived at something of a surfer's metaphysical picture.

A key question about reality is whether or how radically it diverges from its appearance to us. Is it indeed as we experience it? Or are we in error or ignorance of its true nature?

At one level, Kant settled for ignorance. He explained how ordinary objects, like the cup on the table, could have a kind of reality for us, and he made sense of the sciences. But he confusingly still spoke of "things in themselves," of which we know not (except that they somehow are). Sartre, in taking up phenomenology, proceeded on the assumption that there is no relevant difference between *reality* and *reality for us*. We should just see how things show up for us in our general experience, and maybe in the end there's no interesting question of an independent reality.

Our phenomenology of surfing suggests a further wrinkle, an explanation why there is no further gap between appearance and reality to account for. In chapter 4, we said that doing well in a skillful activity is *by its very nature* a way of being related to the world beyond one's head. For all the fun of a virtual reality surfing machine, one would not in fact be surfing, the skilled activity. As we elaborated in chapter 5, this is the know-how of adaptive attunement, which is akin to successful perception. To perceive the world is already to know how to engage what lies beyond one's head in the first instance, already to understand how to adapt one's body to one's environment in action. So surfing is a kind of genuine knowledge. There's no deep difference between "in here, in my head," and "out there, out in the world," no great gap between our experience and reality.

One way to transcend ourselves, then, is simply to be attuned to that sublime reality. We need only do the philosophy of surfing, which attunes us to our attunement, revealing the deep way we are often harmoniously related to what lies beyond.

So we can transcend ourselves on a regular basis in everyday life, especially while surfing, work permitting at least. Having considered the human's being, this book will now turn to political philosophy: What follows for society, our relation to nature, and the future of work?

Part Three

Political Philosophy

7

Society

ESTELLE to GARCIN: Excuse me, have you
    a glass? . . . a pocket-mirror will do.
[Garcin ignores her.]
ESTELLE to INEZ: When I can't see myself
    I wonder if I really truly exist.

—Sartre, *No Exit*

FROM THE SUPER STORM system that rotates around Earth's southern pole, which spins storms northward into the southern oceans for much of the year, the windswept choppy seas gradually separate into bands of swell, and radiate through New Zealand or Tahiti in their many-thousand-mile march through deep ocean toward coastlines as far away as the Northern Hemisphere and California. Their final rise begins as they mount upon a gradually shallowing continental shelf, where the lines of swell refract into bays, beaches, and points, which stand ready to transform them into splendidly peeling breakers. And as the lines mount and crest at the best surf breaks, ending their long journey, they are enthusiastically greeted—by a crawling throng of surfers, who, leaving no wave unmolested, block or cheat or snake each other in a splashing hustle for position, often colliding in a clown-car crash-up derby, dinging surfboards and bodies, and then yelling, grousing, and cursing about all the drop-ins, back paddles, slights, dings, and injuries. "What the fuck, man, I was clearly in position." "Drop in on me again and I'll work you." "Fuck off, man, you don't even live here." "Fuck *you*, bro, let's take it to the beach! No, seriously, fuck yooooouu, man."[1] Welcome to Southern California and the shit-show that is Malibu or Lower Trestles on a hyped swell on a Saturday morning. The green wind-feathered wave faces are defaced, such is the usual unpleasantness, the scuff mark of society.

Why even bother to surf Malibu, with a hundred-plus surfers amped to catch any wave that rolls through? Well, the waves are beautiful, and you paddle out with hopes of nabbing one for yourself. And then you might have waited forty minutes, beat the pack into the exact best position to command right-of-way on a choice set wave, yelled like crazy that yo, yo, yo, hey, hey, yooo, yaaahh, wooooahhhh, you got it, you *got* it, you FREAKING GOT IT . . . and still four people will drop right in. One dude on a soft-top board for relative beginners is sporting a butt-in-the-air, stinkbug stance; another is flailing; another cowboy just doesn't give a yee-haw; and a final interloper, who might be a twelve-year-old Gidget-like chick, you can barely see for all the whitewash splashing you in the face. On a different wave, with your luck going a bit better, maybe only one or two surfers ride in front, staying far enough out on the shoulder to at least let you pump down the line and shellack the lip all mixed up in their board wake. Maybe you get a few sections to yourself after they finally kick out. (It's a long wave, and even the last third of it is worth the wait.) Or maybe your luck keeps going south, and you mainly get burned or catch scraps as you watch others nab great waves all to themselves, some of them burning others right and left, laughing, and preening unapologetically.

In Sartre's play *No Exit*, three co-antagonists find themselves exquisitely matched for the mutual torture of verbal and erotic refusal. In

---

1. Note that here "fuck off" indicates an attitude of alienation, but not radical alienation. A surfer would count as having "fucked off" simply by leaving the zone of competition for waves. He might be back in the thick the next day, with memories of yesterday quickly fading.

the play's closing moments, Garcin, the male character, famously sums up the scene: "There's no need for red-hot pokers. Hell—is other people!"[2] Hell can be three people in a Second Empire drawing room, with a couch, a bronze statue on the mantelpiece, and a door to nowhere. Yet when the room door finally opens, late in the play, no one decides to leave through the solitary passage. Garcin, for one, needs to convince someone, and finally himself, that he is not a coward (he was shot for desertion). For that he needs someone around. Because we see ourselves through the eyes of others, they have power to deny us the identity we'd like for ourselves. And so even the most ordinary relationship, in romance, sex, friendship, or work, is inherently conflictual.

The surfer getting skunked and feeling lowly can of course just exit the water. The thing is, you don't. Eventually, you will just give up and return to the beach. What's surprising, even to oneself, is how long you wait. It is easy to surf mediocre waves alone in California, but of course everyone in the crowd has already passed on that option. So you wait, partly in hope that tensions will ease, which they might, if the pack thins or the sets start coming more consistently. But especially in SoCal, you've also come to accept that crowds require a certain toleration. We don't leave, in part for love of surfing, but also for our deep sociality. And there are in fact real possibilities of reconciliation, ways of making peace in the fair and foul mess that society is. One might call them democracy.

Adaptive Order

Surfing lineups everywhere are organized, even in their more chaotic moments, first and foremost by the rule of right-of-way. The rule itself is more or less the same the world over, but readily adapted to changing conditions. Surfers rely on it in the governance of their common affairs, and they are constantly reinterpreting its meaning,

2. *No Exit* (1947), in *No Exit and Three Other Plays* (New York: Vintage, 1989), p. 45.

depending on wave scarcity or abundance, adjusting their expectations accordingly.

The basic rule says simply that once a surfer is in position on a wave, the others must yield. Who then is "in position"? Often, it is simply the surfer who could most easily catch the wave as it peaks. So the surfer might be sub-optimally situated, a fair bit off from the peak, but you'd still call him or her "in position" by courtesy. It would be an affront to out-paddle him or her in a scramble to the most critical part of the wave and then claim it.

This is true mainly when the crowd is light or the waves consistent (so that everyone is fed). Under such conditions of relative abundance, who is "in position" is easily discerned and usually plain for all to see. As the crowd thickens, or the waves go inconsistent from a long lull or a tide change, the zone for "position" tightens, and it becomes less clear to anyone when right-of-way is held. As abundance turns to scarcity, the move to gain position can become aggressively competitive. Maybe you block the other guy's paddle momentum, forcing him to pull back. He'll be mad about this. If you blocked as a tactic, this would be an affront to courtesy, which forbids flagrant interference. On the other hand, if your interference was inadvertent, just caught up in the hustle, then, you know, so goes a scrum. You'd say, "Sorry, man," less to apologize than to share a moment of regret.

Even in a crowd, you can still find the peaking "money spot," the position in which you know, and everyone can see, and you know that everyone can see, that this wave is most definitely your wave. A sense of satisfaction wells up in these moments; there's nothing like assurances that one's rights are, for the moment, secure. And now if some guy drops in, violating your right to have him yield, you'll have strong and confident grounds for grievance ("WTF, bro, I was so on the money spot!"). Yet getting on the money spot is often more luck than skill, if only because who is in any position is often not obvious in the thick of fast action.

Why Aren't Surfers More Apt to Fight?

This point of unclarity among different people from different points of view, each with his or her own maybe self-serving reading of the situation, is the main cause of quarrels and fights. The guy who was dropped in on protests, "Dude, I was on the inside." The guy who dropped in rejoins, "Yah, but I was already on it farther out. You back paddled" (that is, paddled behind a surfer already in position). When is someone "already on it"? Again, there's often no telling.

If the disputants argue and don't agree, then maybe the exchange of reasons is over, and they fight. After a punch or surfboard jab, the fight is to settle who shall be regarded as Not to Be Messed With, but not, of course, who was originally in the right. Surfers do not believe that might makes right. Yet the contest of posturing, intimidation, or force often does settle right-of-way for the future (de facto if not de jure). The guy who is ever willing to punch, his reputation formed, will thereafter get more waves. For people tend to steer clear of an asshole.[3]

Gray areas are in steady abundance, with the tide changing or the crowd thinning or thickening, so there's ample room to cheat, skulk, or back paddle. The rewards are considerable: you score more and better waves than you could otherwise attain if you chat someone up while secretly doing quick kicks under the water to vie for choice positioning, so as to smile and bolt for the money spot as the good wave rolls in. And what would keep a surfer, of all people, from exploiting easy opportunities to score a great wave?

The answer is that the burned surfer will get pissed and object. Which is to say there's a high risk of being held accountable for one's misconduct. The surfing lineup is a case of "spontaneous order," but not of the market variety that the Nobel laureate libertarian econo-

---

3. This is the guy (they are mainly men) who takes special advantages in cooperative life out of an entrenched sense of entitlement that immunizes him against the complaints of other people. The "special advantages" here would be easy right-of-way; you get whatever wave you paddle for, because people steer clear. See my book *Assholes: A Theory*.

mist F. A. Hayek celebrated. It's an emergent social practice, which no one formally agrees to but nearly everyone follows, for the management of a common pool of resources, in this case waves.[4] Surfers thus more or less cooperate in wave sharing from a "democratic" kind of accountability founded on common reason.

In *Leviathan,* one of the three greatest works of political philosophy of all time, Thomas Hobbes claimed that peace depends on rule by an absolute sovereign (like the British monarch of his day).[5] The sovereign's main qualification is his awesomeness. As a result of his godlike power to "over-awe" all who might contravene his commands, we each enjoy certain assurances: if someone is tempted to kill me, I know that he knows that the sovereign will be coming after him. I can trust his prudence and go about my business. But if I can't be assured the law will actually be enforced, then the fact that you don't know someone is coming after you doesn't mean he isn't. Or just as bad, some person might be thinking that *I* am coming after him, and decide that he'd better try to get the jump on me while I'm sleeping. And of course if I can predict that some guy is thinking this way, then I could prudently do a preventive strike while *he* is sleeping. But of course he'll also predict that this is my thinking, in which case . . . neither of us will rest peacefully. And without the peace of assurance, none of us enjoys the trusty regularity needed for ordinary arts, letters, science, and industry, a condition that inexorably unravels into a hellish "war of all against all," each killing or being killed, while striving for his or her own preservation. With neither the surplus resources nor the time for science, art, letters, or sport, no one rests, and no one surfs, and "the life of man is solitary, poore, nasty, brutish, and short."

There is virtue in surfer adaptability, but if society did suddenly

4. Elinor Ostrom won the Nobel Prize in Economics for her study of "common pool resource" schemes worldwide, in fisheries or forests or even international relations (for example, the successful Montreal Protocol manages the ozone layer by regulating standards for chlorofluorocarbon usage).

5. The other two greatest works ever are Plato's *Republic* and John Rawls's *Theory of Justice,* at least according to the late G. A. Cohen, a fierce Marxist turned socialist critic of all three.

unravel, someone who adapted *too* handily, discovering a Lord-of-the-Flies ruthlessness in his depths, would be more like a sociopath who finally has his chance to kill with impunity than your ordinary joyous surfer who adapts like a virtuoso in the trusty normality of peaceable everyday cooperation. Surfers are conservatives, not for any caution in the face of death, but for love of the familiar ordinariness of civilized life and the hope of enjoying it for longer. Hobbes's war is gnarly and terrifying, but this is not the sublime gnarliness whose appreciation affirms the simple beauty of ordinary life.

If one can conjure up images of the "surfer hippie," "surf Nazi," or even a "Hobbesian surfer" of *Survivor*-style cunning, these are rare birds. After decades of casual observation, my firm unscientific assessment of the global surfer tribe is that while some really are irritating, or dull, oblivious, lazy, self-centered, crassly hedonistic, in trouble with the law, or righteous in bogus entitlement ("locals only, bro. This is our backyard, man"[6]), the vast preponderance of surfers are pretty cool and relatively civilized. Although surf culture certainly has some stupefying effect, for its mindless repetition of clichés and tolerance of dopey or schmucky manners, the especially grating types don't seem to come in numbers out of proportion with the larger human miscreant population. So if you have a low view of humanity, you could count surfers as a relatively wonderful subgroup. They compare favorably with all the egoistic politicians, celebrities, professional athletes, bankers, CEOs, or professors, and to the extent most surfers live by the important maxim to "just be cool," to live and let live, this may even set them apart, as far less flawed than the privileged types who think driving a luxury car means not having to yield to pedestrians at a stop sign. At least in the shifting social dynamics of the wave lineup, even the stereotypically oblivious surfer is less idiot than idiot savant: in certain surprising ways, he's attuned.

6. Or instead of "bro," which is continental American, it may be the South African "bru," or the Hawaiian "brah," or the Australian or Kiwi "mate." There's less variation in the localism BS around the planet.

Surfers do occasionally fight. More often they quarrel, and the interesting question is why the quarrels don't lead to more fights. For the fact is that surfers never descend into Hobbes's all-out war. At such time as two surfers are about to brawl, the other surfers usually work together to contain the dispute. A third party may jump in to make peace, while the rest dutifully keep it mellow, cursing under their breath about how crowds seriously suck. This mainly works beyond the watch of law enforcement, so it seems Hobbes was wrong that stable order could last only in the shadow of the state. Even in "ungoverned spaces" in or around developing countries, where the rule of law is generally weak (for example, in parts of Nicaragua or Indonesia), surfers handle things themselves without devolving into kill-or-be-killed anarchy.[7] In the advanced countries, when fights do go down in the water or on a remote beach, people often won't call the cops or take matters to court. The laws of wave etiquette are "enforced," but in personal, decentralized forms of enforcing accountability.

For its lack of any centralized government, the surfing lineup is akin less to the domestic state than to the "anarchical society" that is international relations. There isn't and most likely won't ever be a global sovereign government. But with various important exceptions, states more or less cooperate. They follow international law and practice in part for their shared ideas and willingness to complain, reason together, discuss, trust and verify, and work out their issues under common public norms and values—all without the formalities of voting and well before talk of war or sanction.[8]

---

7. One village in Nicaragua close to quality surf breaks does have a murder culture, though I wasn't told that it seeps into the water when I was taken through the village harbor on the way to the waves. An even larger murder culture in nearby Guatemala is found in a city inland.

8. See Hedley Bull, *The Anarchical Society: A Study of Order in World Politics* (New York: Columbia University Press, 1977). And on "cooperative sovereignty," see Abram Chayes and Antonia Handler Chayes, *The New Sovereignty: Compliance with International Regulatory Agreements* (Cambridge, Mass.: Harvard University Press, 1995).

So it seems Rousseau was right, and Hobbes mistaken, about the human disposition to cooperate rather than fight. The crowded surfing lineup can be hellish, but then maybe the waves really are epic: sets are rolling in again, and, who knows, a beauty of a wave might just have your name on it. It is only because surfing is completely wonderful, especially at the good breaks on the better waves, that one can bring oneself to accept that, yes, alas, the conflicts are just part of what life is like in sharing a treasured common resource. It isn't just that society is the unfortunate price of conveniently getting a good wave. The practice of wave etiquette also has its own value, as the basis for cooperative peace. In John Stuart Mill's phrase, it brings its own kind of "unity with our fellow creatures," and so, often, easy feelings of bonhomie.

Fluid Democracy

It was in response to Hobbes's authoritarianism that Rousseau gave the world its first modern vision of democracy, a free community of equals, ruled by their common reason.[9] The vision was mainly conjecture and speculation, inspired by his beloved city of Geneva. But his dream traveled well and eventually inspired such important developments as the French and the American Revolutions, the spread of democracy in the twentieth century, the postwar era's "long peace" without world war and with declining hostilities, the stability of capitalism, the reduction in poverty unprecedented in human history, the high standard of living in the advanced societies, and thus the very prosperity that has created time for leisure and crowded surfing lineups.

And yet as Rousseau also explained, if civilization saves us from Hobbes's war of all against all, it brings its own discontentment. The

9. *Of the Social Contract* (1762), in *Rousseau: The Social Contract and Other Later Political Writings,* ed. Victor Gourevitch (Cambridge, U.K.: Cambridge University Press, 1997).

trouble began in the first days of leisure around the campfire. Leisure, for Rousseau, was at once a reward for work and the original source of vice.[10]

Hobbes thought everyone would prefer peace if everyone else is peaceable, and they really would be peaceable provided certain assurances. Rousseau's idea was that this doesn't require an awesome sovereign. What it requires is common interest and a promising signal of good faith. One has to eat, and maybe the two of us in a state of nature would each happily hunt stag together, instead of separately hunting the measly hare we can catch on our own. We wouldn't have to spend all day scrounging, and because stag lasts for a whole week (this is of course before refrigeration), we could work together and then laze and relax! Maybe you seem like-minded and willing to show up for the hunt. If I show and you don't, I get nothing, having passed up my own chance of hunting hare. So I will indeed need assurances, as you will as well, because you'd also be passing up your chance to hunt hare. But with a promise or a promising signal of your firm intentions, which I gladly return, we can get into a cooperative rhythm and get a bit richer together. We could all take our chances on cooperative hunting, steady industry, or investment and rise together in our standard of living.

Which of course frees up time for playing. But, alas, Rousseau tells us, as the bounty of the stag hunt brought new prosperity and the first seasons of leisure, the seeds of inequality and vice were planted:

> Everyone began to look at everyone else and to wish to be looked at himself, and public esteem acquired a price. The one who sang or danced best; the handsomest; the strongest; the most skillful; or the most eloquent came to be most highly regarded. . . . From these first preferences arise vanity and

10. *Discourse on the Origin and the Foundations of Inequality Among Men* (1754), in *The Discourses and Other Early Political Writings,* ed. Victor Gourevitch (Cambridge, U.K.: Cambridge University Press, 1997), pt. 2, para. 16, p. 166.

contempt on the one hand, shame and envy on the other; and the fermentation caused by these new leavens eventually produced compounds fatal to happiness.[11]

Dancing or singing meant not just dancing or singing joyfully for oneself, from a sense of one's worth and happiness that requires no concern for others, as though one were cuddled in motherly arms but self-nurturing. For in a crowd, the singing or dancing in performance also means *comparing* who is the better singer or dancer. Basic needs met, attention turns to the game, to the contest for rank or status, and so how one is scored by the game's score keeping, whether in accolades, smarts, riches, or looking hot and sexy (and reaping the benefits). If one previously valued oneself with no comparison to others, the possibility of self-love now comes with conditions, depending on who is the better, the superior, the winner, and who is the lesser or merely average. Striving in comparative self-regard—what Rousseau calls "amour propre"—we thus find ourselves miserable in relentless competition, with contempt and inequality spoiling the joys of civilization. Whether around the campfire or in the surfing lineup, a conflictual contest for recognition can thus foul the most picturesque of surroundings.

Rousseau's solution is state democracy: a political union in which everyone is recognized as an equal before laws founded upon our common reason, as the law's subjects and equal co-authors. Our equality upheld, no one must struggle for position as inferior or superior. In our main common affairs, we cease striving for position and advantage and carry on working for mutual benefit in common purpose, in a lasting community of free and equal citizens.[12]

But if the surfing lineup runs beyond the reach of the state, why again don't words lead to blows more often? Because it, too, is more or less "democratic," not with votes, voting systems, or collectively made decisions, but with the same presumption that all are to be

---

11. Ibid.
12. *Of the Social Contract.*

counted as equals. In the practice of wave etiquette, all are properly subject to the public expectations of wave sharing, unless some special justification can be provided. Each has powers of enforcement; each has standing to speak up for his or her rights and demand a justification when there is cause for suspecting an infraction of right-of-way or courtesy. And each is rightly held accountable for his or her conduct, being prepared to give an account of it should anyone ask, on terms others could accept in good faith.

A few lineups are frankly authoritarian. When arguments devolve into threats, the local "heavy" (who is often both mean and weighty) steps in to "regulate," usually siding with the other local ("I've never seen you around here before; get outta here!"). Local surfers will tend to get more and better waves due to their superior wave knowledge. And infrequent visitors do owe respect for the going tone as a courtesy. "Localism" goes further, claiming entitlements in the simple fact of residing near a surf break. In California, the rich, middle-aged locals at Lunada Bay, Palos Verdes, yell and punch and throw rocks and slash tires of outsiders under the averted eyes of local police.[13] Yet these and other redoubts of localism are still exceptional cases, which prove the rule of democratic equality.

The surfer asshole also flagrantly rejects the idea that everyone else is his moral equal. He'll drop right in blatantly and then get angry if you complain. He's an asshole, so he just walls out the complaint, assured in bogus entitlement (*"I live here"*). Yet assholes are exceptions, and must be; their ability to exploit the gray areas of cooperative life depends on the cooperation of others. It is only when enough of the others are following the rules of right-of-way and courtesy that one can take special privileges under them. For the asshole, the rules do generally apply, except not to him, or not to locals like him, because he's the "local," or the better—or at least

13. Though legal action is more recently under way. See "Lunada 'Bay Boys' Surfer Gang Hit with Another Class-Action Lawsuit," *Los Angeles Times,* Aug. 5, 2016, http://www.latimes.com/local/lanow/la-me-ln-lunada-bay-boys-lawsuit-20160805 -snap-story.html.

the older—surfer. In this way, he feels morally special, and when others object, he really can feel that he's not being treated fairly. His error is the homage vice pays to virtue, the collective virtue of democratic equality.

In normal surfer practice, before any fights, or threats of punches, the recognition of equality is served in the simple act of voicing a complaint, or flashing a "stink eye" look. Most surfers will actually listen. Some begrudgingly take the point or even apologize. Even after putting up a sham defense to save face, a surfer often won't burn the offended person again, knowing she was right. Ultimately, the constant quarreling is a way of giving and asking for reasons. I wouldn't exactly call it the ideal of Socratic dialectic, but the exchange of words, rather than of fists, is all in the service of common reason, democratic accountability, and mutual respect.

The Look

A squint, a scowl, a darting glance—you are looking at me, and I feel the complaint. It's the Look, as Sartre calls it, a heavy glare of contempt, or at least doubtful questioning. I feel you addressing me, seeking my gaze, as though you're setting a challenge for me to look at you back, eye to eye, and explain myself with a straight face. You see a brazen affront. I actually didn't see you riding along on the wave before I dropped in, but do I dare tell you this if I also didn't exactly look to check? I know you won't buy it; you'll snap back, "You should have fucking looked, you fuck." In which case maybe I'll say something about the section foam blocking my vision, or something else hard to contest.

But why go to all the trouble of rationalization and confabulation? For why should your stink-eye gaze command my attention in the first place? Can't I just not *see* the Look? Must I read a mind into your face? The facial movements on display—why aren't they just muscular spasms, with no connection whatsoever to me and the wave I might or might not have taken at your expense?

For Sartre, the answer goes to our very existence. There are three basic types of being. Being a mere object (an "in-itself"). Being a conscious subject (a "for-itself"). And "being-for-others," which is to say being a conscious being who sees him- or herself through the gaze of another.

In Sartre's famous example, I am peeping into a keyhole, voyeuristically. I hear a creak in the hallway floorboards. Suddenly I feel shame. To feel ashamed is to be ashamed *before* someone for something one has done or who one is, which means I must in that moment presume there is a someone seeing me. I sense you seeing me, therefore you must *be*. A brute object cannot give the Look, so you must be another conscious being, seeing me in a light I may not appreciate. And I, too, must then *be*, another self, viewed within your gaze, however unsavory my identity.

All this could still be an illusion; maybe the creak in the floor was caused by a passing cat, and I am alone in the hallway. Robinson Crusoe might feel shame for a moment, with the being of another intruding his consciousness, seeing himself for the moment as no longer alone on the island. Shame is not proof that other minds really exist, not of the indubitable sort that would convince Descartes. But feeling shame, or pride, might demonstrate that my being for someone else, for an Other, who can give me the Look, comes to me originally, as part of my very being. I think, and therefore I am—in case I needed a reminder. Likewise, in my shame, I suddenly see you seeing me, therefore *you* must be.[14] I see you not simply as a fleshy "in-itself" bag of bones and muscle with a nervous

14. This wouldn't solve the traditional problem of how one could have evidence of another mind. Yet as Thomas Nagel explains, it does speak to the deeper problem of how we could even understand the proposition we might or might not have evidence for, that another mind exists. How, as Sartre puts it, could I understand a "self which is not myself"? This cannot be constructed on the basis of our knowledge of ourselves. As Nagel explains, "The cogito is not a compound built up out of the prior and independent concept of the I together with the idea of thought. Rather, the I is revealed only as the subject of this thought. Similarly, the concept of the Other is extracted from the more basic experience of shame, which is a form of the experience of being seen." "Sartre: The Look and the Problem of Other Minds," in *Secular Philosophy and the Religious Temperament: Essays, 2002–2008* (New York: Oxford University Press, 2010), p. 168.

system; you must be a *someone*, a someone *else* who is looking back at me, in whose eyes I see myself as *another* self.[15]

Even the shameless asshole responds to the Look. Only a psychopath wouldn't be ushered into the perspective of the Other in the face of a stink-eye glare. Maybe he kills someone in order to eat her lunch, because for him people are but objects in the world to be manipulated. He may also be grossly imprudent, a perverse solipsist who fails to see even his future self as real enough to have concern for in the present. For the asshole, by comparison, the Look merely triggers an internal conflict. He is shameless about taking special privileges in the lineup, taking any wave he wants, getting angry when people complain. But his shamelessness is something of an accomplishment, a product of his ready defenses; he's learned to be quick and confident in spontaneous rationalizations to wall out complaints to which he is otherwise susceptible. The psychopath is an object of dread or terror, the asshole merely demoralizing, frustrating, or flummoxing, because he at least has the moral capacities to appreciate a moral entreaty. Which is why we are thrown back into self-doubting. We need reassurance that we really are an equal, to be respected like anyone else, as we don't in a dog or shark attack.[16]

Sartre points out the deep place of shame in our being. He also obscures its moral and social dynamics.[17] While it's clear why the shameless surfer asshole responds to a look of contempt, we don't see how he marshals his own sense of moral confidence. As sug-

15. Actually, if what's recognized is the Other's *freedom*, the idea may be closer to Simone de Beauvoir's version of mutual recognition. In breaking from Sartre, she draws on Hegel's (and perhaps J. G. Fichte's) view that a slave can command a sort of recognition of his basic freedom from his master, simply by speaking to him and being understood. That idea was in turn inspired by Rousseau's provocative claim that being recognized as a political equal "forces us to be free." See Nancy Bauer, *Simone de Beauvoir, Philosophy, and Feminism* (New York: Columbia University Press, 2001), p. 155.

16. On waffling between a demeaning acquiescence and a personally disappointing and ineffectual fit of rage, and how to find a middle path, see my book *Assholes: A Theory*, pp. 120–43.

17. Arthur Danto makes this criticism, noting that shame (perhaps unlike guilt) is essentially a matter of social appearance, in *Jean-Paul Sartre*, p. 122.

gested earlier, he can resort to defensive anger in part for his partial interpretation of his moral rights under the common wave-riding practice. *He lives here,* he thinks, and so he gets special privileges under the rules that otherwise rightly govern wave sharing. He's also not easily embarrassed or humiliated, for being viewed unfavorably, but his lack of shame has a moral aspect.[18]

A contest for recognition with an asshole is its own kind of hell. For all his moral capacity, he's entrenched in a false perspective, and won't really listen, won't really see you as equally real. For Sartre, all human relationships are and must be so conflictual. But is that right, even about surfers? They've found a way out of hell, in wave etiquette. At once a worldwide custom, the morality of a global tribe, and the social embodiment of common human reason, the rules for wave sharing express a common sense of how we are to manage common resources together. Like Rousseau's ideal democracy, the public practice for sharing waves provides a basis for mutual recognition, and therefore peace.

Everyone—even the asshole—more or less knows the rules of right-of-way and courtesy, with a pretty good sense of their basic rationales or purposes. As surfer equals, each with standing to press for the rights afforded to them and to hold others accountable for their conduct, there is a real possibility of voicing and acknowledging an objection, so as to resolve conflict in peaceable (albeit possibly tense) cooperation. Maybe we quarrel. Or maybe someone complains, sort of fairly, and you just say, "Sorry, man, next one is yours." The rules define rights, and so create the possibility of apologizing for an infringement. There is a real possibility of mutually acknowledging our rights and equal worth, and so the possibility of

18. According to the philosopher Casey Hall, shame differs from mere humiliation in its moral aspect: "The belief that characterizes experiences of humiliation is, 'I am in fact seen as lessened or diminished in the eyes of others whether I deserve to be seen in this way or not.' On the other hand the characterizing belief in instances of shame is, 'I deserve to be seen as lessened or diminished in the eyes of others whether I am in fact seen that way or not.' Shame relates to one's values in a way that humiliation need not, and shame has a moral component that humiliation lacks." "Shame, Humiliation, and Punishment in the Liberal State" (Ph.D. diss., UC Irvine, 2013).

peace. We can each then just enjoy the waves. For we can each be reconciled to the crowded societal mess, for the love of waves, and we can all enjoy our enjoying the waves together, in unity with our fellow surfers. Only an hour ago we argued. Now, with the crowd thinning and the sets pumping, we laugh about our common good fortune. "Where is everybody? Man, we are lucky." Whatever we bickered over, it's all good.

Capitalism and Meritocracy

The surfing lineup is highly meritocratic. While no rule singles out any personal merit for special privilege, everyone loves good surfing. So better surfers often get deference. Some even lay claim to it. A visiting pro starts paddling for a wave, with poise and an air of entitlement. His smug expression says, "We all know I'm going to rip this wave, and because excellence is something I know you value, we all know that you're going to yield to my paddling, and maybe watch me surf." Which is not incorrect. The lesser surfer often does yield, and even watches the wave from the back, to see the plumes of spray and the surfboard fins flying in wafting top turns. Because, actually, this pro *really is* going to rip it, and it'll be exciting to see. Because we all love surfing and value its excellence. We're all trying for it ourselves, and we gladly pay homage whenever it happens. Thus the lesser surfer gets fewer waves, and the talented, who certainly don't need the help, take the lion's share of the common resource, by virtue of the lesser surfers' deference.

Welcome then to Lower Trestles.[19] Far from being a retro long-

---

19. That great friend of surfers and the last major liberal environmentalist, the Republican U.S. president Richard Nixon, opened the Trestles area on the north end of Camp Pendleton to the public, after years of MPs confiscating the surfboards of desperate wave-seeking surfers. Nixon had a house—the "Western White House"—there on Cotton's Point. The Secret Service still tried to outlaw surfing while Nixon was in town, for reasons of security (I guess even surfer dudes could incite his paranoia). See David Morris's "Surfing in Nixonland," *New York Times,* Sept. 6, 2010, http://www.nytimes.com/2016/09/06/opinion/surfing-in-nixonland .html?smprod=nytcore-iphone&smid=nytcore-iphone-share.

board paradise like Malibu, "Lowers" is one of the world's high-performance capitals, a hotbed of SoCal talent that's flooded by visiting pros, travelers from the world over, and kids bent on making it big, as more than a few have before them. It can be a piranha scramble when a wave approaches on a crowded day. But if you surf the place a lot, getting super attuned to the wave movements, you can acquire a superior talent for "deep prediction" about where the shifting wall will eventually pop. Then no matter how crowded the place gets, you can often break from the herd and get yourself on the money spot, in which case it's your wave every time.

People still might drop in, to double-check that you've got it. Or maybe you wind up weaving between paddling surfers who, by a norm of courtesy, should really have gotten the hell out of the way, paddling into the foam instead of up and over the wave face. Because they weren't courteous, and because surfing is not slalom, you never quite key into the wave's rhythm. So it goes. Lowers giveth and Lowers taketh away. But if you can out-jockey the pack enough, you'll get plenty of waves to yourself, and because a single wave at Lowers is as good as ten waves most anywhere else for the ample opportunity it affords for your best maneuvers, you're golden. In the thick of what just was or again soon will be conflictual hell, heaven is possible.

Lowers is one of my favorite places on planet Earth. After returning to California from graduate school, I reconciled myself to the SoCal crowds by becoming a wave capitalist. My "talents" now include winning in the Lowers wave distribution system, which makes crowd surfing more wonderful than I would ever have imagined.

This "talent" was once a source of meritocratic quarrel between me and the late Andy Irons, a three-time world champion, while he was on a stopover from the world competitive tour. We both dropped in on a nice set wave. Irons thought the wave was his, but I was on the more critical spot, and so I claimed it, "Yo, yo, yo." He was expecting deference, and though he kicked out courteously, he then confronted me. "What's this 'Yo, yo, yo' . . . sheesh?" he said, sounding pissed. I replied, "Yeah, you know there's no line out here, and I was on the spot." This was true, but not really the relevant truth. The relevant truth was, "Truly, my friend, you of all people do not need my help getting waves." Irons was a tremendous surfer, my better as a surfer in every respect. He wouldn't be so indecent to so brazenly invoke a meritocratic right, not even to say, "Do you know who I am?" (He assumed I knew who he was, as I of course did.) What he said was, "Shit, so much for the aloha spirit and the family style." (He hailed from Kauai.) I shrugged. I thought (but didn't say), "Yeah, that's nice, but you do know this is *Lowers*; we don't do sharing and caring."

That wasn't quite true either. We do give away waves—occasionally. The truth is that I was invoking my own meritocratic right: I won the contest for that wave (and, actually, another wave on which he dropped in), and so I deserved it under our common rules. I beat him that time in the system, fair and square; it didn't matter that he was the better surfer. Procedure trumped quality, and fairness excellence. Anyway, he certainly didn't need my help getting waves. If I'm going to be charitable, I'd rather give a wave to one of the guys who works like crazy, who is out here trying to scrounge together a moment of joy around an oppressive day at his tire sales business. So even meritocracy has limits: procedural merit in wave catching trumps surfing talent. Goodness and beauty come above everything, except for justice.[20]

Fair Sharing

I said, "There's no line out here." Actually, that was only half-true. It was a winner-take-most scramble on that busy morning. Yet more often there *is* something of a line, or at least a fluid practice of line forming, of taking turns among people in roughly the same posi-

20. John Rawls distinguishes such "legitimate expectations" under a practice (of being given a promised reward) from secondary ideas of desert according to moral worth or reward for virtue. *Theory of Justice*, sec. 48.

tion, waiting for roughly the same waves. If someone's been waiting awhile, and now he or she is about to finally get a wave, others will usually yield. "Yeah, you've been waiting," they'll concede. "Go for it!" Maybe they offer an encouraging hoot. They'll do this even if it is the best wave anyone has seen the whole day. Or even the whole year. Or ever. They'll kick themselves in jealousy but still yield. Sometimes they feel pity for the surfer who's been waiting for an hour. Mainly they yield from fairness, for being willing to share fairly.

Yet as for overall wave distribution, the rule of right-of-way itself doesn't care. Its sole concern is the given approaching wave, not how often any given surfer manages to secure position and what distribution of wave counts or quality emerges over a few hours. The rule distributes the common wave resource among otherwise equal claimants, but only in the claim to another wave helping.

Much as at a picnic, everyone would ideally get a goodly share. If a person kept coming back to a common food source, eventually some might ask, "Haven't you had enough? Yeah . . . so maybe save a lamb chop for those who've eaten less." Likewise, while the surfing lineup is a sort of capitalism, it is at bottom egalitarian.

For starters, everyone can in principle claim a wave share. Or at least everyone who can paddle out into the wave zone and get himself or herself into position to claim right-of-way, and then show sufficient competence in wave riding, above a pretty low threshold. (If localism gives general priority to "local" residents, it merely carves out an exception to this background presumption of equal access.)

The cutoff for basic ability can itself be cause for dispute. Although a surfer may be just capable enough to get into position, for being able to paddle, sit on a board, and wait, without a certain level of skill in wave catching and riding, he won't have a rightful turn, because others won't be required to yield. Not without certain assurances. If chances are 90 percent that the guy is going to eat shit as a powerful wave jacks upon the reef, the others can just go, even if he waited a long time in line. Many will yield, for reasons of charity. But they aren't *required* to suffer the high opportunity cost of having missed out on an epic tube. For when the cost of yielding is so high, it is reasonable to ask the incompetent surfer to please go eat shit on the inside, where the waves are small and in abundance and no one else is asked to pass up a good wave. The trouble is that a proper kook may or may not be willing to admit that his surfing does not pass muster. Although eating shit on a wave is often conspicuous, and its manner or frequency may undeniably show a lack of competence to knowing observers, the surfer himself may vigorously deny it. Perhaps the basic joy in surfing movements is confused with excellence in doing them. Or perhaps you need the know-how of surfing to appreciate the know-how you are lacking. What's at stake here when surfers argue is not meritocracy but the scope of cooperative egalitarianism. For if you are indeed basically competent and get yourself in position, you have equal rights. The better surfer must always yield, no matter how good the wave.

Among the basically capable, surfers not only respect the person who has been waiting; they often feel obliged to spontaneously form a line. And the point of forming a line, of lining up, is precisely to bring about a fairer distribution of waves. This is particularly good for the unfortunate. For those otherwise coming up short, one can get in the queue for the best waves and wait one's turn, and, once one holds first position, the wave is one's own. A small bit of wave justice is served.

So the surfing lineup is a kind of democratic egalitarianism, albeit of a fluid variety. For even line forming must be relatively adaptable. The reef passes in the South Pacific (for example, Tavarua, Fiji) have a well-defined takeoff area for the best waves, and there you just take a number. At most surf breaks, there isn't a well-defined takeoff zone because the waves arrive in different places and running a line isn't feasible. Then the norm is catch as catch can, except among all those in rough striking distance, in which case, sort of take turns.

In South Africa, the practice among friends is more concertedly communistic. If you're surfing in roughly the same area, as friends tend to, and one of them has not had a wave since you last did, then for any wave you could both catch, it is seen as your obligation to yield until he or she gets one. You are permitted to take only the waves he or she can't, and even paddling for a wave he or she might catch is a potential betrayal of civility and friendship. As a Lowers surfer, one becomes accustomed to hustling and double-checking whether the guy who *seems* in position really is. Pretty often, people miss waves, or the wave rolls beneath them, and if you've double-checked, keeping an open option to catch it and ride, the wave is yours. I've gotten used to this, and on one occasion it became a bone of contention in South Africa, while surfing the famous Jeffreys Bay with my South African friends Graeme Bird and "Flame."[21] Being an American, a Lowers capitalist no less, I thought it ridiculous to let good waves go to waste for the sake of communism among friends. So when the better waves were approaching and I wasn't first in line, I made sure they were going and went myself if not. But my South African friends, having become accustomed to the comfort of knowing that the next wave is yours without getting hassled by a "Lowers hustler" (as Graeme calls me), complained of my zeal. I should just wait until they go and it is definitely my turn. I deferred to local South African custom but insisted that we debate the limitations of communism as a way of distributing waves. (South Africans tend to be game for vigorous argument.)

"Communism doesn't work" is the familiar critique. That wasn't my point. In some cases, it does, or can, work, among friends or in an especially well-defined lineup such as Tavarua, where wave turns can be effectively counted and shared. In those cases, I agree one is morally obliged to respect a line if it has already formed and initiate formation of a line if not. Yet in many other cases, maybe at most breaks the world over, including the usual day at Lowers, a rigid line-forming practice maybe *could* work, but only at a high opportunity cost in waves lost. Is strict line forming always required?

21. Flame is a pyrotechnician—though only coincidentally. The nickname (his name is Michael Robinson) derives from a surfing accident to his groin in Mozambique. What was then a new surf break was subsequently dubbed "flame balls."

Must any two surfers form a line, and any third get behind? I don't think so. We'd have to have decided to sit close together and to wait for and ride only certain types of waves, taking turns only on those waves. The other waves coming in, however easily caught, would have to go unridden. It's a nice sentiment, all for one and one for all, but my own disposition would be to just not sign up. I'd leave the line area to the others and go chase waves by my own exercise of skill and luck.[22]

There is such a thing as being a capitalist *pig*, however, or one who takes much too much from a common resource. One could do wrong by not "leaving enough and as good for others," in John Locke's phrase, without taking *way* too much. Even if one is being a pig, or a pig across many areas of life, one might not be moved by any sense of entitlement, and so not be an asshole. One can simply be greedy or impulsive, as in grabbing way too many cookies on a picnic table in a moment of weakness. Even in the good ole U. S. of A., but away from supercompetitive Lowers, I have been politely asked to please stop catching so many waves so that others might get more of them. I decided that, yes, I guess I was in fact being a pig.[23] At a picnic, there's such a thing as taking too much from the buffet, even if there's no line, and even if it takes great skill to pile sushi rolls high on a single plate. Surfing's rule of right-of-way only concerns a given wave helping, so it doesn't guard against over-appropriation of a shared resource. And even when a well-defined line for wave sharing won't work at a given break, courtesy still requires giving a few away when you've had plenty. Not from charity, but as a matter of fair sharing. Even if you'd win the larger

22. I've heard of (but never experienced) an arrangement in which one person calls out numbers. Each person takes whatever wave is coming when his or her number is called out. This will only work in a small common wave zone, but the system was presumed to cover the whole surf break. Those who preferred to hunt waves around the margins, without taking a number, were called "scabs." In this scenario, I'd probably wait in line for a few waves and then scab.

23. This was done more from zeal and obliviousness than from any sense of entitlement. I didn't try to defend my greater share, so I hope I was merely being a pig and not an asshole.

share, fair and square, *if* this were a wave-catching contest and not an easy session, you can't just make what's now an easy session into a contest area by changing the tone with aggro paddling, in order to be able to take that greater share. You'd irritate the others, and for good reason. For this to be permissible, you'd need a shared sense that a more competitive footing was required by the lack of waves or increase in surfers. Without that, you're not a pig taking to excess but a boorish and greedy asshole who is merely degrading the easy session for personal advantage.

So surfers have a fluid wave-sharing practice, which they adapt to changing wave circumstances. It's comparable, but still more fluid, than pedestrian practice on a busy city sidewalk. In walking along, we each adjust our walking pace and side steps to accommodate the others, giving way or speeding up, each doing our parts, moment by moment, in a scheme by which each goes his or her own way in a hum of togetherness. Each has rights, to be somewhere, to go somewhere else, to have others watch and coordinate smooth passage as they are approaching. (Only an asshole just walks straight through, in a "No, *you* move" posture.) Much as in the waves, your right over this or that particular location is fluid and ever changing. The spot or trajectory that's definitely now yours here is someone else's only moments later. We thus "surf" the crowd in sidewalk traffic.

We each surf the crowd, but not the street, which isn't constantly changing. The surfing lineup is adaptive in that regard as well. Surfers attune to each other, and together attune to their changing wave environment. They fluidly adapt cooperative expectations to conditions of relative wave abundance and scarcity. In this respect, as I explain presently, the surfing lineup is akin to international relations in a changing global environment.

Attuning Capitalism

Surfers do spontaneously what nations have only begun to do: together adapt their cooperation for their changing global environment. In the "anarchical society" that is international relations, nations do cooperate, more or less, by international law and practice, policy coordination, and diplomacy. But on a planet whose common resources are now shifting from abundance to scarcity, they've been slow to adapt to changing conditions. According to scientific consensus, the atmosphere can only absorb so much of the emissions of economic activity without raising average temperatures in a way that imperils our prosperity, our leisure, and the very future of humanity. If the cause is our old style of capitalism, with its fossil fuels and heat-trapping gases, then the question for all nations is a matter of surfer know-how, of how to attunedly adapt capitalism to the new human condition of ecological scarcity.

What works among a pod of surfers won't necessarily work for anything so large as the basic structure of a whole society, let alone two hundred or so different nations, each with millions of vote-wielding residents. Yet in the big picture, surfer society and international relations are not so different. The surfing lineup, the state, and international law and practice are all forums for the governance of common affairs. And governance is always a matter of historical experimentation with changing circumstances.

Conjectural futurology is a tough business, so it's understandable that Hobbes didn't guess how civilization and prosperity would spread under the rise of democracy. In *Leviathan,* the choice is between a sovereign's awesome rule and a disordered anarchy. But that dichotomy turned out to be facile even by the book's date of publication. The modern state system, which began at the 1648 Treaty of Westphalia (just before *Leviathan's* 1651 publication), ended the very wars that led Hobbes to describe international relations as an anarchical war of kings and princes. Europe was pacified, and not by a superstate sovereign of Europe capable of overawing all of them. Peace came by a truce for mutual benefit and a practice of mutual forbearance. Even without centralized government, the practice stuck and eventually brought peace to the whole globe.

Eventually, at least—because, yes, that whole imperial expansion of the state system didn't exactly go swimmingly. But if you can squint and fast-forward through a centuries-long interlude of colonial conquest, mass slaughter, untold horrors, two world wars that were by far the bloodiest in human history—not exactly growing pains—it's still true that Kant's dream of peace became a reality.[24] Eventually, yes indeed, we got the "long peace" of the postwar era. Which is certainly much better than continued or rising violence. Democratic governments tend not to go to war.[25] But the backstory of modern order and postwar peace begins way back with the early system of states and the Peace of Westphalia. Industrial capitalism finally emerged, and with increasing globalization and the rise of democracy working people could finally climb from poverty and ask by vote and protest not to have to work so much. By the mid-twentieth century, with a new forty-hour workweek, leisure culture flowered. In the blooming culmination of modernity, the leisure revolution began, giving capitalism a new surfer styling.

When Karl Marx predicted the end of capitalism, he imagined people working a few hours in the morning, making adjustments to the labor-saving machines, and then spending the afternoon doing various excellent activities, like fishing, or reading, or spending time with the kids. Capitalism is still very much with us, and Marx was wrong in thinking that it had to end for us to be somewhat freed from constant toil. We now take the forty-hour workweek for granted, which means we all agree that a capitalist system must afford the human person time to rest, relax, and recreate, with weekends off, some semblance of a vacation, and retirement before death.

Only the purest, most hard-core capitalism leaves all matters of time and labor to the market. When social insurance was first established in the 1880s in Otto von Bismarck's Germany, the hope

24. In "Toward Perpetual Peace" (1795), Kant focused on economic integration as the basis for peace, which turns out to be less important than democracy, though perhaps still a contributing factor. Immanuel Kant, *To Perpetual Peace: A Philosophical Sketch* (Indianapolis: Hackett, 2003).
25. Michael W. Doyle, *Liberal Peace: Selected Essays* (New York: Routledge, 2011).

was to improve upon the measly Poor Laws of England by adopting health insurance, pensions, and workers' compensation in order to prove that a system of private property and markets could work for the common good without converting to socialism (Bismarck even banished socialist leaders and banned socialist meetings and mailings).[26]

And so capitalism was adapted according to its presumed point. Why augment the wealth of nations? Why, to relieve poverty, so that one can become secure and prosperous and relax! But by the rising "wealth of nations," Adam Smith officially meant only the annual produce, or the aggregate we now call GDP. Why strive to make that number larger? To most people, this will not sound all that important unless one is actually getting a piece of the growing pie. If Bill Gates walks up to a picnic, the picnic GDP goes way up, but the other picnickers don't get any richer for his mere attendance. And if many people only get the barest "opportunity" to get richer, with slim prospects of getting ahead, despite all the risks and vulnerabilities of being ruled and dominated by ravenous capitalists, then it's fair to say that capitalism will have failed to deliver on its world-historical promise.

The rising wealth of nations is supposed to bring widely shared prosperity. And not just by allowing a worker to exchange longer hours in work for a bit more money. This quickly runs into limits, given the number of hours in a day. For without a goodly measure of "leisure time"—defined by economists as time away from work in the labor market (which may, however, include unpaid household work, child rearing, and work-like activities)—when exactly will you enjoy the fruits of your labors? With a forty-hour workweek, vacations, proper retirement, and other benefits, people have a better balance of money for time—more money earned through less

26. Elizabeth Anderson, "Common Property," *Boston Review,* July 25, 2016, https://bostonreview.net/editors-picks-us-books-ideas/elizabeth-anderson-common-property.

time at work, with permission to take meaningful leisure.[27] And even if the leisure revolution has stalled for at least three decades—Americans, for example, work longer hours to make up for stagnating wages—the grand adaptive experiment can still continue. What's needed is a twenty-first-century attunement of capitalism's market/state balance.

In the mid-1940s, Hayek warned of the road to serfdom under socialism. But for all of his insights about social order and the power of markets,[28] his stark choice between "central planning" and "free markets" was always unimaginative as philosophy.[29] In fact, the postwar economies were on the road to surfdom, even where markets were heavily regulated, as in the United States. Prosperity came to mixed economies, each with its own market/state mix, adapted to its particular circumstances.[30] Talk of "capitalism" and "socialism" can *sound* philosophically deep. In practice, there is no bright line between them and only varying adaptations in changing conditions, which might be more or less "socialistic" in differ-

27. In his Marxist phase, G. A. Cohen argued advanced capitalism is inherently biased against reducing toil and extending leisure. Business competition is inherently biased toward expanding output instead. The bias against leisure is only by "broad empirical generalization," which admits exceptions. I'd say the forty-hour workweek is a huge exception, even if "antagonism" is the rule. *Marx's Theory of History: A Defense* (Oxford: Clarendon Press, 1978), p. 311n1, and the section "A Distinctive Contradiction of Advanced Capitalism."
28. See his wonderful *Law, Legislation, and Liberty,* vol. 1, *Rules and Order* (Chicago: University of Chicago Press, 1973).
29. See his not-so-wonderful *Law, Legislation, and Liberty,* vol. 2, *The Mirage of Social Justice* (Chicago: University of Chicago Press, 1976). He still bought a version of Hobbes's bad dichotomy between the sovereign's rule and anarchy, simply being more bullish about "anarchy," which could generate "spontaneous order." Still, arguably even the purest capitalism must be "embedded" in institutions that regulate property and other rights within judicial, administrative, and legislative systems. See the sociologist Karl Polanyi, *The Great Transformation* (Boston: Beacon Press, 1957).
30. Dani Rodrik, *The Globalization Paradox: Democracy and the Future of the World Economy* (New York: W. W. Norton, 2011); and *One Economics, Many Recipes: Globalization, Institutions, and Economic Growth* (Princeton, N.J.: Princeton University Press, 2007).

ent governance areas, depending on the mix.[31] The United States didn't become a socialist country when it adopted the forty-hour workweek, or when it made national parks or the coastal beaches public property, or when it set up public fire departments, or when it started sending out disability or retirement checks, or when it moved toward nearly universal health insurance. It merely became more mixed. Indeed, the United States entered its golden era of broad-based growth, with low inequality and a widely shared leisure culture, *after* it started making just such attunements.

Will the future be like the past? Maybe not. Modern governance has always been a trial-and-error project. It wouldn't be wise to name any development "the end of history," as Francis Fukuyama famously did, even with liberal capitalist democracy vanquishing its communist foes.[32] The idea of "liberal capitalist democracy" is itself tremendously broad and endlessly flexible and so open for further attunements. The question is simply what governance mix is most attuned to a now quickly changing human condition.

Can We Adapt the Game?

"All that is solid melts into air, all that is holy is profaned." Marx thus lamented rather than praised the adaptability of capitalism. Nothing is so sacred—not religion, not even surfing—that it can't be monetized for profit.

Unless, that is, we ourselves refuse to let capitalism adapt. Which we might do, in the following all-too-realistic doomsday sce-

31. We might define capitalism in general as an economic system mainly of private property that relies largely on markets for the production and allocation of goods, services, and capital. A system that has more public property and relies less on markets would still be capitalism until it shades into a society much further along the spectrum that mainly has public property and largely doesn't rely on markets for economic decisions. Every advanced society today lies somewhere in the middle, as do most developing countries.

32. Francis Fukuyama, *The End of History and the Last Man* (New York: Free Press, 1992).

nario. Suppose we will invariably compete for status. But the status game is already set—as the game of working for ever more money, to pay for ever more consumption-heavy leisure. And yet suppose that unless we can work less on average, spending more time in less ecologically disruptive leisure (among other equally or more urgent measures), we won't curb grave risks of ecological cataclysm. In that case, humanity is hosed. We won't ever ease off the emissions throttle. Short of our getting extremely lucky in the climate casino, disaster will ensue.

Is this a realistic scenario? It may seem a simple matter of human nature. To Hobbes, we have no way of just being, without competing for status; man invariably strives for "vain-glory" in "a perpetual and restless desire of power after power, that ceaseth only in death."[33] Rousseau thought our natures are more flexible and that we willingly cooperate if we feel seen as an equal. Then we can each cease our strivings for relative status ("amour propre") and love ourselves contentedly, without comparison ("amour de soi-meme"). Yet for Rousseau the problems of recognition only get worse in affluence.[34] The troubles around the village campfire were manageable. But the rising wealth of nations brings the rise of property, inequality, and power. Our inflamed feelings of envy, jealousy, and resentment cast a whole society into that hellish contest for recognition that Sartre dramatized so fiendishly.

Rousseau's insight isn't just sour conjecture. In the villages behind Lagundri Bay, on Nias Island (back in Sumatra), the communities regularly interrupt their same-as-it-ever-was poverty, which leaves them without such luxuries as toilets, for a game of *fútbol*/soccer. The ragtag, mismatched, multicolored uniforms leave no discernible difference between the two teams, as families gather, laughing and cheering over sounds of the roaring ocean beneath the nearby cliffs. I assume someone is sort of keeping score. The competing

33. Thomas Hobbes, *Leviathan*, ed. Richard Tuck (Cambridge, U.K.: Cambridge University Press, 1996), 70.
34. *Discourse on the Origin and the Foundations of Inequality Among Men.*

villages do seem to know each other well enough to know roughly who is going in what direction. The players are definitely trying to score into the rickety stick goalposts. It all seems rather unorganized and "inefficient" to a visitor like me from an advanced country. Yet they plainly don't suffer from the advanced worlder's confusion about whether scoring and winning are different and more important than the moment of community, of being all together, smiling and chatting, on an easy golden afternoon.

In "advanced" America on any Saturday morning, on the other hand, after much hoopla and boasting about how, come the weekend, team Arrow Lightning is going to *totally school* the wayward Brown Pandas, the Pandas are forced to dig deep to avoid shameless defeat and salvage the honor of their whole city block and their own esteem and stature. The angst and consternation won't allow people to feel "it's just a game," which is what the *losers* say to cope in humiliating defeat. It can't just be a game, not in the culture of competitive society, where relative fates are set by contest and winners take most. The game can't just be played for its own sake, in easy sporting, not given the high stakes. As for the conflictual struggle for recognition, that persistent source of untold personal misery and social ills, it's game on, whether in sports, paychecks, houses, cars, vacations, smarts, degrees, fame, good looks, and/or social media followers and "likes."

All of which raises the doomsday scenario. With our global climate hanging in the balance, could competitive society be humanity's final undoing? Is not the game already set—the game of working for money, scored in paychecks, cars, and houses, with weekends and vacations for "work-hard-play-hard" ecologically disruptive leisure, instead of easy surfing? Will we thus only worsen the warming problem? Will our perpetual and restless striving to prove our worth cease only in death, block our attunement to the foreboding new condition of scarcity, and literally court the end of human civilization as we know it? It certainly might. Must it? What would be the alternative?

We must search for an answer.

8

Nature

You cannot step in the same river twice.

—Heraclitus

DESERT POINT WILL BE among the first surf breaks to be swamped as sea levels rise with global warming. I'm sure its unusual geo-situation there on the west edge of Lombok, in the Lombok Strait, a southern passage of the Indonesian Throughflow, has something to do with the extraordinary quality of its long, tubing blue-green walls. Indian Ocean swells mount suddenly upon the shallow reef, having traversed the depths of the strait, which is itself a small part of the global heat conveyor belt that regulates our planet's average temperature, as warm freshwater flows through from the Pacific into the Indian Ocean. But the warming trend in that very system won't be kind to Deserts. The spot needs a low and preferably rising tide to turn on, and with the predicted three to fifteen extra feet of water on the reef from rising sea levels, depending on the scenario, the majestically reeling wave walls will be transformed into high-tide-like mush—what French surfers call *merde*.

Nearly all of the world's surf breaks require certain tides if the waves are to be any good for surfing. Whether high, low, or somewhere in the middle, the tidal level at a given time determines how shallow the water is over the reef or sand bottom, and so how the waves refract, mount, and peel as they arrive from deeper water. Although each surf break works under its own set of conditions, which local surfers obsessively track (with sophisticated surf forecasts, which they check and recheck, amid much voyeuristic peering at the waves), a higher tide will leave most breaks fat, shifty, and lethargic.

Even a surfer can fall into despair at the thought that any of this would actually happen. Desert Point and a whole raft of low-tide breaks will be gone with only a few extra feet of water, and most of the half-decent spots we've surfed and loved since our youth will be swamped eventually. What took thousands upon thousands of years to form into just the right wave structure will become *merde,* forever. (Or at least for thousands more years, which comes to the same thing, humanly speaking.)

Structure and Flow

A *flow,* whether a breaking wave, a flowing stream, or the Indonesian Throughflow, always flows *through* something that is not flowing, a *structure* that shapes *how* the flow flows, allowing it to have a flowing dynamic.

In a flowing river, the riverbed shapes the water, perhaps in a bending or switching path. At the beach, the bottom contours and sea level combine to structure and shape how each wave breaks. The various islands and waterways and bottom topography of the Indonesian Throughflow shape the flow of freshwater from the Pacific into the Indian Ocean. Throughout nature, flows depend, physically and metaphysically, on an underlying structure.

People and society are of course part of nature, and so the metaphysics of flow and structure applies to them as well. On a wave, a surfer can go along with a wave's flow only because certain other things are in alignment—only because, as the breaking wave peaks and shifts, certain other structural contours remain relatively fixed. While riding along, a surfer will have given a flowing performance only within the constraints of the wave itself and the rough repertoire of evolving surfing practice. In surfer society, surfers flowingly cooperate, more or less, within the structure of wave etiquette, together adapting to their changing environment, much as societies have always adapted, lest they perish.

And if consciousness itself flows as we feel it must, its subjective feel certainly depends on underlying mental structures. Kant thought that basic "categories" of understanding (space, time, and causation) had to structure any human experience or "intuition," no matter how spontaneous it seemed. Experiencing beauty worked differently, in a "free play" or "free harmony" of thought in imagination, in a freer-flowing consciousness, which is less constrained and more enjoyable than observing a cup on a table. Yet even Sartre was a Kantian at the deepest level. Consciousness flows very freely, but still within our structured physical makeup (our "facticity").

A flow is only as permanent as its underlying structure, and so may or may not be lasting or dependable. For a flow to flow for a time, a structuring relationship has to be there over that span of time. Yet the relationship may itself be dynamic. A structure will give a flow its shape at any instant, or over a stretch of flowing, as when a kink in the riverbed turns the water flow over an afternoon or a week. A flow can also shape its own shaping structure as time passes, as when the flow of river water gradually erodes the kink. The two can change each other in a larger environment, as long as the basic structure/flow relationship doesn't change too much all at once. When big changes come too quickly, we lose the crucial difference between change and disappearance. A big enough flood won't *change* the stream's water flow, but simply wash the whole stream away.

And therein lies the problem of climate change. The relationship between crucial ecological flows and their structures is changing too quickly. Although average temperatures have always varied from epoch to epoch in the planetary scheme of things, the Industrial Revolution brought a sudden burst of heat-trapping emissions. And because the carbon dioxide, methane, and other gases we've pumped up into the atmosphere cannot be fully reabsorbed by natural processes (for example, by sea algae, which is a major carbon sink), they linger and trap the sun's rays, steadily raising average global temperatures. So while our capitalism and sources of energy have created wealth at once unimaginable levels, they have also permanently and radically changed the way our climate and oceans structure earthly life and society.

Here I just stipulate the going scientific consensus about planetary warming trends, their human causes, and the risks that range from major to cataclysmic as givens. I personally take the science at face value. More skeptical readers might note that our present concern is simply the *philosophical* question of ethics under uncertainty. If we assume for the sake of argument that our planet is warming, potentially with catastrophic consequences, the question is, what follows, ethically speaking? It's at least an interesting thought experiment. And if there's any real chance that climate science is onto something major, it seems fair to say we shouldn't slough off any question of our responsibility, like some lazy and oblivious surfer.

"Bru, Don't Stress"

My dear South African friend Graeme, a consummate surfer, isn't excessively sunny as a person. So even aside from the edgy style of South African political argument, I was surprised to hear that in a conversation about the potential end of surfing with his fellow South African surfers, they became rather pissed off by his note of cautious optimism.

The others were apparently voicing existential despair at the very thought of rising sea levels. I'm sure they do worry about the risks of increasing droughts, famines, floods, hurricanes, resource wars, migrations, the millions of deaths to ensue, and the woman on the Bangladeshi floodplains who will be cast to the four winds, having lost everything. But for the moment these surfers, being surfers, were preoccupied with the fact that with rising sea levels, the world's great and half-decent surf breaks will be submerged, indefinitely.

The sea level rise we've already seen doesn't sound so terrible (seventeen centimeters over the last century, and three centimeters per decade lately). The worry is that the levels will increase much, much more, relatively soon, with ice sheet collapse accelerating. No one can say by exactly how much or exactly when; the science involves models of super-complex systems, which are inherently uncertain, even beyond the uncertainty in predicting the future. From the surfer's perspective, the exact details aren't so important; it is enough that for all the uncertainty there's a *profound risk* that sea levels could get *a lot* higher than a couple of extra feet. Apparently, a rise of ten or so feet is now almost certainly inevitable, though the figure of seventeen extra feet is mentioned in various studies. If that isn't disconcerting enough, one might note that when the atmospheric concentration of carbon was last at today's level, the sea level was apparently something like *seventy feet higher,* which obviously bodes ill not just for the quality of waves but for all coastal life on the planet. So if nothing major is done in time to curb the rising global tide, this will ruin pretty much all of the world's surf breaks.

So it should come as no surprise that surfers argue about what to make of this world-historical development. I'm sure Graeme was cool as a cucumber in the argument he relayed to me, as he always is. Being South African, he's well acquainted with the darker side of human nature, as well as nature's terrors. He well knows nature's splendor as well, such as the transfixing beauty of the well-groomed, marching lines of South Africa's Jeffreys Bay (where Graeme and I first became fast friends). And he's been to Indonesia plenty of times (and went back even after getting malaria). He's a respected Durban local, with a top-notch back-side tube-riding act, but also whip smart, articulate, exceptionally polite, and certainly not lacking in the love of waves. He's organized his life around waves as much as any of us, and he'd ultimately be devastated if they were all more or less history.

Even so, in response to all the weeping and gnashing of teeth by the others, Graeme boldly countered: Rising sea levels *will make a few spots a lot better.* Some surf spots that are now too shallow for surfing will get better as sea levels rise, as water fills in over the reefs.

His case in point was a surf break called "the Machine," on the island of Nias, in Lagundri Bay, which I had mentioned to him in relaying the effects of the big 2005 Sumatran earthquake/tsunami after I went to Nias on a surf trip. The quake raised the continental shelf an astonishing *ten* feet above sea level. The famous surf break there in Lagundri Bay (Sorake is its local name) got better, while the reef at the Machine, of what was a beautiful machinelike peeling wave, became too shallow for surfing (except on the largest swells and the year's highest full-moon tides, which rarely happen at the same time). Graeme was saying that the Machine could be surfed again and that a raft of other spots that are now just a bit too shallow, in the Indian Ocean as well as across the South Pacific, would really start cracking.

The audacity in this didn't so much lie in Graeme's predictions. It was the implied *philosophical* perspective. Graeme wasn't questioning climate science or minimizing the threat to most of the world's existing waves. But if only by trying to somehow find some sort of bright spot in a dark and darkening picture, he seemed to be saying that we surfers shouldn't be too worried about the specter of a surfing cataclysm, even if it really does happen. Not only would we still find a wave to surf somewhere, there will still be some kind of grand reckoning in which things can be said to have worked out okay. So we really needn't worry. We can just go with the flow in this whole climate change business, see how things play out, and take things as they come. The waves are good today, aren't they? As Graeme would say, "Bru, don't stress."

Was Graeme just displaying an admirable willingness to adapt as things change, to take things as they come? Isn't that, after all, the quintessential surfer attitude? Equally, shouldn't we prepare ourselves for acquiescence to the end of surfing itself, if that is indeed to happen? The waves are good today. As for the future, whatever happens happens. We surfers, being surfers, will adapt.

That is the Stoic attitude, but I myself don't think it can be the proper surfer position. The very possibility of there being a flow that one can be in, or go with, depends on bigger things that aren't flowing; certain things that have to be there anyway, arranged just so for any flow to be possible. Again think of the way a stream of flowing water depends on a stationary riverbed and flows in one direction or another within the riverbed's relatively fixed contours—its structure. Each surf break depends on all kinds of underlying conditions, from bottom contours to wind direction to sea levels to swells originating from storms far away. Likewise for our natural climatic and oceanic surroundings, which structure almost everything else. When something so grave as the end of surfing as we know it is a real prospect, sunny resignation to that disastrous outcome isn't the right way to think about what "going with the flow" involves. At least not in the sense that seems to have real value, in surfing and in life generally.

It wasn't supposed to be this way. Surely it's all some grand cosmic accident, and not retribution by the gods against humanity's profligate ways. Our forebears went all in for industrial capitalism, unwittingly creating risks of ecological calamity, and we're left to deal with them. So it goes. But if we are now stuck asking how we might sense what is changing and adapt, the so-it-goes attitude just isn't true to the surfer's love of waves. It doesn't square with what the surfer really does know about "going with the flow," in the most important sense.

The surfer knows how to be attuned to a changing natural phenomenon, from a real sense of the value of being in this kind of adaptive relationship. And that partly means having a sense of the structural preconditions for that very relationship. So to the surfer who values the activity of surfing, he or she must also value preserving what creates its very possibility and be willing to adapt our way of life accordingly. Things are already changing, in decidedly gnarly ways. So if surfers are going to stay attuned to the waves and ocean they love, they may have to *actually do something* to stave off a global surfing cataclysm, before the opportunity passes and we lose what chance we may now have.

How then might the surfer make him- or herself useful? Strange as it may sound to those of us saddled with the Protestant work ethic, the surfer can contribute by not working and going surfing instead.

A Convenient Truth

We began our inquiry noting that work as we now practice it creates the gases that are warming up the planet. So one can contribute to the cause of reducing emissions by working less and doing something less ecologically disruptive. Most surfers will happily offer this service to society. And if they hadn't previously thought of surfing as a social contribution, they will boldly keep going surfing in a new spirit of cooperation.

Of course this wouldn't be necessary if we could anticipate a technological fix that removes or drastically reduces the trade-off between emissions and economic production. Yet for all the amazing developments in renewable energy lately, we unfortunately can't expect any or all of them to make the whole problem go away.[1] In the models that project possible outcomes, all of the not utterly awful scenarios on various warming trajectories *already* bank on future tech progress (especially in carbon capture) on a scale that we have no capacity for at the moment.[2]

---

1. The success of renewables is unfortunately also undercutting support for nuclear power in some cases (for example, in California), which is crucial as a clean energy source.
2. Thomas Malthus famously argued that (1) people love making babies, (2) the earth can only produce so much food, and so (3) population growth must outstrip food supply, bringing mass starvation. This didn't happen. The green revolution showed that food production could keep up, because market signals and technology increased resources as growing populations needed. The climate change problem is more radical in scale, scope, and consequence, so we can't blow it off as passé Malthusian doomsdayism.

So if we all worked less overall, spending more leisure time in less disruptive activities, this would be an eminently sensible way to adapt to our more fragile global ecology. It wouldn't be sufficient on its own. But along with other equally or even more urgent measures (carbon taxes, cap and trade, and so on), we could continue the leisure revolution with new vigor.

As noted earlier, this isn't to say the surfer could *simply* cut back the working hours. She really would have to emit less in leisure than she would if she were working. Surfing a wave is itself more or less carbon-free. Yet if the surfer is not already the type to keep her surfing lifestyle simple, by riding a bike to the beach, or at least not doing a lot of driving to check different spots, then she'd also have to learn not to emit as she would if she were working in the labor market. Likewise if one hopes to make the surfer's contribution by other means. One could read a book, take a long walk, have a much-needed nap, play with the kids, chat over coffee with friends, visit the elderly, or help a charity. It's all good, as long as it doesn't worsen the climate change problem as much as if one were working for money.

This is especially important if our personal emissions over our lifetimes do a lot of damage on their own. Then one personally does less harm to others by making the surfer's contribution.[3] But working less and surfing more need only make a *contribution*. Maybe one's personal emissions over a lifetime are only a "drop in the ocean" in the combined emissions of the cars, house lights, or computers of billions of people that are systematically polluting the climate. Yet when it comes to pollution, we say "every little bit counts" for a reason: it is only by each of us doing our bit that a larger practice of forbearance can ever itself make a real difference. Small efforts shared widely often do make a great difference.[4]

3. The eminent philosopher and economist John Broome argues that we have "duty of justice" not to harm others and should reduce our personal emission by buying offsets. *Climate Matters: Ethics in a Warming World* (New York: W. W. Norton, 2012), chap. 5.
4. John Fleck, *Water Is for Fighting Over, and Other Myths About Water in the West* (Washington, D.C.: Island Press, 2016), tells the story of successful piecemeal and small-bore efforts at conservation in the Colorado River basin that added up to

Although it wouldn't despoil a beach to toss a single water bottle into the bushes, you'll still "pack your trash" and uphold a general trash-packing practice that keeps the beach clean. In the same way, working less and surfing (or listening to music or knitting) can be a way of "doing one's bit," a way of participating in a general work/leisure practice that itself makes the warming problem less terrible than it will otherwise be.

The 2008 economic crisis caused high levels of unemployment, forcing people to involuntarily work less and live simply. During that period, carbon emissions dropped markedly. The unemployed worker who sat around the house feeling "good for nothing" could have encouraged himself somewhat; he was at least doing his part on the climate change front. But the evils of joblessness aren't required to lower our emissions overall. We can equally cut back on total work hours if we all work, but all work a lot less, in a much shorter standard workweek.

Suppose we cut the workweek down to the thirty-five hours put in by the lazy Germans. Even that would help greatly. It would help even more to go further, until we've reduced work levels to some lower bound at which an advanced economy won't function. No one knows where exactly that lower bound is. But as something of a rough benchmark, the twentieth-century economist John Maynard Keynes, who, almost ninety years ago, correctly predicted how rich we'd by now become, also thought we'd by now have the workweek down to fifteen hours. (Why we haven't is an interesting question, which I'll come back to.) If that sounds too low to be feasible, let's go with twenty. So the advanced countries move to a twenty-hour workweek and spend the rest in leisure, and the climate change problem becomes less terrible than it will now be.

Even before leisurely living becomes the new normal, one can contribute by easing the way for its normalization. Social trending is

---

a solution in the face of water scarcity, despite warnings of mega-droughts. This is another example of the "common pool resource" systems studied by the Nobel laureate Elinor Ostrom.

unpredictable, but someone has to go first, and because people are influenced in a monkey-see-monkey-do way, others may gradually get on the bandwagon, perhaps with self-styled "influencers" speeding the movement along. And once people have gone ahead in cutting back their work hours, while bragging on social media about all the fun they're having not working, it will become easier to properly standardize a shorter workweek through policy and regulation, with any needed adjustments or appropriate exceptions. In this regard the surfer is a model of civic virtue, and the "workaholic" the new problem child.

But is it not just "lazy" to work less? Is the surfer who works less just too entitled, selfish, or self-indulgent to exert himself for the benefit of others? No, because paid work is not the accurate hallmark of social contribution. Parenting mainly goes unremunerated, but of course does much for society. A surfer who chooses to surf instead of work is *not* lazing or loafing, but actively surfing, and maybe working on her technique. Her contribution lies in her choice of activities, her choice to *surf instead of work* in the labor market, which serves an important social purpose. Odd as it may sound, then, even a choice of lazing or loafing over working for money can likewise contribute to the worthy cause of sparing humanity from a slow-motion cataclysm.

The surfer will nevertheless have duties. The public may want assurances that her leisure emissions really are lower than if she'd worked. So, as with paying one's taxes, the administrative work of civic surfer virtue may not be convenient.[5]

Would the surfer rise to the call of leisurely service too enthusiastically? And might such enthusiasm suggest a certain lack of regard for the true needs of society? Well, parents contribute plenty, and some are more enthusiastic about than exhausted by child rearing. We don't hold their enthusiasm against them, and we don't expect

5. How do we know the surfer is keeping it simple? Our emissions would have to be roughly estimated, to ensure that a contribution is being made. We'd want an unobtrusive method of accounting with easily tracked categories. I assume this is mainly an administrative and technological problem. There could be an app for that.

them to care about the cause of good parenting. While some parents actually contemplate society's need to rear the next generation, if many just want their kid to get ahead in life and provide them security in their dotage, they'd still rightly be honored on Mother's Day or Father's Day. Or think of the caretaker who changes Granny's nappies willingly and without payment for her love of people. We wouldn't discount her service because she performs it enthusiastically, or expect her to have pondered her salutary role in the political economy of elder care. What matters, even to her, will be that Granny stays clean and comfortable. And for that we'll thank her, because if she wasn't performing the service, someone else would have to be paid to do it, and someone will have to make that payment, whether the family or the taxpayer.

So while greenhouse gas emissions may not be foremost in the surfer's mind, the surfer can be thanked and supported for doing his or her bit, for being willing to forgo work and the gases it would emit. We fawn over the capitalist whose rank private greed helps to create jobs and boost GDP. Okay, fine; contribution is measured in expected outcomes rather than by intent. Equally so, the surfer's stoked contribution is still a contribution. Indeed, the surfer who is especially talented at work makes an especially large contribution by not working. If the surfer would be unusually productive had she been working, the fact that she is surfing, instead of working, may mean there is even more work for the others who want or need the opportunity.

Surfers Help Capitalism

The rise of capitalism over the last two hundred or so years has reduced absolute poverty on an astoundingly huge scale, first in the industrialized nations, and lately in developing countries, in South Asia (and especially in China), but also in Latin America (though to a lesser degree in Africa). Nearly every great apologist for capitalism, from Adam Smith to F. A. Hayek, has celebrated its marvelous capacity to reduce poverty. For all of its woes and troubles, this is the main way it has been legitimized as a morally welcome, or at least tolerable, force for world-historical good. It's not only different from slavery, which is unjust and impermissible, but rather wonderful from a humanitarian perspective.

At the same time, now in our new world of ecological scarcity, insofar as we lack a technological fix, we can't assume there is no limit on the global rate of economic growth if we are to avoid disastrous outcomes that are themselves morally unacceptable. Perhaps we aren't personally or even collectively to blame for kicking off the whole process, which is just a huge unforeseen misfortune, like the curtains catching on fire at what would have been a fabulous party. Still, it seems fair to say that all of us—even surfers—have to accept certain responsibilities to adjust from now on.

What to do then? Work as we now define it adds to the emissions problem significantly, so we at the very least have to rethink its role in our lives, along with success, reward, and what contributes to society. And as suggested earlier, while there is no one easy fix, it turns out that one eminently sensible adaptation is to shorten the workweek. We can nearly all work, but work a lot less, with basic income support, pensions, and so forth, to ensure that our leisure time is meaningful. Indeed, we may be *forced* to work a lot less soon enough, if or when robots start taking our jobs more quickly than we can find new work for displaced people to do. In any case we *already* have good reason to cut back the workweek voluntarily.

Among the possible climate adaptations, this one is certainly the surfer's favorite. That isn't simply a sporting preference. Consider again that capitalism's basic source of legitimacy as a way of organizing social life is its ability to eliminate want. If that's true, then the developing countries should fairly claim the lion's share of what growth possibilities there are. That in turn means the advanced societies probably can't grow at the rates they've been growing, not without busting through an obligatory global emissions limit. But then working less and surfing more is not just a social contribution for making the warming problem less bad than it would otherwise be. It is also a way of upholding capitalism's claim to moral legitimacy.

If we did work less in the rich world, we'd be honoring the harder work of billions of very poor people all across the developing world who are climbing their way from privation to meeting basic needs to a middle-class income, or something close. Even aside from future generations, the ethical question is what we owe to the bustling, hustling developing worlders who are making good on capitalism's promise to eliminate want, by pulling themselves up by their boot-straps. But if economic growth has global limits, and there is only so much work that can be done, then it seems only fair for us advanced worlders to work less in order to free up opportunities for developing countries, which can continue on a path of "convergence" up to our high standard of living.

Surely we can't insist that poor people *stay* in poverty simply so that *we* can work for a bit more money instead. We say we honor hard work in solemn tones; so why not let them do it? Why deny them the opportunity? Can't they reasonably ask us to learn to be content in our affluence? Is work so important that we should insist on doing any amount of it—whatever the consequences for others?

Our grand surfer-philosophico argument might be stated in three main premises. Leisure capitalism will be necessary in the advanced world for the following reasons:

First, *there's no easy fix*. We can't now expect a technological remedy that adequately mitigates the trade-off between eco-nomic activity and terrible, unacceptable ecological outcomes. So we are morally obliged to limit the global rate of economic growth. (If we can still *hope and pray* we stumble into a tech fix, we can't now *expect* it, at least not with good reason, short of wishful thinking.)

Second, *developing countries should get the lion's share of remaining growth*. The moral legitimacy of capitalism consists in its power to eliminate poverty. In that case, the lion's share of growth possibilities should be used by the developing world. Given a limit on the global rate of growth, advanced countries must grow a lot less.

Third, *working less in the advanced countries is by no means objectionable*. If advanced countries must grow a lot less, then among other measures people can work a lot less, on average. A sensible arrangement would standardize work/leisure hours according to some new, much lower average, say of twenty hours per week, with ample vacations and time off for parental leave and similar contingencies. This is feasible, and otherwise unobjectionable—in part because all but the incurable workaholics among us would be just as happy.

These premises don't seem *obviously* mistaken. If they are correct, we've got an argument that advanced societies will have to move to full-on leisure capitalism in one form or another. So the premises are there for you to assess for yourself, as you see things. You can reject the conclusion, but then you should explain where the argument has gone wrong. If you don't reject one of the premises on the basis of good reasons—because maybe they seem plausible— then you're stuck with the conclusion: leisure must be capitalism's future.[6]

Being Fortunate

Yet isn't capitalism itself really the problem? Hasn't the whole eco-convulsion unmasked its fatal, delegitimizing flaws, laying bare its soul of greed and disrespect, much as the über-Left from Karl Marx

6. Suppose I offer this argument: surfers are heroes if people must work less; people must work less; so surfers are heroes. The conclusion would follow by dint of logical necessity (in this case, the rule called *modus ponens*). Then you could deny that surfers are heroes, but you'd have to reject one of the two premises, on pain of believing things that cannot all be true. And if you can't fault any of the premises, you're stuck with the argument's conclusion: surfers are heroes! The argument stated in the main text can likewise be stated as a logically valid argument.

to Naomi Klein have been saying all along?[7] Not according to the surfer: capitalism instead needs certain fine-tuning.

Humanity opted for capitalism a while back, and surfers should be grateful for it. You don't surf much if you're living hand to mouth, sloshing around in the rice paddies in order to feed rice to the kids (as some surfers in the developing world still must). We inherited the enormous wealth created since the Industrial Revolution. Along with a forty-hour workweek, we can thank capitalism for giving us the possibility of meaningful leisure and surfing.

Alas, Americans aren't quite so fortunate as the lazy Germans, who work only thirty-five hours per week on average, along with six-week paid vacations, while sharply segregating work from leisure, so that free time feels free. By some estimates, they work less than the supposedly lazy Greeks. Still, the fact is that all of us in the advanced countries were fortunate enough to have been born into the present world-historical sweet spot. We get the benefits of relative wealth and leisure, and even if the climate risks do ripen into an ecological cataclysm, when the shit *really* starts hitting the fan, most of us will be safely dead. The real cost of our affluence will fall mainly to our children, their children, their children, and so on and so forth, after our blessed lives are long over. In life, there's certainly nothing like good timing. But being so breathtakingly fortunate isn't any sort of reason to refuse to take action, especially if that means getting comfortable with one kind of inaction.

The surfer makes a social contribution to the moral legitimacy of capitalism in a world of scarcity, by freeing up work opportunities for others, especially the three billion or so very poor people all across the developing world. If the "price" of abundance is our being asked to forgo what further riches we'd have in a more gung ho capitalism, and take more leisure instead, shouldn't we still count ourselves extraordinarily fortunate, world historically speaking?

7. Naomi Klein, *This Changes Everything: Capitalism vs. the Climate* (New York: Simon & Schuster, 2014). If she doesn't quite make this strong claim, the suggestion is at least that we look for something radically different.

In fact, being fortunate as we are, one question we might ask ourselves is whether we can *refuse* to adapt, without being pretty unreasonable. Can we children of affluence really complain of being asked to work less and go surfing, not for our own happiness, but for the seemingly worthy cause of reducing risks of serious harm to living and future people, with the potential upside of not prematurely ending human civilization?

It depends. Is a great sacrifice being asked of us? Then maybe we could reasonably object. I can't be expected to part with one of my eyes so that a blind person can become sighted by an eye transplant. Even for that very worthy cause, *that* sacrifice is not morally required of me. Yet our climate situation isn't quite this sort of case. What's at stake is the very moral legitimacy of capitalism. And surely the advanced countries could be asked to give up *something* for the moral legitimacy of the very system that has made us rich. Why shouldn't we have to at least "sacrifice" by slowing growth and getting a bit less rich?

Actually, a slow-growth, "de-growth" economy might not entail sacrifice for anyone. What we lose in money, we gain in time. We are fortunate to have become rich enough to have a real alternative to work. The surfer will happily take less money for more time in meaningful leisure. But it isn't just the surfer; perhaps most or nearly all of us could in theory be just as happy, or even happier, working less if we really could manage a decent standard of living. We might thus adapt to climate change without an overall sacrifice.

And if we have no overall sacrifice to complain of, we are most *definitely* obliged to adapt. It would be patently unreasonable for us to object or dig in or drag our feet. Think of how the argument would play if future people could speak. They'd say to us, "I don't mean to embarrass you, but you do realize that you are passing emissions, which is really quite foul for those of us historically downwind. If it's all the same to you, could you please choose less gaseous activities instead. Seriously, please contain yourself; we aren't asking much, or indeed anything, of you. Truly, it really is or should be *all the same to you.*" Not even a surfer would begrudge that moral argument. And short of workaholism, why wouldn't working less and lazing or surfing or tending the garden leave us happier, or about as happy, or not too much unhappier?

Surfers are going to love the new capitalism. Wouldn't almost anyone? We needn't assume the hippie or French view of the good life that one should "work to live" rather than "live to work" (even if some surfers share that position). Let's grant that it's perfectly honorable to love one's work and make it central to one's life and identity. What's asked of us is merely that we do less of it for an eminently worthy purpose. And who couldn't use some extra leisure time for tennis, or reading the classics, or playing with the kids?

So the climate change fiasco doesn't *have* to be the complete cosmic, world-historical bummer that is shaping up before us. Humanity has a real possibility of a decent future, in which there is more leisure and much surfing. A surfer philosophy of life and society holds a convenient truth: life can be better for all of us.

Leisure Capitalism Is Efficient

It may seem ridiculous to think that a surfer can fulfill his or her civic duty without sacrificing anything at all. Work less and surf more—twist my arm.

Surfers will suddenly hear the solemn call of service. But aren't we obliged to *sacrifice,* and maybe even suffer, for the urgent cause of averting the portending cataclysm? Is it not frankly unserious to ask for *nothing* from the world-historically privileged?

Well, no. No overall sacrifice is necessary, according to such surfer exotica as basic economic theory. In general, efficiency is achieved (for example, in a "perfectly competitive" economy) only when no one is made worse off (for example, because people suffer costs, or "negative externalities"). But climate change is the Godzilla of all negative externalities.[8] Our current form of capitalism is *inefficient*, in the sense of the classical economist Vilfredo Pareto, who defined "efficiency" as benefiting some while leaving no one worse off.

Present and future people are made worse off for our emissions. But there are ways of avoiding this without making anyone else any worse off. We just reduce the costs to future generations and then compensate ourselves.[9] That is, we'll have to emit less in order to reduce those costs, using less of the resources from which we now benefit. That would leave *us* worse off, unless we somehow compensate ourselves. But we *can* compensate ourselves in various ways.[10]

One especially pleasant way is for us to simply work less and take more leisure. So, yes, in working less, we lose money we would have made, but we'd also gain from the benefits of enjoying more time free. And if the gains in leisure from spending extra time in the waves or on the soccer/*fútbol* field are considerable enough to leave us no worse off on balance, then efficiency is achieved. And aren't they considerable enough? The surfer will certainly take less money for more time in meaningful leisure. So the surfer is a model for leisure capitalism's efficiency.[11]

---

8. On why this is a matter of "social and moral preferences," see the godfather of neoclassical economics, the Nobel laureate Kenneth Arrow and his "Political and Economic Evaluation of Social Effects and Externalities," in *Frontiers of Quantitative Economics,* ed. Michael D. Intriligator (Amsterdam: North Holland, 1971), pp. 3–23.

9. Duncan Foley, "The Economic Fundamentals of Global Warming," in *Twenty-First Century Macroeconomics: Responding to the Climate Challenge,* ed. Jonathan M. Harris and Neva R. Goodwin (London: Edward Elgar, 2009); Broome, *Climate Matters,* chap. 3.

10. John Broome and Duncan Foley, "A World Climate Bank," MS, describe various ways future generations can, as it were, pay us for the benefit they receive in emissions reduction. We in the present can simply leave them fewer nice things than they'd otherwise inherit. So, for example, we might divert investments now headed for conventional capital, which they stand to inherit, over to green infrastructure, which reduces emissions and costs to them. They inherit less, but as "payment" for the present cost of emissions reductions for their benefit, leaving them no worse off for the swap. This could work with no new expenditure, leaving us no worse off.

11. The surfer's "utility function," in this case the way a surfer would trade time for money, explains how compensation is possible. The workaholic will have different preferences, which we return to in the next chapter.

Humankind will still have to be lucky enough to avoid the entirely possible worst-case scenarios, which perhaps are already happening in slow motion. We might have already crossed any number of tipping points after which things quickly go from bad to awful to even worse. We really don't know that we aren't soon to have biblical floods washing over the continents, in which case the surfer has no special wisdom. I can't predict that life *will* be better for all of us, or that surfer philosophy will wash over and refresh the foulness of Washington, D.C., politics. Thankfully, the philosopher can think through what *ought* to happen, however the political winds are blowing. The surfer observation is that the whole problem *can* work out better for all of us if, and only if, a lot of us become a lot more willing to go with the flow and make certain adjustments. And because no sacrifice need be asked of us, a lot more of us might well become willing to dutifully adapt.

Oddly, world politics has mostly ignored that rather convenient idea, even though it might have more easily won a political consensus.[12] Certain influential economists argued that we should ask present people to sacrifice, because this promotes the greatest welfare overall.[13] That is, we should go for the greatest overall benefit, measured in a cost-benefit analysis that factors in all people, present and future, weighing the expected gains and losses to each in view of population estimates over *n* generations, while "discounting" benefits at some rate to people in the further future. The problem is that there are *a lot* of future people coming down the pike, all of whom could benefit. Benefits to us living people matter as well, but the question is then how much we should give up and leave for the

12. The 2016 Paris agreement is something of a consensus, but everything still depends on whether enough countries can faithfully follow through on emissions cuts. Support for this may depend on whether countries feel they are sacrificing a present generation's interests instead of simply seeking efficiency.

13. Nicholas Stern, *The Economics of Climate Science: The Stern Review* (Cambridge, U.K.: Cambridge University Press, 2007); and William Nordhaus, *A Question of Balance: Weighing Options on Global Warming Policies* (New Haven, Conn.: Yale University Press, 2008), which says on pp. 179–80 that the "optimal" strategy involves sacrifice rather than mere efficiency (or "optimal-plus-deficit").

many, many, many future generations. Yet people generally aren't so altruistic as to be very concerned to maximize the sum of all human satisfactions, especially not with any real (albeit discounted) worry about people n-generations down the road. It isn't just surfers; people generally aren't keen to sacrifice as "overall welfare" would require.[14]

But then insisting upon sacrifice makes the perfect the enemy of the good—or in this case the friend of the catastrophic.[15] People are more likely to accept an efficient capitalism, free from sacrifice, with more time for surfing or papermaking. We might already have missed our chance to keep emissions at "safe" levels. If we still have a chance at averting disaster, and we can at least significantly reduce the risks, isn't efficiency good enough?

Some Practicalities

How feasible would it be to cut back the workweek, if not all the way to twenty hours, then still far enough back to move the needle on our collective emissions? The details are of course for professional economists. Yet in broad outline, a new, super-advanced capitalism and shorter workweek might look something like the slow-growth periods to which we've recently become accustomed.

For starters, growing *less* than we now do probably won't require the "end of growth." Like some contemporary "green economists," John Stuart Mill long ago proposed a no-growth "stationary state"

14. This is a famous problem with utilitarianism, the view that the right action, or just institution, is the one that maximizes welfare overall. Although "everyone counts for one, and no one more than one," as Jeremy Bentham put it, we figure out what is right by simply toting up the sum total of harm and benefit for our different options and then choosing the highest total. We might have to sacrifice some poor soul, or even ourselves, for the greater good, for instance, by giving up an eye so that a blind person can become sighted. This isn't "above and beyond the call of duty," but morally required if indeed it would promote the greatest overall welfare. I for one don't accept this view because of its rather outrageous implications, including its unreasonable demands. John Stuart Mill proposes a utilitarianism of rules that include commonsense morality, but it suffers from its own problems.
15. This is Broome's view, *Climate Matters,* p. 47.

for the long run. He may or may not be right about the very long run. At least for the foreseeable future, the advanced countries will probably need to keep a positive growth rate, if only so that developing countries can keep growing and keep reducing poverty. Countries develop in large part by the march of technology, shared by way of international trade, which is often driven by universities, public investment, and entrepreneurialism in the advanced world. So, much of this activity would have to continue, along with essential services, fire and police departments, sanitation, government, and the like—albeit, if possible, with a larger number of workers so that each worker could take a shorter workweek.

The idea of very slow growth in the rich world is hardly unrealistic. It's already happening. Japan, the United States, and Europe have seen historically low growth rates lately (in part due to financial crises). Some economists suggest low growth may well be the new normal for the advanced countries, either due to chronic underinvestment ("secular stagnation")[16] or because the big gains in productivity from technology have already been harvested. The washing machine did wonders for freeing up time for other things, the Internet much less so, and the trend of diminishing gains may continue in the future.[17] Artificial intelligence may soon free up time in huge amounts, while taking most of our jobs (a matter we return to in the next chapter). At any rate, we can no longer expect high growth rates by historical standards in the rich world, whether for lack of opportunity or by deliberate choice to ease off the throttle.[18]

---

16. See the articles by the Harvard economist Larry Summers at http://larrysummers.com/category/secular-stagnation/.

17. Robert J. Gordon, *The Rise and Fall of American Growth* (Princeton, N.J.: Princeton University Press, 2016).

18. The choice to ease up on growth in a shorter workweek might require stimulating the economy at the same time, to at least keep a positive growth rate. We'd have the usual methods—monetary policy, public investment, tax cuts, or even the reduction of inequality (because those with less are more likely to spend). But the assumption wouldn't be that more growth over the long run is better, as we assume today. Any such measures would be justified by a (low) target rate.

How might that look as the new normal? Well, maybe things economical just take twice as long. What was once done by one worker is now done by two. Each worker is as or more productive in a given hour but while putting in fewer hours at work. And so maybe the new iPhone appears every four years instead of every two. And maybe wages rise to the same average level in twice as many years. One will have to save longer to buy a home or opt for a smaller place. But home prices may not rise as quickly as well. Retirement savings won't rise as high, either, but then many may willingly put off full retirement for putting in fewer hours anyhow. We could still of course cultivate a strong twenty-hour work ethic and take pride in our work. And, rest assured, with proper coordination of work schedules and flexible hours, milk or gasoline would still be available at odd hours.[19]

The forty-hour workweek took hold as an institution in a gradual way. The twenty-hour workweek could likewise be phased in, leaving plenty of time to plan and adjust. Our fears of loss or decline often underestimate our adaptability. We often normalize to new circumstances much more quickly than we would predict for ourselves, returning to a baseline level of happiness. So we'd normalize to a slower pace. Many will be genuinely happier for working less. Those who aren't will revert to their baseline level of happiness or unhappiness. In time, then, we might look back upon our growth-anxious era the way we now look back on the go-go 1980s and 1990s—as frenzied and somewhat out of touch.

Surely working less wouldn't doom the Republic. Would we be *so* unhappy? Could we *really* complain? (I mean, reasonably.) In a well-managed economy, we could all have assurances of a decent income and (slowly) rising prospects. How well different social groups could adapt would of course depend on how wealth is distributed. Everyone would require enough of an income for secure and meaning-

---

19. A man I met in Tahiti, who once traveled to the United States, mentioned the availability of milk at odd hours as a chief way the United States is wonderful compared with Tahiti (where you have to plan your milk run). I tried to explain the downside of a have-it-now culture, but to no avail.

ful leisure, in many cases with a basic income supplement to their wages from work.[20] Yet surely most people could get used to a shorter workweek and more leisurely standard of living in principle. It would be especially easy if nearly everyone else was working less and surfing or camping or socializing more often.

But is trimming the *workweek* really necessary? Aren't there better ways of adapting? We could instead work as much as or *more* than we now do, in order to get as rich as possible, and target and tax highly consumptive activities, whether in work or in leisure. We'd discourage consumptive activities, leaving people to otherwise work or laze as they will. And if we are curbing emissions, we wouldn't want to throw the growth baby out with the warming bathwater, would we?

This is the current conventional wisdom, and it can seem smart and savvy. The approach is very concerned about not missing out on a chance to get richer, but not especially cautious about the grave risks that imperil vast numbers of present and future people. We certainly should put a "price on carbon" and heavily tax gross emitters. But will we have the taxes right? Maybe. Or maybe not. We won't know we've done enough to stave off the risks until after a long period, in the wake of decisions many decades before.[21] We have a limited range of policy options relative to the enormity of the risks, with no chance of repeating the experiment. So it seems wise to bet on a broader, surer slate of measures and make pretty darn sure we're doing enough to rein emissions in. Instead of betting the farm on tax policy, or any one approach, shouldn't we diversify and hedge, like any shrewd investor? And would we be *so* unhappy in

20. Tax receipts would also decline if we cut back the workweek, but we would of course know this ahead of time and hopefully plan public finances accordingly. Financial crises are thought to require deep cuts in services in part because a budgetary imbalance comes unexpectedly. I return to how a basic income might be paid for over the longer run in the next chapter.
21. This is one advantage of a global "cap" on emissions, shared over all nations (for example, at a level to keep us below two extra degrees of average warming), which permits greater caution than various carbon taxes. But then of course there are many ways for different nations to meet their specific reduction targets.

leisure, getting ever richer at a slower pace? If not, why not play it relatively safe?

Welcome to the climate casino, which we seem to have stumbled into and which appears to have no exit. Surfers are risk takers, at least when the risks are manageable and gambling might bring some worthy good. When you might get the best tube ride of your life, you go hard paddling into a jacking wave, throwing yourself over the ledge of the vertical face, taking a calculated chance of being paralyzed in a bounce off the reef. Such accidents do happen, but chances are you'll make the drop, and the tube you'll score, if you score it, will be absolutely epic.

Yet in the climate casino, the stakes are rather different. The risks are greater with a modest upside. Should we double down on growth, going for the extra GDP margin, allowing increased climate risks? Well, suppose we gamble and get lucky. The warming trend is contained, and what is the "upside" for having taken greater risks of calamity? More work. We keep working ever harder, with the same long hours, getting a bit richer than we'll anyway become. But suppose by comparison that we instead decide to play it safer, cutting back the workweek and taking other cautious measures, being pretty damn sure of climate security. The "downside" for our relative precaution? Less work! We become less rich than we otherwise would. But that's fine by the surfer. Many, maybe most, of us will be just as happy to leave the climate casino and gamble (or gambol) out in the waves (or in skydiving, the stock market, or a real casino) during our extra time in leisure.[22]

---

22. This argument for precaution doesn't turn on any strong version of the set of ideas confusingly called "the precautionary principle." One sound idea is just that uncertainty does not justify inaction. The present argument recommends action (taking more leisure). A different idea recommends avoiding grave risks while paying no attention to the benefits of being less careful. I paid attention to the benefits and claimed they were in this case limited.

The Awful

If that's already a good enough reason for caution in the climate casino, there is of course another: the sheer awfulness of what ensues, should our luck go south.

When Graeme relayed his optimism about the creation of new waves with rising sea levels, he seemed unnerved. He was looking to me for validation. Because he's a beloved friend, I found myself wanting to be conciliatory. I admitted that the Machine would probably get good again, at least for a while, after sea levels rose to some modest extent. I even agreed that if we get really lucky, the increase won't be so dramatic. Maybe we'll only lose spots like Deserts, which need the lowest of the low tides. Still, although I didn't make a big stink at the time, the way I really felt was exactly as Graeme's perturbed countrymen: the whole thing is a complete disaster.

To be more precise about my immediate sense of the matter, what I was thinking was that if things keep going as they're going, the whole thing stands to be an *unmitigatable* complete disaster. Graeme is probably right that rising sea levels won't bring the End of Surfing as Such. But it would surely bring the End of Surfing as We Know It, and I just couldn't see any overall way of looking at things, any master cost-benefit calculation, in which a global surfing dystopia could be said to have worked out okay in the end. If there's any upside, it just wouldn't matter; it's finally irrelevant.

Think about how you'd feel about the death of your child. Say your child was killed in some wrongful accident, and you now stand to win $50,000 or $500,000 in a wrongful death settlement. Would you console yourself with thoughts about the money? You surely wouldn't say to yourself, "Well, if my child hadn't died, I wouldn't have got the money, which I'm really glad to have." You instead say something like "I'd give it all back in a second to have him alive." You'd say the money is *irrelevant*.

That's the idea behind the more extreme example that flashed through my mind when Graeme and I spoke. When we consider the Holocaust, there's something terribly wrong with considering all of the good things that might have come of it. That's so even if the presumed good things really are good things, things such as your very existence. Maybe your parents wouldn't have met in an alternative history in which Hitler never comes to power, and you, as the particular individual you are, are never brought into being. Still, in finding the Holocaust horrible, and thinking it should never have happened, you don't thereby have to regret that you are alive, as though your existence, too, should never have happened. You just don't have to think of yourself at all, and probably shouldn't. When considering that kind of terrible event, you are beside the point. After weeping and sorrow, the appropriate response to reflection upon the Holocaust is not any kind of cost-benefit calculation, not pros and cons, but silence.

Something like that was my immediate reaction to Graeme's comment: it just won't change things in any grand reckoning that a few surf breaks somehow survive, while a few other new ones are temporarily created (and then perhaps swamped again), if most of the world's surf breaks really do become swampy, unsurfable crap, indefinitely. If a surfing cataclysm really comes to pass, it will be the Desecration of All Things Good and Holy. In an event of such extraordinary gnarliness, there will be no relevant upside to be spoken of.

Of course, if the Machine did come back to life, surfers would be all over it. I'm sure few surfers would be so inconsolable about the loss of the *other* waves that they couldn't bring themselves to rapturously enjoy what spots remain when the conditions came together. Given the joy of surfing excellent Indonesian waves, the crew might take a few days to relapse into a despondent state. What's harder to see is how serious surfers would be other than inconsolable the rest of the time, even if they found a supposed substitute activity. (Wave pools inland are now producing very good waves, but the thought of *only* surfing wave pools is itself disturbing.) While most surfers won't die because of rising sea levels, the loss of the world's good and half-decent surf breaks really can feel deeply personal, in a way akin to death. It can feel as though life has lost its point. I'm sure there are lots of ways to be happy. But what is the point of being happy if you can't go ocean surfing, if the world has become an utterly befouled mess?

The concern here is to protect what is valuable, in a way that should silence certain purely self-interested calculations. I have to admit, I have consoled myself in the fact that I for one will be dead by the time things really go south. But I don't have kids, and of course the consolation weakens for those who care about the future being left for their children and grandchildren. Timing-wise, a lot of us have been breathtakingly fortunate to have been born into the wake of the Industrial Revolution, to enjoy both prosperity and leisure. And cosmically unfair as it may be, for many people roughly my age and older, chances are good that we'll carry the lightest of burdens to prevent the catastrophes that the Industrial Revolution is slowly visiting upon vast numbers of living and future people. We'll be long gone, having enjoyed what has been a pretty kick-ass party, having taken no real responsibility for cleaning up after ourselves. So maybe surfers aren't the most altruistic lot, but when the question is how to feel about the whole course of world history, I'm sure most surfers will agree that their personal fortunes aren't entirely relevant. Most surfers feel fortunate and deeply grateful to have wound up surfers. They love and cherish the good waves they've tasted or dreamed of since they were kids, and so find great sorrow in the idea that they may be disappearing, permanently. And to prevent that unspeakable outcome, they are willing to adapt. Especially if it means working less and surfing more often. I bet they'd gladly sacrifice a bit as well.

To the surfer, then, we're obliged not to foul the climate as much as we now are, and not just because we could do it without sacrifice. We also ought to protect Surfing as We Know It, because we should respect the natural order for what it is.

In other words, surfers are *conservatives*.[23] The natural world in respect of surf breaks is assumed to have great value, in the sense that we have very good reason to respect it for the way it is. There is what is given, outside human intervention, including the land, sea, and climate, in all its constant motion. And even if we could replace the whole natural order with something better, we should not try to. We should accept it for the given it is, paying our respects, taking care not to mess with it, for instance, by putting it at significant risk of massive degradation.

Surfers love and cherish the deep way we are related to and depend on what surrounds us, which includes the way the flow of ordinary life and surfing is structured by its natural environment. This relationship benefits people in the most basic way. Humanity, and so human benefit, wouldn't be possible without it. Nature matters for people to be people, for ordinary life to keep its structuring preconditions, and this foundation of human natural existence is itself a proper object of deep respect. We can respect it by preserving it, even if we must get a bit less rich.[24]

In the climate casino, this should weigh heavily into the scales of decision. Science can tell us the (very) rough odds, the rough probability of different climate change scenarios, albeit with a lot of unquantifiable uncertainty. But then what risks shall we take? We certainly shouldn't bank on what seems most likely to happen. If we thought modest warming, mild disasters, and medium death tolls were the most likely outcome, we shouldn't stop worrying about *worse* outcomes, which could also realistically happen. Although the house of a randomly selected person is not likely to catch fire, it would be foolish for him not to buy a fire extinguisher. The sheer

23. Of the sort defended by G. A. Cohen, "Rescuing Conservatism: A Defense of Existing Value," in *Reasons and Recognition: Essays on the Philosophy of T. M. Scanlon,* eds. R. Jay Wallace, Rahul Kumar, and Samuel Freeman (New York: Oxford University Press, 2011).
24. This doesn't imply "deep ecology," the view that nature has its own holistic value, quite independently of humanity. On the present argument, respect is for human life and its relational foundation, in the deep way forms of natural order make it possible. The value of nature per se is a further and different question.

awfulness of a fire that burns the guy's house down is a good enough reason for him to reduce the risk by buying the extinguisher, even if that isn't the most likely outcome, or is even rather unlikely.

Foolishness aside, taking certain risks can also be a kind of wrongdoing. I morally shouldn't play Russian roulette on someone's head. One bullet. Six chambers. Spin the cylinder. My target would have a rather good, five-in-six chance of living. Even so, I'm doing something wrong in pulling the trigger, even if the gun goes "click." If the person lives, I couldn't say, "No harm, no foul, bro." There was indeed a foul; he was wronged the moment I placed him at a pretty significant, one-in-six risk of death. That's something he could reasonably ask me not to have done, especially not just for the sake of fun or revenge or a show of dominance. Or if you prefer a less dramatic example, think of a driver who unnecessarily buzzes a bystander, leaving the woman unharmed, after putting her at a heightened risk of getting clipped. He's culpably negligent, and he really should be more careful. The woman could reasonably complain of being exposed to such increased risks when the driver could just slow down a bit.

In the same way, people who must live here on Earth in later generations could reasonably complain of our heating up the climate. We've already created the risks. Even if the whole problem blows over (some self-correcting feature of the global climatic system might be triggered), the wrong will have already been done. If we do nothing and hope for the best, we're akin to the negligent driver who could slow down a bit, but just keeps stepping on the gas pedal.[25]

The prospect of the End of Surfing as We Know It is cause for dread, but not just for surfers: it reflects a profound alteration of basic ways the natural world structures human life. The risks of disruption are not simply risks of personal injury. What's disrupted is a relationship of fundamental importance, between people and

25. For this sort of argument about financial or ecological crises, see my "Distinctive Significance of Systemic Risk," *Ratio Juris* (forthcoming), or at http://www.faculty .uci.edu/profile.cfm?faculty_id=4884.

nature, which should itself be the object of our respect. The potential for such a truly awful outcome should then weigh down the scales of decision, suggesting relative caution in the face of risk. Whatever it is we think we might gain from putting the whole order of human life in jeopardy, the value of any such upside must diminish, or be silenced, in the face of respecting what is. As for us, we can work less and learn to live simply, taking the cautious course.[26]

I suppose most surfers haven't quite thought through all of this eminently surfer reasoning. I bet nearly all of them will be amenable to it. At the moment, the state of surfer opinion about climate change is the usual state of advanced-worlder confusion. Surfers have deep sympathies with sustainability causes, and while some are taking concerted action (for example, in the Surfrider Foundation), most just aren't sure what to do about the fact that surfboards and wet suits and driving to check waves and jet travel to far-flung breaks are not ecologically friendly. There are efforts at "green" surfer products, much as in the wider economy. But surfers are as mixed up as anyone in the fossil-fueled economy we all still depend on.

So it would certainly be understandable if non-surfers found all this leisure capitalism business counterintuitive, or maybe crazy. All human beings before us (save perhaps the flood surfer, Noah) could safely assume a natural world that's just there to be used. John Locke, who had a big influence on the U.S. founding fathers, went so far as to say that the world was created by God and granted to humanity with the express purpose of its being used *as much as possible* for human benefit. Each person was to leave "enough and as good" in the commons for others, but the world was still there for the taking. The point of having nature was human well-being.

26. This doesn't rule out further sacrifice in view of the awful stakes, though I haven't defended it. Perhaps we are required to radically reallocate labor into green projects and work even more than we now do on tech, renewables, sinks, and so on. But we should at least efficiently work less and take leisure instead and reallocate investment from conventional capital to green industry at no new cost.

Locke made a lot of each person's own use of resources (for example, fencing off a plot of land for farming), without worrying too much about what might happen when large numbers of people started using them in a complex system. This made it seem as though there would always be "enough and as good" resources for others, in which case there's no big worry about conservation for future people. This turned out to be sorely mistaken. Now good stewardship does require careful conservation of scarce ecological resources: the good steward would do such things as work less and surf more in order to leave enough and as good for future generations. The Protestant work ethic assumed the righteous could just keep working, being cleansed in sanctification. Nowadays being faithful in God's grant as Locke understood it looks more like an ocean cleansing in regular surfing.

That point certainly isn't obvious; one can see why people might feel confused. The old-style capitalism put us out of attunement with the world's available resources. Science only realized the extent of it relatively recently, and it takes a long while for society to become more attuned to the new world it inhabits—and created.

9

Work

It is the interest of every man to live
as much at his ease as he can.

—Adam Smith, *The Wealth of Nations*

MIKE LEFEVRE, A STEELWORKER out of Chicago, put his finger on
the working person's discontentment. "It isn't that the average working guy is dumb. He's tired, that's all." Lefevre offers a solution:

> If I had a twenty-hour workweek, I'd get to know my kids
> better, my wife better. Some kid invited me to go on a college
> campus. On a Saturday. It was summertime. Hell, if I have
> a choice of taking my wife and kids to a picnic or going to
> a college campus, it's gonna be the picnic. But if I worked a
> twenty-hour week, I could do both.[1]

The good life, for most working people, always seems just over
the horizon. The average surfer can certainly relate. Most surfers
work a conventional workweek. The Australians who put in long
weeks and months down in the mines, and then fly up to Indonesia
to surf during their free weeks, work as hard as anyone. Only a
relative few surfers get paid to surf. While the top professionals are
now fetching huge salaries, most pros have short-lived careers doing
what is in truth marketing for a surf brand, after which they find

1. Studs Terkel, *Working* (New York: Pantheon, 1972), pp. xxxiii–xxxiv.

another job in the surf industry or some other field. The youthful surfer in search of bodacious living quickly sees that the single most important decisions in life are what line of work to go into, whether to have kids, and how to find an understanding spouse. Get any of those choices wrong, and a life devoted to regular surfing becomes impossible, for simple lack of hours in the day.

So the average surfer would certainly second Lefevre's point about the pinching choice we're all asked to make between meaningful leisure and work for money, when we could all run on an easier schedule. Respect must be paid to the surfer weekend warrior, who never misses a Saturday. But as with any pursuit of excellence, surfing requires patient, devoted attention, and goodly swaths of time, and timing, especially if one is to score decent waves and progress in one's approach to a variety of waves. With all due respect for the joys of work, after paying the bills, the forty-hour workweek still takes up too much of the most precious good a mortal has—one's days and hours alive.

The Degradation of Work and Leisure

Is work losing its meaning in our technological age? As Matthew Crawford explains, in the early capitalism of the eighteenth century, pay was by piece rate.[2] This ran into a difficulty: increasing the rate wouldn't boost worker output. Workers would just produce less, now meeting fixed needs with less work. This sounds eminently sensible to a surfer. Definitely keep the time free! But productive efficiency ruled, and in place of the old Puritan moralism of Ben Franklin—"be frugal and free"—we got "consumption engineering" that induced a sense of want, mistaken for need. With incessant advertisements and consumer debt, you came to really want all the cool new stuff, and you could have it all now and pay later, by borrowing against your future time. Once indebted, workers were locked into ever more specialized work, and with its hyper-

2. *Shop Class as Soulcraft*, p. 43.

refinement whole trades based in broad know-how gradually disappeared, along with their engaged kind of human meaning.

With work ever more uninteresting, and time ever squeezed, "leisure" then became what you do for its own sake, without being paid. At the same time, as Crawford puts it, good work became

> work that maximizes one's means for pursuing [leisure] activities, where life becomes meaningful. The mortgage broker works hard all year, then he goes and climbs Mount Everest. The exaggerated psychic content of his summer vacation sustains him through the fall, winter, and spring.

We thus came to feel what Crawford calls a "disconnect" between work life and leisure life. The two are a "transaction between subselves, rather than . . . the intelligibly linked parts of a coherent life."[3]

Crawford proposes a "tighter connection" between work and leisure. Work is best done as vocation in "wholehearted activity," experienced as intrinsically good, in a community based on the common recognition of this value.[4] Work, in other words, would be more like life at the repair shop. As he explains from personal experience, the exercise of mechanical skill is a kind of excellence performed in a community of the like-minded, and the mechanical basis for motorcycle riding, "a kingly sport that is like war made beautiful."[5]

I'd say we can certainly affirm trades work and encourage its pursuit, even alongside college, as Crawford suggests. But that alone wouldn't address the modern worker's discontentment, which isn't about any particular kind of work or its lack. The trouble isn't the general division of labor. As Crawford would agree, more refined roles can enhance the meaning of one's work. One can write a book

3. Ibid., p. 181, also for the quoted extract.
4. Ibid., p. 193.
5. Ibid., p. 196.

without having to design or print it oneself, or fix motorcycles without having to build parts or pave roads. Even hyper-specialized work can be meaningful; you can focus on getting an architectural plan subpart or computer algorithm just right. And as a matter of economics, specialization on a large scale is after all what makes us rich, with time to spare for surfing or motorcycle maintenance.

Nor is Crawford objecting to leisure, per se. The tradesperson needs free time, to laze and/or work when inspiration strikes, as much as anyone else. And mountain climbing and especially surfing of course involve just the sort of situated, embodied know-how that Crawford celebrates for its meaning. So the trouble, in part, is that there's too little time for things like surfing and motorcycle repair—which, after all, is done for the sake of a "kingly sport." But in that case a tighter connection between one's leisure and work might just mean having more of one's time freed, in order to be free to attend to the variety of things that matter most.

The basic problem, the surfer will tell you, is the worker's time pinch. Even that fine adage about life, "do what you love," has come to mean getting paid to do it, for you won't have enough time for it unless you do it as work. Most of us can find some sort of meaning even at a job taken mainly to pay the bills, and ideally we'd each find a job we can do wholeheartedly. But with all due respect for the forty-hour workweek, the key question for society is whether we have enough time to work for enough money *and* spend time with our family *and* exercise our skills at games or sports *and* serve our community *and* perform all the miscellaneous activities of adult life (for example, laundry, keeping the finances, cooking). Not to mention practicing the lost art of loafing.[6] After you work to pay the bills, there's not enough time left for the dedicated practice that gets you attuned to and enthralled by much of anything else.

Fortunately, "stacked" schedules aren't inevitable. We could all

---

6. Here is George Carlin: "When does a kid ever get to sit in the yard with a stick anymore? You know? Just sit there with a fucking stick. Do today's kids even know what a stick is? You sit in the yard with a fucking stick . . . and you dig a fucking hole. You know? And you look at the hole, and you look at the stick."

work, but a lot less, in a twenty-hour workweek. We can all have more freedom, the freedom in having more of our time free.

A Culture for Being?

For Sartre, we are striving in our very freedom, always at work in constructing an identity. Odd as this sounds coming from a quintessential Frenchman, often to be found socializing at the Café de Flore, we are saddled with something like the Protestant work ethic by our very free nature. In the Protestant version, you at least get something for all your efforts. After an onerous struggle toward virtue and self-perfection, through self-denial and hard labor, you gradually receive sanctification and the public sign of God's blessing in the emblems of prosperity you can now afford to purchase. Yet even if personal perfection and riches are overrated, there is at least *something* to shoot for. Sartre's project of anguished self-creation gives us nothing but responsibility. For all the constant work of self-making and remaking, with no really valuable purpose beyond the ones we've simply chosen, not even freedom is your reward. For you already had freedom, in the very human condition that saddled you with ceaseless existential labors in the first place.

This brings us to a main result of our inquiry. Sartre seems mistaken about human nature. He puts freedom before flow. The surfer suggests that flow comes first. Flow is a matter of attunement to what lies beyond the self, and it is through attunement that we find full freedom and contented peace.

Angst is not our natural state but socially induced, by a cultural requirement such as the Protestant work ethic. For Sartre, our anxious culture simply reflects our anxious selves. Our need to be seen, loved, validated, and Instagram "liked"; our ceaseless preoccupation with self-presentation in social media postings, fashion choices, and displays of wealth, of sex appeal, of intellectual plaudits, or of taste—these are mainly public expressions of our "being-for-others" that anyway would haunt our private thoughts. We each hope to recognize ourselves in the gaze of others but find ourselves in fraught, even hellish, conflict, always denied mutual recognition and lasting peace. For the surfer, our natures and our social dynamics are less fixed. Our attunement to others or to our natural environment can certainly be spoiled in a confused culture. But it can equally be eased and drawn forth in cooperative practice. Our driven, time-is-money work culture is a disability for living. But we can lessen the demands of work, in a shorter workweek, and our anxieties can be reduced. The surfer's lightness about being could be for all of us.

In his 1776 *The Wealth of Nations,* the masterpiece that justified industrial capitalism, Adam Smith claimed that people are inherently lazy, interested mainly in "ease." Their nature is not to be constantly at work, not even the work of constructing a respectable identity. Which is why the lazy worker must be cajoled to labor, in the promise of money or the threat of starvation. The worker's discontentment is a product of capitalist culture, but necessary if society is to grow rich.

When Smith celebrated the pin factory, his famous exemplar of capitalist productivity, he made it clear that the efficient assembly line keeps the worker's mind from drifting to something more interesting. Mind-numbing tedium is exactly why more units get produced: the worker isn't losing time switching his or her focus from one task to another. This is "efficient," because no time is "wasted" on variety or stimulation or complexity, not to mention worker sanity. (The worker who goes bonkers is easily replaced.) As a line worker and spot welder for Ford Motor Company once explained, as late as the early 1970s, "There is no letup. The line is always running. . . . It's not like . . . if you lift something, carry it for a little while, lay it down, and go back—while you're going back, you're actually catching a breather. Ford has a better idea . . . of getting all the work possible out of your worn body for eight hours."[7]

---

7. Terkel, *Working,* p. 165. Note that earlier Ford had a big role in establishing the forty-hour workweek in the United States.

If Sartre is mistaken that angst goes to our very being, Smith goes wrong in the other direction, in seeing people as naturally indolent. Which brings us to another major result of our inquiry. Not even surfers are lazy by nature. Being a person is mainly a matter of *doing*, of adaptively responding, in perception and action. But being is not *just* doing, in constant striving. For active engagement can reliably bring its own way of ease. This can come in life as it does in surfing. Skillful, fluent action brings harmonious feeling, self-transcendence, and a contented peace, through active attunement to the world's natural changes and to others in cooperation.

Smith said that "the real price of everything . . . is the toil and trouble of acquiring it." Before the Industrial Revolution, when the better part of necessary labor *was* toil and trouble, people of course needed to be paid. But the success of capitalism has made our chores less onerous. The hardest of shit work—albeit with *plenty* of exceptions—is now mostly done for us, by technology or sweatshop workers in developing countries. Now, for much of the advanced world, work can be interesting, so why bother doing grueling or unpleasant things? If people have become averse to toil and trouble, it hardly follows that they are lazy by nature, interested mainly in ease. As Mike Lefevre put it, they're tired, that's all. If they had more time for leisure, beyond rest and recuperation, they'd find greater zeal for skillful, creative pursuits. Or maybe they understand how to live from love, like a surfer who paddles for long hours from the love of waves. They'll "work hard" in the thrall of meaningful projects but just can't get the juices flowing in grueling, grinding, unnecessary toil and trouble. Maybe that's not being lazy but having respect for oneself, for the value of one's limited time in life.

When Baudelaire said "work is less boring than pleasure," he must not have gotten wind of the utter tedium of assembly-line work or of many office jobs. Both work and leisure can be either boring or interesting. Leisure time can be wasted. People mindlessly watch *a lot* of TV when they could be surfing, or reading, or strolling. The remedy isn't necessarily more work in the labor market. What's lacking is a deeper, more committed lazing, which one can do by lying back and resting, or listening carefully to good music, or taking that walk, or heading to the beach.

Some people actually brag that they "work hard, play hard," and go hard for the pleasures of the moment in so-called leisure (perhaps in hard partying, compulsive sex, or extreme sports). Life can become only more tedious when "leisure" is supposed to involve obsessive workouts and hot yoga, with eager strivers boasting on social media, while the rest of us wonder if just coasting is still possible. Loafing or passively "vegetating" *should* be "boring"; the whole point is to disengage the active faculties, for rest and repair. Surfing during leisure, on the other hand, is especially absorbing. The sublime way it relates one to outer things, in fluid, skillful movement, is a big part of its joyousness. It's why surfing is worthy of a life's devotion, while mere resting or constant loafing maybe isn't.

Work, too, can be very interesting. The exercise of skill may have its own meaning. It may present a real challenge, or an occasion for common purpose, or fulfill one's deepest innermost drives for mastery and status. Yet if work has value in these ways, it tells against our long workweek in paid labor. For work can equally have such value outside the labor market without money payment. Think of raising a child or performing community service or creating art for its own sake. Or spending time out in the waves, while refining the Protestant virtues of hard work, discipline, and thrifty efficiency in your surfing technique.

If work or leisure can be either boring or interesting, the key problem is lack of time to find out which is which and their proper mix. The problem is how to have our time freed for getting attuned.

Workplaces arrange for "hard work," or at least its appearance, by making sure that fellow employees are in the same building, where they can be monitored. Yet there is no immediate connection between being seen working and being creative, or forcing oneself to work and producing something important. Lazing often works better. Maybe I don't feel like getting up from the couch to read an important article one afternoon; I'd have to force myself to get up and sit at the computer. So I just lie there staring at my smart phone and read the article while lying around, cogitating while couch lazing. And then maybe I have my best ideas all week (whereupon my collaborators later compliment me for my "hard work").

Capitalism runs on innovation, and face-to-face collaboration is admittedly key for getting group flow started. But actual creative exchange is only a very small part of the conventional workweek. Lately even business has come to see that leisure and idle time are as important as time in the office for fostering creativity. Certainly the CEO, who is supposed to keep an eye on the big market picture instead of meddling in detailed business, should live more like the surfer or the artist. Likewise, the employee skilled in the humanistic arts—the world of ideas, texts, culture, craft, performance, social meanings, law, and history—will be keen to reframe old problems and find fresh solutions, so that firm innovation keeps up with the competition. And as with any creative endeavor, the mind is most productive when it's afforded time for the ebb and flow of trial and error, rigor and imagination, focus and meandering, in collaborative discussions but also in private daydreaming.

Workplaces have become more fun, flexible, and enticing, and the digital age has made work somewhat less tied to the office. Yet enlightened management has often come at the high price of compromising time that used to be respected as free. Less and less time is *protected* from intrusion, from impatient e-mail, sent by people wondering *what you could possibly be doing* if not addressing business right away. (Fortunately, one can't take the phone into the water while surfing, at least not yet.) Hurried expectations make it ever harder to just turn the damn phone off, or be away for two hours freely, without scurrying back to the beach to digitally check in. For the unfortunate fact remains that, in the new Protestant work ethic, for the digital age, leisure is but another resource. Creativity is but another part of business, just another way of being "productive."

Yet for all the dignity in work, the surfer will tell you that freedom isn't just a means of producing further things. The human being should be free to have his or her thoughts, letting the mind go where it wanders, having an easy daydream, getting creative, maybe while flowing through the foot traffic in a big city with no particular place to be. As Sartre would say, we humans are free in flowing reflection. So enabling human imagination, in and out of work, has its own dignity.

The main cause of leisure's degradation is the spillover from a strenuous, amped-up pace of work. For the Stoics, the resulting anxieties are a simple matter of personal responsibility. How I direct my attention is always up to me. Whatever the cultural messages, it's my own fault if I'm constantly distracted, unable to concentrate, by the hard-to-resist, attention-sucking technology that we're still barely learning to manage. I should just work harder at attention discipline. Earlier I argued against being so controlling. We are part of a world, and our surroundings can make it harder or easier to be attuned. As social creatures, we are influenced by others in our thinking, and our culture shapes what we attend to, what we can attune ourselves to, and how readily. A twenty-hour workweek and a more leisurely style of capitalism would certainly be an improvement. The time and the mind would become freer.

Searching for Lost Time

R.J. is a surfer from San Clemente, California, and he doesn't mind his job waiting tables. He barely pays his pricey twelve-hundred-dollar rent for a small apartment on his nineteen-hundred-dollar paycheck, working long hours at minimum wage with just good enough tips. But of course he has his health, and the restaurant is down by the pier, overlooking the ocean. Life is pretty good, and he's not complaining—except that, when the waves are really cracking, he often has to work, in eyeshot of the waves he is not surfing. A customer is irritated about the mustard on her burger, and, over her shoulder, just in the distance, lines of swell are pouring in, and peeling off, with the worldly perfection he once thought would organize his whole existence. A lot of his life has been spent transfixed in appreciation of waves in just those moments, especially on the good days like today. Now his main way of coping is to look away.

Just so, the average surfer sitting in a desk chair, staring at a computer, falling behind on e-mail, awash in daydreams, can slip into bummed despair. But the source of despair is a sense of absence, an awareness of time being lost, for being in the wrong place.

Freud approved of wakeful dreaming, as a way of coping with under-stimulation. Reality can be boring. Seeking pleasure, we dream. Yet at least some of the daydreams are less about entertainment than self-discovery. A photograph or video can draw forth a flood of memories of saturated green and silver speeding moments, of roaring along in or around the tube, or of sliding along the wind-groomed wave face. It may be a classic "Proustian moment": a genuine memory comes unbidden, suddenly, from places forgotten. One sees again one's life's real meaning, as once envisaged when one knew life could be wonderful. A sense of self recovered, the latest BS work issue, of money, of personal status, of vanity, can simply pass through in the stream of experience, over one's shoulder, into the past and forgotten, replaced by a simpler, singularly meaningful persistence. Yet the daydreams can also be wishful, beyond the reach of events that actually happened. As the poet Rainer Maria Rilke says,

> You think of all the traveled lands,
> the images and tattered strands
> of all the women you could not hold.
>
> And suddenly you realize: there's nothing there.
> You rise to your feet, and before you appear
> the fear and form and empty prayer
> of the absence of another year.[8]

8. "Memory," trans. Paul Weinfield, at https://paulweinfieldtranslations.wordpress.com/2014/09/21/rainer-maria-rilke-memory/. The philosopher Mark Rowlands

Maybe the surf photographs or videos nicely color a lived experience long lost to time, or recolor a longing for perfection, which will never quite come to fruition—not even or not quite on a pricey boat trip in the otherworldly surf of the Mentawai Islands. But no matter. The sharpest loss of all is not of past time forgotten, in time's ineluctable passing. It is of time now being lost, here in the present, *in this very moment at work,* a moment now not being spent *wet* in the waves.

Work Can Be Inefficient, Wasteful

The Stoic philosopher Seneca once noted a particular kind of stupidity. "People are frugal in guarding their personal property; but as soon as it comes to squandering time they are most wasteful of the one thing in which it is right to be stingy." And it isn't that life is short in duration, so that one must *carpe diem,* as though there's no tomorrow to plan for or invest in. "It is not that we have a short time to live, but that we waste a lot of it. . . . We are not given a short life but we make it short, and we are not ill-supplied but wasteful of it. . . . Life is long if you know how to use it."[9]

Because work is where most of us spend most of our time, aside from sleep and meeting basic needs, the efficiency-minded economist would surely look there first for possible waste. In modern economic jargon, any time spent in work has an "opportunity cost" that must be counted, as long as one values what one might have done with the time instead. The more one values surfing, gardening, or getting to know one's husband or wife—all of which takes time—the higher the opportunity cost of work for money is, measured in time forgone in a limited life span. Because a person only has so much time in a life, there's some point at which the cost becomes *inefficient,* even *wasteful* of an essentially scarce resource, given the

---

argues that Rilke is onto a distinctive, embodied mental type, in "Rilkean Memories," at http://miami.academia.edu/MarkRowlands.

9. *On the Shortness of Life,* trans. C. D. N. Costa (New York: Penguin Books, 1997).

greater value of what one could have instead of working for a bit more money. Thus the "workaholic," who doesn't count the cost of work, can easily squander the most precious of resources: the mortal being's time alive.

The source of our discontentment is not work itself. It is how much we are asked to work during our limited time in life, when we could all run on an easier schedule. With so little time for everything else, the long hours at work leave one feeling stuck in the wrong place, trying not to think of what one could do if we instead instituted a twenty-hour workweek.

As noted in the last chapter, Keynes correctly predicted how very rich capitalism would make us by now. In fact we're richer overall than he guessed in his 1930 essay, "Economic Possibilities for Our Grandchildren."[10] Now even the worst off in the rich world are on average better off than the vast part of all human beings, ever, including the vast majority of people now living.[11] Keynes also predicted—this time incorrectly—that we would by now have scaled work way back. The rich world is five times richer than in 1930, but we work on average only a fifth less. Keynes wondered, once people have left poverty, why would they keep working for money, given the marginal inefficiency of extra work? We might wonder as well: Why again are we working so much?

Economists cite several possible (not incompatible) factors.[12] (1) We just like work, find it interesting, and like a challenge. (2) We want to buy quality stuff as it is innovated (for example, a plasma TV, the new iPhone). (3) We are led to want things by consumption engineering through advertisement and status comparisons. (4) We work to keep up with the Joneses, who are also working more and trying to get richer, to keep up with the Smiths. As Rousseau would

10. Lorenzo Pecchi and Gustavo Piga, eds., *Revisiting Keynes: Economic Possibilities of Our Grandchildren* (Cambridge, Mass.: MIT Press, 2008).

11. As a rule, according to development economists, the bottom 20 percent of the advanced-world income distribution is better off in absolute terms than 80 percent of the developing world.

12. See Pecchi and Piga, *Revisiting Keynes.*

explain, if we fall too far behind, or can't keep far enough in front, we won't love ourselves as much.

These are not the best reasons for working, given the time we give up. We can have all of these motives and still work less, striving, consuming, rising, and comparing at a slower pace, in a slower race. Why the frenzied rush?[13] And how could any or all of such reasons justify working as much as we do, unless we ignore the considerable value of the leisure time we forgo?

Put things this way: Are we prepared to curse our grandchildren with unnecessary labor? We wouldn't, right? Well, *we* are the "grandchildren" of our laboring forebears in past generations. And shall we refuse their gift to us of time free? Are we so dull or ungrateful, so hungry for money or status, as to not receive the opportunity as the gift it is? (Must one be a surfer to grasp the point?) Why work like crazy, especially if the very richest are collecting nearly all of the economic gains, as they have been for several decades? Might a more relaxed way of working together be both more efficient and morally better, given that work for money is so very *expensive* in lost time?

The magic of capitalism is to create plenty from scarcity, by efficiently converting any unit of time into money. Yet it can do that, with equal efficiency, by creating more time for a given amount of money, or more money for a given amount of time. We can choose either, depending on what we value most. We don't *have* to use up the scarce time we have in life to create ever more wealth, which we'll then leave to grandchildren who already stand to be vastly richer than we are on average.

The surfer firmly favors *time efficiency*: never waste time in work for money, unless the money will go to an especially worthy or fine cause, or you happen to know (given the surf forecast) that you won't be missing waves. A surfer-friendly leisure capitalism would

13. Important but ultimately unsuccessful jeremiads about the shallowness of conventional economic life include John Kenneth Galbraith, *The Affluent Society* (Boston: Houghton Mifflin, 1958); and Charles Reich, *The Greening of America* (New York: Random House, 1970), which praised skiing.

be time efficient as well. For some specified (perhaps rising) level of wealth, the economy uses less and less time to create that acceptable standard of living. It *economizes on time,* freeing up ever more of it, being efficient with respect to the *value of time,* rather than the lesser value of creating even more wealth.

Aristotle noted that a person will need sufficient resources in order "to do fine things." Surfing is a very fine thing to do with one's limited time in life, and one won't surf much or very well if one hasn't eaten or rested or found the funds to buy or make a surfboard. But beyond gaining a half-decent income, which may require time in work, the cost of every action or commitment can be measured in the amount of time it takes, given the potentially more important things you could be doing instead. It is easy to miss the good waves, or just not have enough time for a decent session on a regular basis. And as for how to further allocate life's most precious of resources—one's time in life—trading time for further money can quickly become very expensive. So why not put capitalism to work for us, harnessing the magic of markets and technology so that less and less time is lost to work? First lift the curse of Adam, freeing mankind from gruel and toil. Then lift the curse of Adam Smith and create more and more time for surfing and other self-transcending pursuits.

The opposite of time efficiency is *money efficiency*: all time is valued in money and spent as productively as possible in money-making. It is only *wasted* on pure leisure, which is a forgone opportunity for money production. And while you can't work constantly, for needing a break now and again, vacations, leisure, and relaxation are to be limited to *optimal resting,* lasting no longer than necessary to recoup the energy required to maximize one's money holdings over a lifetime.

Thus businesses compete with each other for margins measured in abstract money values, while the money hungry compete with each other in a status contest scored in dollar or euro amounts, or homes or cars or boats known for their price tags. The players often speak fondly of "efficiency," but the loose words, used with an air of sophisticated necessity, mask an ethical judgment of what is relatively important. Because money-hungry business counts costs only in what increases money, it won't count what you or your loved ones give up in exchange for your time at work (unless it brings the firm money). The firm, and people who think like the firm, don't care about the charity you didn't serve, the time you didn't spend with the kids, or the waves you missed. Which is not a concern for "efficiency" as such but a value judgment about the relative unimportance of your time away from work.

Money efficiency is at bottom insane and, in the limit, repugnant. Thankfully, almost no one really believes in it (not in the pure form just stated). Even those who mouth the words "time is money" aren't usually questioning the need for some basic social limits on how much people work. You get to *retire* at some point. There's a *workweek*, with periodic paid *holidays*. Children should *play* and *learn* rather than work through their youths. Some days you should go to a *wedding* or a *party*. If you make it big now, you can *stop working* in freedom and do *whatever you want*. You angle for a big payday in hopes of *early retirement*, to play more *golf*, when life can finally be lived. Then it won't matter that the time on the greens could be cashed in for money. One will frankly admit what the companies won't: that there's such a thing as having enough—that enough can be enough.[14] Because what else is life for, except for doing fine things? If an uncle who spent nearly all of his time on work for money was telling you on his deathbed that his life has gone to waste, despite a huge, now un-spendable bank account, you might feel sad the realization came late, but also think, well, you know, you sort of have a point.

So when the money hungry say that "time is money," feeling very sophisticated for making such a sophisticated statement about the metaphysics of time, they are confused. Time is *time*. Money is *money*. Time is not money, and time is properly fungible for money

---

14. On this theme, see Robert Skidelsky and Edward Skidelsky, *How Much Is Enough? Money and the Good Life* (New York: Other Press, 2012).

only within certain socially sequestered times of a person's life (for example, in one's prime, working years, but not on a Sunday). Much of our culture is simply confused in this way. And in that case a surfer cannot afford to go with the cultural flow. In a money-hungry hustle that dismisses how much a person surfs, and has no concern for whether a person's life is wasted on work, the one thing to strenuously protect is your time.

Is the Workaholic a Parasite?

In a 1932 essay called "In Praise of Idleness," British philosopher Bertrand Russell argued that working less would make us all happier. "A great deal of harm is being done in the modern world by the belief in the virtuousness of work," he claimed. "The road to happiness and prosperity lies in an organized diminution of work."[15]

Yet the argument from happiness, by itself, is insufficient. What Russell calls "belief in the virtuousness of work" is a religious/moral doctrine—the mighty Protestant work ethic—which just assumes that happiness isn't everything from a moral perspective. And that is surely right in some sense. If I've promised to be at work, I should definitely show up, even on a great day for the beach, even if I'd be much happier surfing than sitting through an admin meeting. I shouldn't be unfaithful in my work, with people counting on me. The Protestant work ethic must be answered in kind. There must be a plainly *moral* argument for a lighter workweek.[16]

We gave a moral argument in the last chapter. The surfer who works less and surfs more makes a contribution to the moral legitimacy of capitalism on a changing planet. Leisure capitalism is an efficient way of fulfilling our moral obligation to reduce the profound risks of ecological change. So the surfer is not a lazy, mooch-

15. "In Praise of Idleness," *Harper's Magazine*, Oct. 1932, http://harpers.org/archive/1932/10/in-praise-of-idleness/. Skidelsky and Skidelsky also argue from the value of happiness in *How Much Is Enough?*
16. The happiness argument is moral if we assume utilitarianism, as economists often do.

ing, sponging, freebie-taking freeloader. Surfers mostly work, but they'll happily contribute to our adaptation on a changing planet, by working less and leading an exemplary life of non-eco-consumption.

In the bizarro world we're now entering, the main troublemaker is the *workaholic,* here defined as the person who can't dial back work below some (low) average, without being miserable. For the sake of his or her anxious, striving kind of "happiness," the climate change problem is being made worse than it has to be.

Some emissions are largely unavoidable, but one's lifestyle choices can be more or less in sync with larger trends. The workaholic sets a bad example, making it only tougher for the rest of us to dial back to a lower average workweek. For those struggling to let go of the old work culture, it is only harder to learn to stop judging one's self-worth by the invidious comparison. If we must compare ourselves, we can do it on a lower "playing field," on the golf course or basketball court, or with lower absolute incomes. But the workaholic is driving the standards up, encouraging others to work more to keep up. So we should ask, why isn't the workaholic a parasite, for not doing more on the ecological front, for pushing the burden of adaptation onto others?

Well, it wouldn't be cool to morally condemn a person for an unfortunate disability in taking it easy. We accommodate alcoholics, drug addicts, and the mildly disabled. We could also make special arrangements for those who by compulsion must work more than a suitably low average.

Many people who are now workaholics will surely get the hang of leisure with a bit of practice, after a cultural detox period. As noted in the last chapter, we underestimate our ability to adapt, and many will find themselves just as happy working less. Many will take to new activities, finding that they can equally exert themselves and develop their skills in sport, art projects, or reading books. And some who retain a firm preference for work may simply be mistaken about their own happiness. As we saw in chapter 4, the ancients saw the good life for a person as a bundle of objective goods. A person's preferences can be mistaken or irrelevant for how well his or her own life goes, perhaps for being unduly influenced by a money-hungry culture of workaholic enablers.

Others may clearheadedly insist that they *love* their work. Their lives would feel empty and meaningless without it. The exercise of skill brings deep satsfiaction, and maybe life feels drab beyond the office or the factory, where friendships forged in common labor are especially sweet. Which is understandable, and why it would be unreasonable to ask people to forgo work entirely. Surely workaholics could be asked to work a tad less for the sake of climate adaptation—though even that won't be necessary if enough of us are willing to do our part and spend the day at the beach to average out their overwork. As long as enough others contribute to society by working *below* the low average in order to free up work opportunities in accord with the normal total, the incorrigible workaholic could keep working like crazy. Yet for every workaholic, a surfer must be surfing to "offset" the workaholic's overworking if the workaholic way of life is to be morally acceptable in an advanced capitalist society.

This wouldn't require a "surfer class" that never works, like the leisure class that now exists among the rich. Even the surfer who "offsets" the emissions of the workaholic might still have to put in some baseline number of work hours. So the workaholic wouldn't be an unforgivable parasite. Yet his or her chosen way of life is still, in one way, parasitic on the surfer's making his or her own kind of contribution to society.[17]

All of this suggests that leisure capitalism can be an efficient way of meeting our moral obligations after all. Even incorrigible workaholics wouldn't have to be made worse off. They can be accom-

---

17. I wouldn't say an incorrigible workaholic acts wrongly. One isn't personally obliged to cut back on work without assurances that enough others are doing likewise in a larger work practice that moves the needle on the climate problem. The issue here is less personal responsibility than what does or does not contribute to our living up to our collective obligations to stop creating risks of eco-catastrophe. How individual responsibility is assigned is a further, complicated question.

modated, as long as enough other people have the surfer's "utility function," which trades time for enough money to have meaningful leisure, but then places great and increasing weight on the value of time relative to money.[18] Then workaholic and surfer alike can adapt together in civic friendship.

Basic Income as Fair Return

Given the amazing recent advances in robotics and artificial intelligence, we can now credibly consider the terrifying (if far-off) possibility of self-reproducing psychopathic robots that start wars and take over the world. At the same time, on the potential upside of a robot explosion, they could do any work we didn't want to.[19]

Alas, they'd also do work we might really like to do. Are robots coming for our jobs? Yes seems to be the increasingly credible answer. The question is not "whether" but "when." According to the MIT professors Erik Brynjolfsson and Andrew McAfee, the future of work could well be permanent technological unemployment on a large scale.[20]

In many cases, machines will likely complement humans rather than completely substitute for their work.[21] Deep Blue beat Kasparov, but amateur chess players using computers beat Deep Blue by "coaching" computers to look into deep positions. And computers probably won't ever come up with good new ideas or concepts, as scientists, journalists, chefs, engineers, artists, and philosophers

18. I mean "utility function" in the way economists do, except the preferences for time versus money are a measure of objective goods, or, if you prefer, idealized preferences instead of actual preferences. For survey-based evidence that happier people do prefer time over money, see Hal Herschfield, Cassie Mogilner, and Uri Barnea, "People Who Choose Time over Money Are Happier," *Social Psychology and Personality Science* 7, no. 7 (2016), pp. 697–706.
19. On said explosive "singularity," see David J. Chalmers, "The Singularity: A Philosophical Analysis," http://consc.net/papers/singularity.pdf.
20. *The Second Machine Age: Work, Progress, and Prosperity in a Time of Brilliant Technologies* (New York: W. W. Norton, 2014).
21. Ibid., pp. 189–91.

do. As Picasso said of computers, "But they are useless. They can only give you answers." So there will always be creative work to do. (In which case philosophy or humanistic study is the ideal college major.)

Still, robots or computers need only be capable of doing the routinized part of a job. That alone would reduce the overall number of experts required in an industry, in which case jobs would become scarce. And computers now seem capable of even sophisticated "cognitive" tasks such as reading complicated texts and discerning narrative patterns or even stylistic differences. By some estimates, half of U.S. jobs are automatable, including much of white-collar work. That might be fine if retraining and reemployment could keep up. But in fact jobs have already started being replaced faster than displaced workers can find new work. In the 1990s, Brynjolfsson and McAfee note, employment grew alongside productivity. After that, they decoupled. Brynjolfsson and McAfee explain what this might mean:

> As digital labor becomes more pervasive, capable, and powerful, companies will be increasingly unwilling to pay people wages that they'll accept and that will allow them to maintain the standard of living to which they've become accustomed. When this happens, they remain unemployed. This is bad news for the economy, since unemployed people don't create much demand for goods and overall growth slows down. Weak demand can lead to further deterioration in wages and unemployment as well as less investment in human capital and in equipment, and a vicious cycle can take hold.[22]

Nor can we simply bring home jobs we've "offshored" to the developing world. The jobs sent abroad tend to be of the routine, manual sort, which are most readily automated. Even in the sweatshops of China, robots are increasingly depriving very poor people of a key

22. Ibid., p. 232.

ladder out of poverty.[23] And among the jobs now being "re-shored," many come back in automated form, in worker-less factories.

Martin Ford, futurist and author of *Rise of the Robots*, worries about a "techno-feudalism" in which a very rich plutocracy doesn't exploit the working class, but leaves it superfluous. The best we could hope for, he suggests, would be a "collective form of semi-retirement." Most people would live off a basic income paid for at least in part by taxes on the superrich.[24]

Suppose robots, in endless supply, could do everything. What would that mean for the larger economy? Brynjolfsson and McAfee explain,

> The owners of the androids and other capital assets or natural resources would capture all the value in the economy, and do all the consuming. Those with no assets would have only their labor to sell, and their labor would be worthless.[25]

Although robots may never top a good chef, if they get pretty good at cooking, the competition will drive down culinary wages, except for a few "superstar" chefs. We'd get the same result in other industries. Most everyone would be out of work, have no income, and so no money to spend. Soon enough, with no one buying the goods or services on offer, there'd be lesser or no income for the robot owners as well.

The natural solution, Brynjolfsson and McAfee suggest, is to give people money, in a basic income payment. A deposit just appears in everyone's bank account each month. The surfer will content-edly go surfing. The mechanic can work on motorcycles, for money or for free, as he or she pleases. And the capitalist who owns the

23. For my heavily qualified defense of sweatshops, see my *Fairness in Practice*, chap. 10.
24. *Rise of the Robots: Technology and the Threat of a Jobless Future* (New York: Basic Books, 2015). Ford's comments are reported by Elizabeth Kolbert, "Our Automated Future," *New Yorker*, Dec. 19 and 26, 2016, http://www.newyorker.com/magazine/2016/12/19/our-automated-future.
25. *Second Machine Age*, p. 181.

robots will gladly pay a high tax to cover the basic income for every-one, simply to make money. For if people have no money to spend, there's no money for the capitalist to make, no reason to invest, and his or her "assets" become worthless as well. A basic income might then be welcome all around.

Figures on both right and left have supported a basic income because it offers a simple fix to income poverty.[26] The new trends and speculation about technological change offer a further reason: it may soon be needed not only to meet basic needs but to give capi-talists a marketplace. Climate adaptation is yet another reason: our urgent need to adapt, starting now—meaning *yesterday*—supplies its own rationale for basic income. Working less and keeping it sim-ple in leisure are social contributions. Because working less means having a lower income, a basic income payment is fair return for that sacrifice.

John Rawls rejected this idea. Reciprocity is at the heart of his magisterial theory of justice, but with conditions attached: one must work the standard workweek. Rawls singles out Malibu surfers: "So those who surf all day off Malibu must find a way to support them-selves and would not be entitled to public funds."[27]

In one of the rare occasions in human history that surfers became

26. This is the idea supported by such wild-eyed Bolsheviks as the twentieth-century libertarian economist Milton Friedman, the arch-free-market booster F. A. Hayek, the think-tank conservative Charles Murray, and the former GOP U.S. president Richard Nixon. The idea has also found support on the left from Thomas Paine, Bertrand Russell, Martin Luther King Jr., and the economists James Tobin, Paul Samuelson, and John Kenneth Galbraith. The Right tends to want to replace the social insurance programs commonly found across the advanced world. The Left sees basic income as a mere supplement. Although this is a major point of disagreement about how to pay for basic income, the Right and the Left can agree on the idea in principle.

27. As Rawls explains his thinking (and people like me pay careful attention to exactly what Rawls was thinking), there are different approaches. One is to "assume that everyone works a standard working day." Another is to "include in the index of primary goods [the things one can claim from society] a certain amount of leisure time, say, sixteen hours per day if the standard working day is eight hours. Those who do no work have eight extra hours of leisure and we count those eight extra hours as equivalent to the index of the least advantaged who do work a standard day. Surfers must somehow support themselves." *Justice as Fairness,* p. 179. The quoted

a bone of philosophical contention, the philosopher Philippe Van Parijs argued to the contrary that "surfers should be fed."[28] A basic income should be *unconditional,* because social justice is not finally about reciprocity and its conditions. What justice requires is freedom, that everyone is able to pursue his or her own ideas of the good life. Because a liberal society must be officially neutral about the good life, it can't disfavor the Malibu surfer without undue discrimination. If the "lazy" aren't "excited about the prospect of a high income and [have] decided to take it easy" according to their best notion of what is best for them, well, they should still receive the highest sustainable basic income, with no attached conditions. Who, after all, is the *government* to tell them how to live?

As for the surfer view of the matter, I expect most surfers would be fine with the government discriminating against the workaholic, who really could be encouraged to take it easier. When it comes to staving off risks of a changing climate, his or her notion of the good life might seem too consumptive to be especially reasonable.

And yet the surfer would certainly say that Malibu surfers disinclined to work should be fed, rather than denied public funds. A basic income can be paid *as reciprocity.* Rawls didn't quite think through the climate change problem (which heated up late in his lifetime). The surfer who works less and lives simply is indeed making a contribution to an important national and international effort at adaptation. And while man shall not live by bread alone, any time out of the labor market is of course premised on one's ability to eat. "Leisure" time away from work while hungry and homeless and restless won't allow for much meaningful surfing. So for the surfer's contribution in living simply, a basic income—like the Australian "dole"—would be fair return.[29] Not that surfers would have to be

line in the text was from an earlier version of these remarks in "The Priority of Right and Ideas of the Good," *Philosophy and Public Affairs* 17, no. 4 (1988), p. 257n7.

28. "Why Surfers Should Be Fed," *Philosophy and Public Affairs* 20, no. 2 (Spring 1991), pp. 101–31.

29. Australia added residency conditions to its "dole," which many a surfer had been taking to live like a king in Indonesia. This hobbles a pretty effective foreign aid program, which helps Indonesians work their way out of poverty. Even on

paid as well as, say, bankers. Yet they certainly do more good for society than the financial market speculator who helps precipitate a sudden collapse and vast economic calamity.[30]

"The Pursuit of Happiness"

Lest this all seem un-American, the value of leisure arguably goes back to the Declaration of Independence. John Locke said that we have natural rights to "life, liberty, and property." The U.S. founders adapted this to "life, liberty, and the pursuit of happiness." They swapped "the pursuit of happiness" for "property," but why? According to some historians, the idea of happiness had gained new currency in the era due to reports of surfing from the South Pacific.[31]

In the late eighteenth century, during the French Revolution, a radical notion caught on. Happiness was not just an idea but something one could attain and enjoy in one's earthly existence, a possibility that came to be associated with a newly discovered place, Tahiti. Napoleon himself wrote about the general question, like a would-be Rousseau, before he decided to become emperor. And while the French explorers were especially concerned to note titillating sexual adventures in Tahiti's sultry, erotic paradise, the British explorers showed particular interest in surfing.

One crew member of James Cook's vessel wrote of the activity for the first time, on May 29, 1769: "All seemed most entertaind with their strange diversion." Later travelers would marvel that the surfer locals "effected what to us appeared to be supernatural,

---

Bali, once beyond the touristic areas, vendors can have trouble finding change for a fifty-thousand-rupiah note (a bit less than five dollars). One could think of Aussie surfers in Indo as working ambassadors of sorts.

30. Actually, people in finance doing socially unproductive work (when it is unproductive) would do well to just move to more productive work, such as school teaching or science research. This is another way workaholics could contribute without cutting back their hours.

31. See Westwick and Neushul, *World in the Curl*, p. 22; and Andy Martin, "Surfing the Revolution: The Fatal Impact of the Pacific on Europe," *Eighteenth-Century Studies* 41, no. 2 (2008), pp. 141–47. (The quotations below in the text are documented in Martin's article.)

merely by the application of such powers as they have in common with us." The suggestion was that the visitors could do it, too, and so should try it. Which they did. After one successful canoe surf, one observer wrote, "I could not help concluding that this man felt the most supreme pleasure while he was driven on so fast and so smoothly by the sea."

The question then became how such transcendent happiness—"the most supreme pleasure"—could be lived out in the Northern Hemisphere. And with the era's revolutionary fervor, the British settlers in the new America threw off Europe's class and power struggles in hopes of remaking themselves by their own ideas of transcendent happiness. (Which of course eventually included surfing, after it was introduced by Hawaii's Duke Kahanamoku in 1912 in New Jersey's Atlantic City and soon after in Southern California.)

American capitalism is not originally or inevitably about getting ever richer. It's about life and liberty for creative, transcendent activity, in industry and in leisure. Self-reliant yeomen farmers were never asked to toil in meaningless labor. Many approximated Marx's ideal for diverse, interesting, autonomous work from an American love of free, creative activity. Two hundred or so years later, our modern capitalist economy is a different animal, but fresh adaptations could flow from the same founding values.

Locke himself saw nothing wrong with "drudgery" and servitude (though not full-on slavery) for those with little or no property in a laissez-faire market. American democracy affirms a happier, more energized liberty. In the new human condition, leaving people to the whims of the labor market without meaningful leisure is thus not only undemocratic but un-American. We remain shackled by a rigid work ethic for a bygone era. A twenty-hour workweek would unleash a dynamic flood of free, creative activity in art, surfing, entrepreneurialism, charity, and republican service.

Technology then really could work for the worker. With the help of computers and the Internet, the average worker has been producing more and more for each hour of work without getting a raise (on average, adjusting for inflation), even as corporate profits and executive pay have soared over the same period. Marx called this "theft," a violation of the worker's rights of property over the fruit of his or her labor power.[32] One could instead call it "inequitable": the worker does not receive his or her fair share of the surplus created in part by his or her technology-aided work. And if that still sounds too "Marxist," because things work best, on balance, when wages are left to the market (perhaps beyond a minimum wage), an alternative solution is *surfer equity*: the worker can be paid in time. Just pay the same wage and ask for less time at work. Then the more efficiently the person works, the more time he or she has to surf (or paint garden gnomes, or sculpt, or basket weave).

Machines have always displaced workers, and economists have long assured us that this is all to the good, at least as long as the workers can be readily reemployed. The gains in productivity lift all boats with steadily rising wages, at least eventually. In the meantime, however, workers have the meta-job of constantly adapting, skillfully moving from one job to another, retraining and retooling, somehow paying the bills in the interim. A "flexible," free labor market is supposed to be good for all of us in the economist's "long run," except that people have to live through the short or medium run as well, and working-age people are still waiting: they haven't on average been getting pay increases for all the coping in recent decades. Wages aren't steadily rising across the class spectrum. For all the wonders of "disruption," all the coping might feel a bit more like surfing if the worker could at least count on a basic income.

Then the worker could live more like the investor who spends

---

32. Marx also thought the worker was forced to work in order to eat. The capitalist can hire and fire at will, with an abundant supply of replacement workers, so the wage bargain is exploitative of the worker's inferior bargaining position: she can't just walk, for need of money for basic necessities. (Farming in self-sufficiency isn't an option without land and property, so she's forced to labor at the will and whim of property holders.) Once a worker was hired, Marx saw market wages as theft, a violation of the worker's natural property rights to the fruit of her labor power. That idea is highly controversial, even as "libertarian" foes such as Robert Nozick often grant a similar premise of natural self-ownership. A different problem is that the "labor theory of value," Marx's analysis of what the worker contributes, never completely panned out.

the morning at the café monitoring the market news and looking for investment bargains. In America, the land of equal opportunity, we surely should encourage worker participation in capitalist risk taking and entrepreneurialism. To that end, we could give everyone a "capital grant" on his or her eighteenth birthday, which could be saved for a return or invested in a new opportunity. And if we like, we could add a longer-standing "capital account" for each person, funded by contributions from any work or by a government payment for those who do important voluntary service.[33]

Sartre presumably shared the French or American hippie view that one should "work to live" rather than "live to work." That is a view about the good life, but the surfer's reasons for working less aren't simply about personal happiness or autonomy, as Marx suggested. They're about our together being attuned to the human condition and adapting capitalism to its new moment. Marx was wrong to think that capitalism had to end for workers to enjoy autonomous, self-directed, non-alienated meaningful labor with plenty of time free. We can continue the leisure revolution *within* capitalism, with a lighter workweek that affords the time in leisure and lazing needed to be creative—not just for the CEO, entrepreneur, or artist, but for everyone.

Voltaire said that "work saves a man from three great evils: boredom, vice, and need." Basic income only addresses need. So is work necessary for other reasons? Surfers are neither bored nor vicious. They're enthralled and rather virtuous (at least athletically speaking). Their issue is need and getting a fair shake. The surfer's ques-

---

33. This raises the question of how high a basic income (along with any other social benefits, including Social Security) should be. What minimum share of the social surplus, along with wages for twenty hours of work, would a surfer fairly receive? Or, otherwise put, what inequality in overall prospects (counting time and money), if any, would be unfair? Whatever the truth of the matter, I don't sense any distinctively "surfer" position on this controversial question. As suggested in chapter 7, the surfing lineup is tolerant of wave-count inequality but still has general norms for fair sharing. It's a mash-up of capitalism and egalitarianism. Surfers would have qualms with large economic or political inequalities that impede surfer values of societal climate adaptation and time efficiency, but the extent to which that is a real problem might itself be cause for disagreement.

tion isn't whether we should work. It's whether we work too much in order to have a fair standard of living. As Brynjolfsson and McAfee note, work will always be a principal source of "self-worth, community, engagement, healthy values, structure, and dignity."[34] Yet none of these values say *how much* we should work, given its expensive cost in time free. We can pay healthy respect to those values and work a lot less.

For those who would still like a lot of stuff, a basic income would at least help fund a bit more leisure. If one worries that surfers won't work enough, we could set social expectations to encourage the right low measure of work. A basic income payment could gradually phase out as income increases, so the minimum guarantee comes without a disincentive to work. (The United States already has a modest version of just this sort of "socialism," in the earned income tax credit, a negative income tax supported by Republicans and devised by the libertarian Milton Friedman.[35])

And how do we pay for all this? Taxes, of course, though not necessarily income taxes. The question would be which taxes could fund the social support necessary for everyone to have an attractive standard of leisurely living along with income from twenty hours of work. The answer, for starters, is that a basic income could be partially funded by taxes that already fund less productive government expenditures (such as farm subsidies). Some existing social support might also be diverted (how much might depend on one's political leanings). If that alone would provide a very modest income, even alongside wages for twenty hours of work, a higher payment can then be funded by taxes that are anyway a good idea. Carbon taxes are needed to curb emissions, and they raise considerable new revenue. Extreme wealth should probably be taxed further, with postmortem "death taxes" on large estates, lest we reverse the leisure revolution and devolve into what the economist Thomas Piketty calls "patrimonial capitalism," an undemocratic system in which

34. *Second Machine Age*, p. 235.
35. See ibid., pp. 237–41.

leisure and wealth come largely by birth and inheritance instead of being shared widely.[36] A tax on financial transactions à la Nobel laureate economist James Tobin would do much to "make banking safe again," prevent financial crises, steady the rise of longer-term standards of living, and maybe "make bankers pay." While the main goal is to curb a dangerous activity, even a small tax on a huge volume of financial transactions raises enormous sums.[37] International tax agreements would also be needed to more effectively curb tax evasion and repatriate funds.[38] The revenue from a variety of such sources (including further taxes on consumption) could be sufficient even without raising taxes on personal income. Income taxes might be raised as necessary, or also cut in order to encourage people to work less. Then less work would be necessary to earn up to a targeted standard of living.[39]

The "doomsday scenario" presented at the end of chapter 7 posed an important question: If humans invariably compete for status, are we locked into ever more work for money and consumption-heavy leisure, thus courting ecological disaster? We now have an answer: greedy or status conscious as we are, we can strive and compare at a slower pace, in a slower race, in more leisurely, sporting contests.

Rousseau may be right that we cannot but live through the eyes of others in order to love ourselves. Yet we aren't stuck with today's

36. *Capital in the Twenty-First Century* (Cambridge, Mass.: Harvard University Press, 2014).
37. I argue from precaution for a "Tobin tax" in chap. 8 of my *Fairness in Practice*. There I don't take a position on what to do with its considerable revenue.
38. See Gabriel Zucman, *The Hidden Wealth of Nations: The Scourge of Tax Havens,* trans. Teresa Lavender Fagan (Chicago: University of Chicago Press, 2015); and for a philosopher's treatment, see Peter Dietsch, *Catching Capital: The Ethics of Tax Competition* (New York: Oxford University Press, 2015).
39. The conventional rationale for lowering income taxes—to encourage work or investment—might apply in certain cases (for example, encouraging people to earn up to the median income level while counting their basic income payment). Yet again the larger goal would be not to create as much growth as possible but to steady it at a "safe" level.

contest of riches, fame, power, or beauty by way of remunerated work. The contest can instead be for the most interesting leisure activity, the most skilled display of athletic or artistic talent, or the most creative mix of leisure, service, and work. Today's game can be torn down as the basis for our identities and decomposed into a variety of sports-like microcultures, in which we spend more of our time immersed. Then a rich plurality of comparisons could give everyone a real chance at being content with him- or herself. We assess and value ourselves on various bases, which vary by the cultures we identify with and the fellows whose respect we value. Culture can change. So we can change the game and do our part in changing it.

So maybe I'm a decent surfer. And a decent philosopher. I'm part of two subcultures. Maybe I couldn't be happy with myself if I only had the one or the other. If I scored myself solely by the standards of either, being consumed with my status, perhaps I'd have long lost sight of why I ever wanted to give my life to each totally wonderful activity in the first place. But maybe I like myself well enough living in both, because neither is the lodestar of my identity. As Sartre says, I am free to define myself. Who am I? I am a surfer/philosopher from California who is over six feet tall and right-handed. If that's who I am, I'll have almost no one to compare myself with, no one with respect to whom I could decide that I'm not measuring up. I can love myself, as myself, in easy acceptance. And as for the very few philosophers who've tried surfing, or the very few surfers who dabble in hard-core philosophy, why would I wish to compare myself with my soul mates? If we had an afternoon together, we'd just go surfing and discuss Sartre.

So it's at least possible for all of us to more easily love ourselves in a blooming, buzzing variety of leisure and work pursuits, with ample free, flexible time for one's own creative concoction. In a more leisurely capitalism, we'd have a less competitive way of life. We'd all work, but a lot less, and we'd spend more of our time getting attuned, living from love, practicing for its own sake, and transcending status preoccupation for a happier contentment.

—

Less than a hundred years later, our world today is much more like Keynes's vision than the world of his own day. The times change rapidly. The leisure revolution began, with surfers on the vanguard. We could help finish the job, maybe as soon as this century. Surfers number themselves among humanity's fortunate daughters and sons. Might all of us rich worlders catch on? If enough of us learn to attunedly adapt, in due appreciation for our common fortune, might an easier future actually happen?

It is possible.

Under a Fortunate Sun

A philosopher: Why is there something
rather than nothing?
God: If there was nothing, you'd still be complaining.

—a joke by the philosopher Sidney Morgenbesser

WHAT IS THE MEANING of life? To answer, consider a parable:

> A seeker has heard the wisest guru in all of India lives atop
> India's highest mountain, so the seeker tracks over a hill in
> Delhi until he reaches the fabled mountain. It's incredibly
> steep, and more than once, he slips and falls. By the time he
> reaches the top, he's full of cuts and bruises. But there's the
> guru, sitting cross-legged in front of his cave.
>
> Oh, wise guru, the seeker says, I have come to ask you what
> the secret of life is. Ah, yes, the secret of life, the guru says.
> The secret of life is a teacup. A teacup? I came all the way up
> here to find the meaning of life and you tell me it's a teacup?
> The guru shrugs, so maybe it isn't a teacup.[1]

At parties, when I'm asked what I do for work and I say that I
do ethics and political philosophy, I'm often cheekily asked, "Okay,
then what is the meaning of life?" The question is supposed to be

---

1. As told by Thomas Cathcart, at http://www.npr.org/templates/story/story.php
?storyId=10158510.

impossible to answer, so I usually quip, "Oh, that one is easy." I then do what philosophers often do and draw attention to the nature of the question, so as to change it.

If my fellow partygoer will bear with me, I propose that we first answer a different question: "What are the meaning*s*, plural, of life?" If that's the question, I say, then we just enumerate the many different ways life can have meaning. Easy, right? Friendship. Worthy projects. Creative activity. Music. Surfing. Nice parties. Or whatever—the list can be as long as we like. Maybe we won't start to disagree until pretty far down the list.

I then ask why there should be any further question of *the* meaning of life. Why must there be any one meaning of life that is the singular overarching meaning, which somehow explains the rest?

That tends to dispel the allure of Sartre's or Camus's existential skepticism. The meaning of a person's life can be given by a simple list. The harder part is how to creatively balance all the different values as a life unfolds. But that can be left for each of us to work out in our freedom. My suggestion is that "the meaning of life" can be *nothing more than the various ways life is meaningful to us,* where each of us lives by some individual mix of the many different things worth doing in a life. You can't "have it all," of course, so you have to choose. Except you choose not in a spirit of absurdity, as Sartre says, but in overabundance. There are just too many ways to put together a meaningful life, so you must find the one that suits you best.

So the original question about *the* meaning of life is actually easy to answer, because mis-framed. It only *seems* difficult because we mistakenly assume that there has to be one meaning that explains all the rest. The meaning of life can be simple. (Though not as simple as a teacup; rather, there seem to be a whole lot of teacups.)

Yet the hoary old question can feel forceful when we step back from life under the sun and ponder the vast cosmos. Human history is but a blink in time. Soon we will all be dead, ages before the universe disperses into a cool gas as the result of entropy.

Yet this concern for size is confused in its own way, as Thomas Nagel explains: "If our lives are absurd given our present size, why would they be any less absurd if we filled the universe (either because we were larger or because the universe was smaller)?"[2] Would life be more meaningful if we were a hundred or a thousand times as large? No. Size just doesn't matter, in this case.

At the same time, seeing ourselves from a View from Nowhere (as Nagel calls it) invites the idea that one could intelligibly tell a cosmic story about how all of life could have meaning. But then the question is how much should turn on any such giant super meaning. Suppose a life of human struggle is rewarded by postmortem attendance at an eternal banquet, with heavenly cheeses, wines, dishes, and great company. Then the meaning of a person's life, spent like this for all of eternity, would depend on the value of a nice party. And if "nice parties" was already on your meanings list, the question would be whether you'd want a nice party to last forever. If you happen to be the introverted type who prefers to attend such events quickly and slip away before feeling emotionally drained, this particular super meaning might not add a lot of extra meaning to your earthly existence.

Maybe there's some other super meaning more to one's liking. Or maybe not. Either way, life under the sun is splendidly full of meaning. And if you're still really bothered or unappreciative of that important fact, well, then I might refer you to the philosopher Sidney Morgenbesser's joke about the cosmological argument, which suggests a certain lack of gratitude for the blessed goodness that we've got. ("Why is there something rather than nothing? If there was nothing, you'd still be complaining.")

My saying such things is more than enough to sour an otherwise pleasant conversation at a party. For maybe all the philosophical maneuvers don't speak for a human yen to be "part of something bigger," a longing, however inexpressible, for life itself to have enough meaning so that there is meaning in being part of it. But actually, we can admit this style of meaning as well. Depending on what cosmic or world-historical stories you find plausible, just put

2. "The Absurd," p. 12.

your favored super meaning down on the long meanings list. Sartre would deny the absolute correctness of any grand narrative beyond the stories we tell ourselves, but surfers wouldn't grind an ax. As a surfer might say, "Who knows? The world is a pretty interesting place."

What would be satisfying to have is some sort of story, a narrative, about how bigger things fit together, in a way that might touch upon our daily doings and somehow make sense of them. The nice thing about a narrative is that the same events are open to telling and retelling, with all sorts of interesting variations. There's a lot of latitude in storytelling, and the question might be not so much whether a given narrative is the one true meaning as whether it makes for a good story.

Speaking to a sense of nihilism in a secular age, the philosophers Hubert Dreyfus and Sean Kelly point to the collective meaning felt at sporting events. As with ancient life and sport, as handed down to us through the Olympics, the common appreciation of great skill, displayed in a stadium that reflects the best of a city, brings a possibility of self-transcendence. They explain,

> We have been arguing that the basic phenomenon of Homeric polytheism—the whooshing up that focuses one for a while and then lets one go—is still available in American culture today. . . . [T]he moment of exultation in a ballgame . . . offers what autonomy cannot: a sense that you are participating in something that transcends what you can contribute to it.[3]

They point to Lou Gehrig's famous speech, after his record-setting career for the Yankees was ended by what would be a fatal, wasting disease, where he said, "Fans, for the past two weeks you have been reading about a bad break I got. Yet today I consider

3. *All Things Shining: Reading the Western Classics to Find Meaning in a Secular Age* (New York: Free Press, 2011), p. 205.

myself the luckiest man on the face of the earth." To thunderous applause, he found meaning in gratitude in a sacred community of fellow sports fans.

Of course, as Dreyfus and Kelly note, this is also the "whooshing" of the crowd whipped up by the authoritarian at a political rally, who incites nativism and worse in dangerous self-aggrandizement. Crowds can be really exalting or really dangerous. If Lower Trestles is one of my favorite places on our fine planet, some days the crowd is too much; I want to be home and read in peace. And crowd dynamics don't seem necessary for us to meaningfully do things together. Democracy can bring a solemn sense of common purpose, even to the lone voter in the voting booth as he or she helps to decide our common fate as a nation. The Olympics every four years can be not only a contest of skill and celebration of human excellence but an ongoing gesture toward the ancients, our forebears, and every country, in view of our common sporting nature as humans.

Yet being part of a collective enterprise could never be more than one source of meaning among many on a long list. It wouldn't diminish the meaning in going into the wild, for solitude and communion with nature, in order to escape, if only for a time, from both the bad and the good in the demands of society.

So our list of meanings can grow longer, still more inclusive, to cover big parts of human history. Maybe human life is akin to a chain novel, fashion show, or other creative community. We make history, together, as we go along, each contributing our bit before our deaths. Surfers go surfing, but it's more than just surfing if the act of leisure is a joyous culmination of the Industrial Revolution and another step in the progress of the leisure revolution—that great change in capitalism that started in the twentieth century and could well be completed in the twenty-first.

A super narrative could also be cosmic. Friedrich Nietzsche, who saw his own life and philosophy as an exercise in creative self-expression, went for an atheistic version of eternal recurrence: all of history had already happened an infinite number of times and would repeat itself an infinite number of times in the future. As Thomas Nagel explains, for Nietzsche this meant the sanctification of life, even without religion,

> for it made every moment of life eternal. The past has not ceased to exist, and the present is not vanishing as we live through it. Every moment of our being is real forever. And the *Übermensch* is the being whose capacity for self-affirmation will enable him to rejoice at this thought.[4]

This is one way to avoid the usual finality of death and gain a kind of life eternal. Which is all good if death is a big worry to you. Yet the *Übermensch* doesn't have some special presence denied to others. It only takes a surfer to rejoice stokedly in a full presence with a wave, on a day that could be any day. The sanctification of life can come easy, without all the heady metaphysics.

But if we're doing surfer aesthetics, I suppose infinite repetition would be a bit monotonous. Much more intriguing would be an eternal cycle of reincarnations, as in a cosmic wave moving from past through the present to the future and somehow rolling through all over again. Once you've been good enough to be born as a human surfer, if you keep snaking waves and can't just be cool and share, you're at risk of sliding back into your prior cow existence, which will most certainly not permit surfing. (Becoming a dolphin, by contrast, might be considered a promotion.) But I'm pretty sure this won't convince the asshole surfer, whose very experience as a surfer doesn't imply any such spiritual metaphysic. And even if it did, he wouldn't listen to religion or philosophy. Or he'd just uncritically read Nietzsche and think he's an *Übermensch*.

Because surfing is open to different spiritualizations, one could instead go for a monotheistic meta-narrative that posits a creative God behind the sun who is planning big things and using us as

4. "Nietzsche's Self-Creation," in *Secular Philosophy and the Religious Temperament*, p. 38.

her creative medium. Maybe a great artist with true knowledge of the Beautiful wouldn't plan history according to a meticulous script. She'd merely shape the human play of events, with subtle gestures on the canvas of time. Or maybe, as in the Christian version, God runs the show and then steps onto the stage for a live performance, a demonstration of love for humanity that does what simple morality itself cannot: effect reconciliation between God and humanity and among people themselves. (Simple morality doesn't require one to forgive.)

No surfer would object to the sentiment, being all for bonhomie. The surfer would, however, have certain questions if this super plan is supposed to include moving from life under the sun, with real water and real waves, to bliss in a heaven somewhere above. Above where? The other side of the sun? Won't it be rather chilly out there wherever, away from our fine planet? Will the surf *ever* be good? Will there even be waves? The surfer might wonder whether disembodied heaven is a fully intelligible concept, even if people call it a "banquet" or a "party." And if the concept of eternal life turns out to be intelligible, because the nonmaterial can somehow also be spatial and temporal, then, well, surfers like a good party. It'd be a shame to miss out—especially if the alternative is just cooling off in the grave, not doing any real surfing, anyway. A good party is a very fine thing to be around for if one has a bit more time after one's time under the sun. That's probably reason enough to drop any metaphysical qualms about exactly what sort of airy "being" there might be in a radically weird reality.

Back here under the sun, if we look quickly over the last thousand or so years and forward to the coming centuries, human history is its own grand story. History is of course a work in progress, but our story, the story of most living people, is already one of enormous fortune. We are the beneficiaries of the abundant forms of human progress, including the likely end of world war; the dramatic decline of violence, including personal violence; the unprecedented reduction of poverty; the eradication of major diseases; the dramatic increase in literacy and education; and major improvements in racial and gender equality and in health and life spans. There is much to be grateful for. And if *gratitude* must assume an agent or agents to be credited, the agent could be God, or Hegel's Absolute Spirit, or the better angels of society, or liberal social planning. And if one resists all such personification, the alternative attitude could be a more impersonal sense of appreciation and celebration of profound fortune. In any case, we really can be stoked to be part of where history has brought us.

Woody Allen quipped, "I don't want to achieve immortality through my work, I want to achieve immortality through not dying. I don't want to live on in the hearts of my countrymen, I want to live on in my apartment." But on the assumption that all of us will physically die, with no survivors, the philosopher Samuel Scheffler points out that many of the things we value now depend on the existence of future people after our death.[5]

Even if our own life spans were no shorter for it, many of our activities would come to seem much less important to us if we came to know that an asteroid would destroy the planet soon after our death. Or, as in P. D. James's novel *The Children of Men,* if humankind became infertile, and we knew the current youngest generation would be the last to ever come into existence, we wouldn't attach the same value to such things as finding a cure for cancer, research in science, technology, or medicine, and construction of new buildings or infrastructure. Even art, music, literature, and history would have less value to us in the knowledge that their audiences would soon disappear. Few of us alive would say, with complete indifference, "I won't be here; so what?" Just so, few surfers would not be indifferent to the End of Surfing as We Know It, despite the convenient fact that the sea levels will rise significantly only after their deaths. The surfer values a relationship of adaptive attunement to what lies beyond, even independently of his or her experience. And the doomsday scenarios show that we value our relation to future people, even if we won't be around to experience them.

5. *Death and the Afterlife* (New York: Oxford University Press, 2013).

So the surfer can intelligibly surf, not only to surf a wave, but to stay on the cusp of humanity's adaptation on a warming planet, potentially for the benefit of millions or even billions of people. One can surf a wave and surf history in one and the same deed. Surfers aren't so pretentious as to paddle out thinking such a thing. If we asked a surfer what he's doing this afternoon and he gave *this* explanation, we'd chuckle about his comic grandiosity. Still, he wouldn't be wrong about his (and our) historical moment.

Yet any story is the story it is in part for its ending. So what we decide to do or not to do now will make a difference to what our lives will have amounted to. How will our lives or age be judged in looking back from the future? What is it that we will have done with our enormous privilege?

We living people are enjoying the carbon-based prosperity party. And though we'll be dead before our emissions completely befoul the global ecology, if we don't take rather dramatic steps to control their production, our story will be one of having indulged in the feast and skipped out on the check, without paying our bit, let alone helping with the dishes.

This really would not be cool. It would be a gross human failure, or, if you will, a great stain, or sin. In Faust's gamble with the devil, humanity will have lost.

Faust, in Goethe's telling, sells his soul to Mephistopheles for greater earthly powers but then does terrible things and barely escapes damnation (because he has nevertheless "striven greatly"). Likewise, the Faustian project of capitalism aims its amazing powers toward such things as reducing poverty, promoting freedom, and enabling science, the arts, and leisurely surfing. Yet it also induces morally questionable motives of self-interest, which can run amok and imperil the larger good that justifies adopting capitalism in the first place. Bringing disaster to vast numbers of present and future people by our profligate actions certainly would not spare us from just Judgment. We would only escape damnation because enough of us have, like Faust, "striven greatly" for a morally half-decent kind of capitalism, which shows some concern for the impending befouling of life and society.

So the choice is still ours: Shall we personally enjoy a bit more time in the sun and on the water, to do our part in a more leisurely style of capitalism that shares our fortunes with our children and their children? Suppose we did together work less, forgoing ever-greater riches, spending a lot more time in leisure. Suppose this was the "price" of our adapting to a changing planet, so as to pay, as it were, for the world-historical process that made us rich. Now, there's a good story! Capitalism wouldn't have been such a bad idea after all. We'd have *won* Faust's bargain with the devil, achieving worldly power and wealth without forfeiting our souls. We'd be breathtakingly fortunate, saving our souls, along with civilization, by soul surfing.

I must admit, the carbon-based prosperity party was way more fun before we knew we may be majorly hosing future generations. It's a huge world-historical buzz kill and may or may not be the sort of hangover that just goes away.

We receive the sun's good light and heat as always but now trap it in the atmosphere, fouling up the delicate ebb and flow of heat transfer that originally brought a teeming ocean, habitable terrestrial life, and in time humanity itself, spread among the continents. As the world's climate changes before our eyes, as scientists increasingly fear wild and uncharted ecological damage, if we avoid certain deep philosophical questions about the human condition and responsible actions, we will have sealed our fates, having written our head-in-the-sand story.

A more meaningful ending would have us facing up, heroically, to the biggest questions. If we've enjoyed a world of ecological abundance until relatively recently, what does it mean if the human condition itself is quickly changing—if the whole Industrial Revolution party, after having made a lot of us amazingly prosperous, is over? We became accustomed to a logic of capitalism that worked (if imperfectly) in a world of ecological abundance. But that just isn't our world any longer, and if we really are entering a new human condition, in which ecological resources are becoming much scarcer than they've been, then at the very least, we'd interrogate the old way of thinking and let go of it. It might be too little, too late already, but the story would at least be one of adaptation.

But if we are willing to adapt, maybe we'd make a heroic effort. We'd worry, what the hell do we do—what *should* we do—in a world in which ecological resources are *a lot* scarcer than they have been? Just party on?

The answer, this book has claimed, is yes! We should party on— in a different kind of partying. Instead of getting ever richer, we go surfing (each in his or her own way), in a more leisurely style of capitalism, in which we all work, but a lot less.

I, for one, am down for it.

Predictably so, you might say. I am, after all, a surfer. And hasn't this book offered a comically grandiose rationalization for skipping school or work and hitting the waves? Maybe. But maybe not. The question is a philosophical one, for all of us to judge, and judge afresh. Occasionally, there are new things under the sun to consider. And as for whether or how we consider this inordinately consequential question, be assured, we will be judged by God or history.

Acknowledgments

Years after I completed graduate school, my former adviser, the eminent philosopher T. M. "Tim" Scanlon, was visiting Southern California. As we strolled along the bluff overlooking the ocean in Santa Monica, catching up and talking philosophy, he asked me whether the small breakers below were any good. I explained that although the winds were blowing nicely offshore, one condition needed for good waves, the waves still weren't especially good. Tim immediately related this to certain philosophical claims in value theory about "good-making features" that I'd defended over a decade before. It occurred to me for the first time that for all these years Tim was tracking how my own philosophical views flowed from my life as a surfer more perceptively than I myself was. I hope this book, in part an exercise in self-understanding, brings to fruition what Tim has always seen in my thinking.

It is one of the great privileges of my life to have studied with a master, to have benefited from his generosity of spirit and faithful mentorship, especially in philosophical friendship with someone of such unusual decency. As much as or more than anyone, Tim is responsible for my life in philosophy, so this book of philosophy owes an enormous debt to him.

Gerry Howard, my editor, had a major role in every part of the book, from its naming and framing, to its content and structure, to its tone and flourishes. It takes an extraordinary kind of editor to take a chance on refreshing an olden style of philosophical treatise, now long out of fashion in both academia and the larger culture. I might not have pushed my luck creatively without the confidence I gained from his wise guidance.

I am as ever grateful to my agents, Donald Lamm and Melissa Chinchillo, without whom I would never have tried out pop philosophy. I owe a special debt of gratitude to Bill Bracken, for his extensive comments and discussion of Heidegger and Sartre, to David Sussman, who first pointed me to Sartre's comments about waterskiing, and to Marshall Cohen, for his years of friendship, all-afternoon conversations, writing instruction, and unflagging support.

Christine Korsgaard, alongside Tim, has been the most important influence on my thought and philosophical development, even long after she and Tim supervised my dissertation. I should also acknowledge my other teachers at Harvard University: Jim Pryor, my third dissertation committee member; Hilary Putnam, who taught many of my early courses; along with Arthur Applbaum, Stanley Cavell, Richard Heck, Robert Nozick, Derek Parfit, Charles Parsons, Dominic Scott, and Amartya Sen. And for my rich undergraduate education at Westmont College, I am grateful to Robert Wennberg, Jim Taylor, Stan Obitts, Jim Mannoia, and Robert Gundry.

For their comments or conversation, or their support, I thank Arash Abizadeh, Conor Anderson, Chris Armstrong, Ray Assar, Christian Barry, Matthew Begley, Larry Berger, Graeme Bird and Kerstin Mass, Danielle Bjelic, Michael Blake, Tom Blush, Nic Bommarito, Matthew Braham, John Broome, Simona Capisani, David Chalmers, Christina Chuang, Richard Claughton, Konrad Clemmans, Annalisa Coliva, Percy Cottle, Casey Dahm, Brett Detmers, Greg Drude, Michael Duncan, Luca Ferrero, Edward Feuer, Mark Fiocco, Nathan Fulton, Roberto Fumagalli, Pablo Gilabert, Margaret Gilbert, David Theo Goldberg, John Gotti, the Gratteri family, Sean Greenberg, Lori Gruen, Sarah Hannan, Nicole Hassoun, Matt Hayden, Jacob Heim, Jeff Helmreich, Pamela Hieronymi, Fiona Hill, Louis-Philippe Hodgson, Jeff Howard, Lucy and Kyle Hughes, Alex, Alin, Elizabeth, and Wendy James, Mark Johnson, Nicholas Jolley, A J Julius, Sunny Karnani, Erin Kelly, Bonnie Kent, Louise Kleszyk, Rahul Kumar, Seth Lazar, Chad Lee-Stronach, David Lefkowitz, R. J. Leland, Jacob Levy, Susanne Lier, Penn Maddy, Pietro Maffetone, Robert May, Brad McHose, Violet McKeon, Marco Meyer, Cordell Miller, Darrel Moellendorf, Robert Montgomery, Jeff and Debbie Mulligan, Thomas Nagel, Shmulik Nili, Kieran Oberman, Dan and Michelle Oberto, Martin O'Neill, Knox Pedan, Casey Perin, Jesse and Elaine Pike, Daniel Pilchman, David Plunkett, Andrei Poama, Enzo Porcelli, Duncan Pritchard, Tim Quick, Ankita Raturi, Michael Real, Rob Reich, Mark Reiff, Johan Reyneke, Nick Riggle, Robin Risque, Mathias Risse, Jake Ross, Nicolas Rossi and Ximena Da Silva, Eben Sadie, Lucy, Sarah, and Jessie Scanlon, Karl Schafer, Ricky Schaffer, Tamar Schapiro, Steven Scheid, Martin Schwab, Greg Shaffer, Tommie Shelby, Ken Simons, Brian Skyrms, Angela Smith, David W. Smith, Richard Smith, Cristiana Sogno, Jiewuh Song, Lucho Soto, Nic Southwood, Dan Speak, Lombard Steyn, Una Stojnic, Sharon Street, David Tannenbaum, Paul Tannenbaum, Peter and Sally Tannenbaum, Stevie and Diane Thompson, Amanda Trefethen, Dov Waisman, Philip Walsh, Roger Walsh, Andrew Walton, Damien Wao, Matt and Denise Weaver, Ralph Wedgwood, Leif Wenar, Andrew Williams, Larry Wilson, an audience at Avemetric Inc., and my 2016 course at UC Irvine on ethics and the exercise of skill. I apologize to anyone I might have forgotten; the book is still better because we talked.

Finally—although I'm starting to think she won't ever work less than she does, despite all my arguments—I thank Kendra Gratteri for her love and enthusiastic support.

Glossary

Absurd: 1. Lack of reason, value, or meaning. 2. A conspicuous gap between pretense and reality (Nagel).

Adapt: 1. To change one's attitudes or actions in accord with a change in one's circumstances. 2. To change with one's circumstances by virtue of bodily sensing and know-how. 3. To embrace or value change in new circumstances, for intrinsic or extrinsic reasons ("change is good"; "surfing is all about adaptation"). 4. To alter an object designed for a purpose for a further end, as when a hammer is used as an art display or doorstop.

Adaptation: The basis for evolution according to biology. See also Adapt; Adaptive attunement.

Adaptive attunement: 1. Both being attuned and adaptively acting. Perception and bodily action are linked inextricably. 2. The essence of surfing. 3. The human's being or nature (see also Adapt; Adaptation; Attunement; Social attunement).

Aerial: Launching into the air above a wave. Usually done with a head of speed, launched from wave's lip (see Lip). Now a staple of high-performance surfing, done in many variations, often with a full or partial bodily rotation (for example, "air-to-reverse," "360 air").

Amour propre (Rousseau): Comparative self-regard, especially in seeing oneself as rightly viewed as superior or inferior in the eyes of others. The source of vice. The cause of civilization's ills.

Analytic philosophy: A method of philosophy prominent in Anglo-American academic departments of philosophy. Places a premium on clarity and defines terms and uses logic to carefully structure and clarify rival positions and arguments. Origins in logical positivism (see Logical positivists/empiricists).

Anarchical society: Social order without centralized, sovereign government. Examples include the surfing lineup and international relations.

Appropriation (Sartre): Using something for one's purposes in order to own, master, or possess it, as a slave is possessed by his or her owner.

Asshole: The guy (assholes are mainly men) who takes special advantages in cooperative life out of an entrenched sense of entitlement that immunizes him against the complaints of other people. In surfing: the "special advantages" are easy right-of-way (see Right-of-way); you get whatever wave you paddle for, because people steer clear. Contrasts with attunement to others or social flow. See Amour propre; Flow; Social attunement.

Attunement: 1. Being "in tune" or "in sync" with a pattern that emerges over time. 2. Becoming more attuned in small increments of increasing sensitivity. 3. Being fully attuned, perhaps only temporarily. See also Adaptive attunement; Adapt; Flow; Social attunement.

Authoritarianism: Rule by an unaccountable sovereign. Secures order by way of orders backed by threats of violence (Hobbes). Contrasts with democracy (see Democracy).

Awesome (the olden sense): An apt object of awe, in fear or respect, admiration, wonder, or apprehension. Especially as regards the sublime. See Sublime.

Awesome (a newer sense): Welcome and surprising breaks from the mundane in ordinary life. Especially as pertaining to the sublimely beautiful (see Sublimely Beautiful).

Awesome (a newer social sense): A virtue of people in social relations. As defined by the philosopher Nick Riggle in *On Being Awesome*, one who creates "social openings" by breaking out of the usual roles, in order to express his or her individuality and open a door for mutual appreciation. The opposite of "sucking" (as in "you suck, man"), the refusal to take up such social openings.

Back paddling: To paddle behind a surfer already in position (see Asshole; In position; Right-of-way).

Bad faith (Sartre): A person's treating him- or herself as just another object in the world. Failing to assume one's responsibility for choosing what to do or who to be. Failing to meet the demands of "authenticity," of owning up to one's freedom. See also Freedom (Sartre).

Basic income: A cash payment given to everyone, whether or not one works. Reciprocity for the contribution of not working (see Surfer's contribution). Can gradually phase out as income increases so that there is no disincentive to work. Can be funded by taxes that now fund less productive government expenditures, and some existing social support, and new carbon taxes, estate taxes, financial transactions taxes, and consumption taxes. May or may not require raising taxes on personal income.

Bathymetry: 1. The study of submarine topography. 2. In surfing: the propensity of underwater bottom contours of rock or sand, depth or curvature, to influence wave formation, refraction, and quality. A structural precondition for well-formed waves (see also Flow/structure). Something surfers have a keen intuitive sense of, because they are able to predict where or how an approaching wave will break, in order to paddle into position (see In position; Intuition).

Beautiful: 1. What brings pleasure or enjoyment, in contrast with the "delight" associated with the sublime (Burke). (See Sublime; Sublimely Beautiful.) 2. The appropriate object of enjoyment in freewheeling imagination, whatever one's actual opinions or feelings (Kant). 3. An otherworldly, eternal fact (Plato).

Being: 1. Existing. 2. Existing as a conscious subject, perhaps as self-conscious. 3. An embodied conscious subject engaged in particular circumstances, as made intelligible by a culture (Heidegger's "being-in-the-world"). 4. Adapting to changing surroundings (see Adaptation; Adaptive attunement). 5. Presence with oneself, for example, in contented resting, lazing, or loafing. 6. Presence with one's surroundings and self-transcendence, for example, the "being in doing" in archery or surfing (see Self-transcendence). 7. Our being saddled with perpetual labors of self-creation by virtue of self-consciousness—"being as (just) doing." See also Three types of being (Sartre).

Buddhism: A large family of views and religious practices inspired by Siddhartha Gautama, including Zen. Ascetic versions strive for the abnegation of all desire and radical loss of the very idea of the self. See also Middle way.

Bummed: Melancholy, disappointment, or mild sadness. The opposite of being stoked (see Stoke).

Capitalism: An economic system that consists mainly of private property and that relies largely on markets for the production and allocation of goods, services, and capital. Laissez-faire ("hands off") capitalism with an ultra-minimal state, for basic security and judicial functions, is an extreme version. Differs from socialism as a matter of degree (see Socialism). See also Leisure capitalism.

Carving: Turning on a wave, especially in a critical section, in a radical or attuned way.

Compatibilism: Freedom is compatible with determinism (see Determinism). 1. Determinism and indeterminism are *irrelevant* to our freedom and moral responsibility (Strawson; the surfer). 2. Freedom *requires* determinism, because one would otherwise be too unpredictable to count as the sane, rational, free author of an action for which one could be praised or blamed (Hume).

Consciousness: 1. The subjective, inner, experiential life of the mind.

Conservativism: What is given and valuable should be accepted or even cherished for what it is. Even if we could replace it with something better, we shouldn't try to, but instead pay our respects, taking care not to mess with it, for instance, by putting it at significant risk of massive degradation.

Continental philosophy: A style of philosophy originating in continental Europe, especially post-Kant. In Anglo-American countries, often practiced in academic disciplines of literature or critical theory. Key figures include Hegel, Nietzsche, Husserl, Heidegger, Sartre, Merleau-Ponty.

Contribution: Doing something that helps to serve an important societal purpose. Needn't be done enthusiastically or wholeheartedly; a matter of expected outcomes rather than intent. Examples include parenting; elder care; artistic work; working less and surfing more in order to help make climate change less terrible than it otherwise will be.

Control (according to the surfer): 1. Bodily coordination. 2. Efficacy that comes from heightened attunement. 3. Bodily coordination that is efficacious because of its heightened attunement. Something you shouldn't consciously try for (except to address a specific body-control problem). For comparison, see Appropriation (Sartre).

Cope: To adapt to an unwelcome situation of necessity, rather than for its own sake. Aim is to make one's situation less bad than it would otherwise be. May be skillfully or unskillfully done.

Curl: The leading, moving edge of a breaking wave, at the point where the top of the wave curls over the wave face (see Lip; Wave face). May or may not form a tube (see Tube).

Cutback: A fast turn toward the curl of the wave, often on its shoulder (see Curl; Shoulder). May involve a large, fast rotation through the shouldering wave face back up into the curl, combined with a snap performed on the white water (the "roundhouse") (See Snap).

Democracy: 1. A form of centralized government and voting procedures. 2. Society as a free community of equals, ruled by their common reason for mutual benefit, each being at once the law's subject and equal co-author (Rousseau). 3. Cooperation as equals in a social practice. Accountability founded on shared ideas, the willingness to complain, reason together, discuss, trust and verify, and work out issues under common public norms and values—all without the formalities of voting and well before talk of war or sanction. Contrasts with authoritarianism (see Authoritarianism).

Determinism: The world is a deterministic system. Every event that occurs could not have been different given the world's initial conditions and the laws of nature, or divine providence.

Ecological scarcity: The limited supply of environmental services, for example, the atmosphere's ability to absorb carbon or methane emissions without warming on average. Limited such that continued use of resources (of absorptive capacity) creates risks of injury to present and future people. Contrasts with ecological abundance, in which case using as much as one likes still leaves (in Locke's phrase) "enough and as good" for others.

Efficiency: 1. Benefiting some while leaving no one worse off (Pareto). Contrasts with sacrifice, which leaves some worse off. An example of efficiency without sacrifice: adapting to the new world of ecological scarcity by adopting a shorter workweek (see Ecological scarcity; Leisure capitalism; Surfer's utility function). 2. Advancing a valued goal in the least costly manner, for example, maintaining a decent standard of living while spending the least possible amount of time in work (see also Money efficiency; Time efficiency).

Egalitarianism: 1. Everyone counts as an equal. 2. In surfing: everyone of sufficient competence can claim a wave share under the rules of right-of-way. Does not require equal wave distribution—though one can count as a pig for catching too many waves (see Pig). See also Democracy; Right-of-way; Wave etiquette.

Epic: 1. A term of enthusiastic endorsement. 2. Of remarkable quality, for example, in wave conditions, a particular surfed wave, or a particular maneuver. 3. Rightly remembered, of sufficient quality for the record books. 4. Of ideal form, as though Plato's eternal forms were for the moment manifest in sensuous reality.

Epistemology: The study of knowledge, including its definability, proposed definitions, the nature of justification, evidence, and virtue or rationality in regulating one's beliefs.

Eternal recurrence: All of history has already happened an infinite number of times and will repeat itself an infinite number of times in the future (Nietzsche).

Eudaimonia: The ancient Greek term for human flourishing, for doing well as a person. Understood by Plato and Aristotle as an objective list theory of happiness. See Objective list theory.

Experientialism (about happiness): The quality of a person's experience, even when illusory, is all that matters for how well or badly his or her life goes.

Facticity (Sartre): The facts of one's situation, including one's body.

Fade: A slow, anticipatory cutback (see Cutback). Often done from the shoulder to a steepening part of the wave face, in order to position oneself for a newly forming wave section, for example, in anticipation of a tube (see Pitching; Shoulder; Tube; Tube ride; Wave face).

Flow: 1. The attuned exercise of skill. 2. A way of relating to what lies beyond oneself. Contrasts with the experiential state of "flow" (see Flow, experiential). See also Adaptive attunement; Self-transcendence; Social attunement.

Flow, experiential: Defined by Mihaly Csikszentmihalyi as "optimal experience" marked by feelings of control, mastery of our fates, exhilaration, and deep enjoyment. By comparison, see Flow.

Flow/structure: A flow (for example, a breaking wave or a flowing stream) always flows through something that is not flowing, a structure that shapes how the flow flows, allowing it to have a flowing dynamic. (See also Bathymetry; Indonesian Throughflow.) The relationship may itself be dynamic, as long as the basic structure/flow relationship doesn't change too much all at once. That our climate is asked to absorb emissions too quickly is the basic problem of climate change (see Ecological scarcity).

Foam ball: A rolling ball of foam inside the tube of a wave (see Tube). Can disrupt a surfer's travel in the tube as turbulent water releases the surfboard fins from the wave (see also Tube ride).

Freedom (Sartre): 1. The fact of our self-consciousness (see Being; Consciousness; Self-consciousness; Three types of being). 2. Our predicament in having to choose in absurdity, without reason, or sufficient reason. 3. What requires us to constantly construct a self (see also Bad faith). 4. Being such as to use, own, or master something or someone; see Appropriation. 5. Why determinism must be false. See Determinism; Incompatibilism; Radical freedom.

Freedom (according to the surfer): 1. The basic rationality and self-consciousness that makes one the morally responsible author of one's actions and aptly blamed or thanked for them. 2. An achievement, or way of success in action, by doing something worthy of the life you are leading. (See also Meaning.) 3. Being efficacious without control, precisely by giving up any need for it, through adaptive attunement (see Adaptive attunement; Control). 4. The social or political liberty to define one's life given an array of worthy options, given a real option of meaningful leisure (see Basic income; Leisure capitalism). See also Compatibilism.

Game play: To voluntarily attempt to overcome unnecessary obstacles. In Bernard Suits's full definition, to attempt to achieve a specific state of affairs, using only means permitted by rules, where the rules prohibit use of more efficient in favor of less efficient means, and where the rules are accepted just because they make possible such activity. See also Play; Sports.

Gnarly: 1. Especially dangerous, radical, or terrible. 2. One form of the sublime. 3. A particularly skilled or radical maneuver (as in "gnarly turn, bro!"). Contrasts with the beautiful (see also Beautiful; Sublimely beautiful).

Going with the flow: A desirable way of living, for example, walking a city street, in a work project, in the day's tasks, and as a general way to live, with less anxiety, less striving, and a certain graceful success. See also Adaptive attunement; Flow; Flow, experiential; Social attunement.

Happiness: See *Eudaimonia;* Experientialism; Hedonism; Objective list theory; Preference satisfaction.

Hedonism: Happiness consists entirely in having pleasure and avoiding pain, or the greatest overall balance of pleasurable experience.

Incompatibilism: Freedom is not compatible with the deterministic world suggested by macro-level physics (or Calvinist predestination theology). If determinism holds (see Determinism), we are not free. If we are free, determinism cannot hold (see Radical freedom). See also Compatibilism.

Indonesian Throughflow: Located in the southern part of the Indonesian archipelago, an essential part of the global heat conveyor belt that regulates the average temperature of the planet's atmosphere.

In position: Being the surfer who could most easily catch the wave as it peaks, for being either closest to the peak or the farthest out (as in "I was in position, man; back off"). May or may not be easily discerned and plain for all to see, and thus the cause of quarrel. See also Back paddle; Money spot; Right-of-way; Wave etiquette.

Intentional arc (Merleau-Ponty): An accumulation of past experience and skilled bodily dispositions that now inclines me to respond in one way rather than another, given my general purposes. Flexible general capacities of movement, spontaneously refined in response to a new situation, given feedback about what seems to work over time. See also Perception; Reason.

Intentionality: "Aboutness," or being of or about something else. A key feature of thought or other mental states, for example, my thought is about something else, say, Indonesia.

Intuition: 1. Fast thinking or sensing. 2. Doing by know-how without being able to articulate one's reasons. 3. Bodily perception of one's environment (see Intentional arc; Perception). 4. Proprioceptive awareness of one's body, beyond the five senses. 5. The rational basis for a moral judgment, which might be articulated as a more general principle (Rawls). See also Reason; Reflective equilibrium.

Know-how: Knowledge of how to perform a kind of activity. The ability to perform according to certain standards, either of basic competence or of success. May or may not be the same as knowledge-that (see Knowing-that).

Knowing-that: Knowledge of a proposition, which can be true or false, via belief. May or may not be the same as know-how (see Know-how).

Leisure: 1. Any time away from work in the labor market, as defined in economic theory. 2. Passively resting, relaxing, lazing, loafing, taking it easy. 3. Time spent in active pastimes, such as games, sports, or charitable service. May or may not be done in a "leisurely" manner and may or may not be "work" (see Work).

Leisure capitalism: Capitalism with a relatively short workweek. A way of efficiently adapting, without sacrifice, to ecological scarcity. See Ecological scarcity; Efficiency; Surfer's utility function. See also Capitalism; Leisure revolution.

Leisure revolution: What began with institution of the forty-hour workweek, whose explicit purpose was to create time for leisure (of twenty-four hours in a day, "eight for work, eight for sleep, and eight for leisure"). A major move within capitalism circa 1940 away from laissez-faire capitalism (see Capitalism). Might be continued by further cutting back the workweek in the present century, given ecological scarcity (see Ecological scarcity).

Lip: The leading edge of a wave's curl (see Curl). The edge of a peeling tube (see Tube), or the feathering or breaking top of a wave face (see Wave face). Often the site of maneuvering, for example, the "off the lip," which includes various ways of rebounding or snapping off the breaking top of a wave face (see Snap).

Localism: The ideology wherein surfers claim entitlement to wave right-of-way in the simple fact of residing near a surf break. Often confused, especially by locals, with more defensible notions. For example, locals tend to catch more and better waves for their superior wave knowledge. Also, infrequent visitors have a duty to show respect for the going tone of a surf break as a matter of courtesy.

Logical positivists/empiricists: The early to mid-twentieth-century school developed by the Vienna Circle (Moritz Schlick, Otto Neurath, Rudolf Carnap, and Hans Reichenbach, among others). Proposed theories of logic and language to explain how the empirical sciences were possible. Maintained that meaningful claims must be verified or tested in sense experience. Regarded ethical and religious claims (which can't be so verified) as cognitively meaningless, neither true nor false. Contrasts with ethical truth and objective truth (see Objective).

Look: See Stink eye; The Look.

Meaning: 1. Simple value (for example, the value of play). 2. A person's choice of projects among a rich set of values. 3. A basis for peace, reconciliation, zestful engagement in life (see Reconciliation). 4. Narrative, for example, a cosmic or historical story. By comparison, see Absurd; Freedom (Sartre).

Metaphysics: The study of what is real and what it is like very generally speaking, especially as discerned other than by the empirical sciences, such as physics. See also Reality.

Middle way (Siddhartha Gautama): To be as happy as you can be by being willing to be as unhappy as you are. See also Buddhism.

Money efficiency: All time is valued in money and spent as productively as possible in moneymaking. It is wasted on pure leisure, a forgone opportunity for money production. Opposite of "time efficiency" (see Time efficiency).

Money spot: The position on a wave such that you know, and everyone can see, and you know that everyone can see, that this wave is most definitely your wave (see In position).

Mush/*Merde*: A formless, breaking wave that lacks a steep wave face. See also Bummed.

Objective: 1. Values: good or bad aside from one's beliefs or preferences. 2. Truth: the truth of a judgment (for example, in ethics or aesthetics) is invariant with respect to ways our particular thoughts or feelings might have been different. 3. An otherworldly, eternal reality (Plato). See also Reality.

Objective list theory (of happiness): The quality of a person's life is determined by his or her possession of certain goods. The goods are given by a list, for example, health, success in one's projects, enjoyment, harmonious relations to what lies beyond. Their value for the person is objective, quite aside from his or her beliefs or desires.

Opportunity cost: What one might have gained in making a different choice. The value of a forgone alternative. For instance, in choosing to work more hours, the (opportunity) cost is the loss of time one could have spent surfing or playing with the kids.

Peak: A wave that is about to break, which juts upward, forming a triangular, peak-like shape.

Perception (according to the surfer): Being embodied in a particular situation and knowing how to attunedly adapt one's body to one's environment. Seeing does not always come before action. Action also shapes seeing. Understanding sensory-motor movements—the moving of the eyes, turning of the head, or walking forward to reach and touch is not just the way we perceive. It is the very nature of perceptual awareness. See also Adaptive attunement; Attunement; Intentional arc.

Phenomenology: A method pioneered by the German philosopher Edmund

Husserl that looks at what our ordinary experience is like. Also hopes to discern a quasi-universal "logic" that is "implicit" in ordinary experience. Though originally developed in continental Europe (see Continental philosophy), now central to much of analytic philosophy. See also Analytic philosophy; Reflective equilibrium.

Pig: One who takes too much of a common resource. May or may not be an asshole (see Asshole).

Pitching: A wave lip that juts forward beyond a wave's face (see Lip; Wave face). May or may not form a tube (see Tube). The opposite of a mushy wave (see Mush/*Merde*).

Play: 1. Playfulness or spontaneity, for example, in jazz or surfing. 2. Acting on an imaginative pretense, for its own sake, as in child's play. 3. Suits's definition: any intrinsically valued activity. 4. Kant: the "free play" of one's faculties in imagination, in a "free harmony" of thought and feeling, especially in the apprehension of beauty. 5. Huizinga: transforming routine and ritual into the realm of the beautiful and the sacred. See also Game play; Sports.

Preference satisfaction (theories of happiness): Happiness is getting what you want. Preferences may be actual or hypothetical (for example, preferences one would have with more information).

Pump: A way of gaining speed on a wave. Done by a combination of shifting or releasing one's weight and weaving the surfboard in an up and down motion.

Radical freedom: Freedom that is incompatible with a deterministic universe (see Determinism; Incompatibilism). See Freedom (according to Sartre). For comparison, see Compatibilism; Freedom (according to the surfer).

Reality: 1. What is. 2. Ordinary: What is by ordinary standards. Especially as regards what can't be completely shaken in anything recognizable as an ordinary human life. 3. Personal: One's bodily sense of space, in one's own possibilities of bodily movement in a situation, in relation to certain possible tasks (Merleau-Ponty). 4. The impersonal world of physics.

Reason (according to the surfer): Thought in action guided by embodied, situational perceptions and by past practice. (See Intentional arc; Perception.) 1. Slow and calculative deliberation. 2. Quick and spontaneous thinking, the know-how of reason in practice. Contrasts with affect or emotion. See also Intuition; Reflective equilibrium.

Reconciliation: Finding peace through acceptance, of the world, of oneself, or both. Based for the surfer in stoke (see Stoke).

Reflective equilibrium: An ideal state of intellectual coherence (Rawls). Achieved by a process that considers ethical or other "intuitions" and fashions them into a body of knowledge through reflection. Explicates principles or theories that explain intuitions and then adjusts or prunes either the intuitions or the principles or theories until they all fit into a coherent, holistically satisfying system. See also Intuition; Reason.

Right-of-way: Once a surfer is in position on a wave, others must yield. See also Back paddle; In position; Wave etiquette. Violations of right-of-way called being "snaked," "burned," "cut off," "robbed."

Rippable: A wave that is highly suitable for high-performance surfing. See also Aerial; Carving; Cutback; Fade; Pump; Snap; Tube ride.

Self-consciousness: Being conscious of oneself (see Consciousness). The self may appear in the focus of one's experience, or its periphery or background. Contrasts with self-transcendence (see Flow; Self-transcendence).

Self-transcendence: To go beyond the self. 1. Ordinary: the ordinary loss of self-awareness while "absorbed" in a skilled activity. Can be fluid and a matter of degree. Possible because practice and habituation conserve attention, freeing it for other uses. 2. Relational: the ordinary loss of self-awareness in a relationship that preserves one's metaphysical identity as a distinct self. 3. Radical: there is no such thing as the self, or the realization of this fact.

Shoulder: The sloping, tapering part of a wave face (see Wave face). Contrasts with a steep wave face or the breaking curl (see Curl).

Snap: A maneuver performed on the lip of the wave's curl (see Curl; Lip). The surfboard is placed, often vertically, on the wave lip and then turned quickly in the opposite direction. The tail of the surfboard may break free ("tail slide") or break out of the top of the wave ("tail waft").

Social attunement: The social form of adaptive attunement. Staying attuned to other people and responding fluently in each new moment of cooperation, for example, in a conversation, a meeting at work, or a crowded city street. Brings a sense of harmonious social connection and a sense of peace. See also Adaptive attunement; Flow. Compare the asshole (see Asshole).

Socialism: An economic system composed mainly of public property that largely does not rely on markets. Differs from capitalism as a matter of degree. See also Capitalism.

Soul surfing: 1. Surfing with a soulful vibe and style, without regard to expectations of performance, usually away from a crowd. 2. Working less and surfing more under leisure capitalism and winning Faust's bargain with the devil. Achieving worldly power and wealth without forfeiting our souls. 3. Basis for reconciliation (see Reconciliation).

Sports: A kind of play, done for its own sake (see Play). Defined by "constitutive rules" that specify a kind of sporting activity. Generally less constrained by rules than game play. Can be made into a game, which may or may not be competitive; the players may or may not accept rules that define scoring and winning in a contest of skill. See also Game play.

Stink eye: 1. Looking askance at someone else. 2. A way of enforcing the rules of wave etiquette (see Wave etiquette). 3. A demand for justification, an assertion of one's equality, or a claim to respect. 4. A challenge to look back, eye to eye, and explain oneself in good faith. See also Democracy; The Look.

Stoicism: 1. A school in late antiquity that includes Cicero, Epictetus, and Seneca. 2. The most distinguished practical philosophy of how to live. 3. A stoic is one who controls his or her mind in order to maintain a steady tranquillity and detachment, accepting his or her circumstances as beyond his or her control. 4. One who adjusts his or her desires to his or her circumstances.

Stoke: 1. Feelings of excitement. 2. Heightened sense of harmonious dependence. 3. Basis for reconciliation (see Reconciliation).

Structure/flow: See Flow/structure.

Sublime: 1. A feeling of terror from a safe distance, along with a sense of pleasurable "delight" in being relieved of pain or fear (Burke). 2. "Delight" that involves admiration or respect and "submission, prostration, and . . . utter impotence" (Kant). 3. Something beyond feeling (for example, the ocean) that is the appropriate object of admiration, respect, or sober wonderment, without utter impotence (the surfer). See also Beautiful; Gnarly; Sublimely beautiful; Sublimely gnarly.

Sublimely beautiful: Both sublime and beautiful. A possibility that was obscured in Edmund Burke's 1757 treatise, *A Philosophical Enquiry into the Origin of Our Ideas of the Sublime and Beautiful,* which presented the sublime and the beautiful as normally opposed, or mixed only in exceptional cases. Contrasts with the sublimely gnarly (see Sublimely gnarly).

Sublimely gnarly: Both sublime and gnarly, as opposed to sublime and beautiful. See Beautiful; Gnarly, Sublime; Sublimely beautiful.

Surfer: 1. "The surfer": a way of referring to what surfers have in common, a widely shared sensibility about life and existence. Especially for purposes of asking what the surfer might appreciate above and beyond the technicalities of wave riding. 2. One who holds "the surfer position" on an issue, that is, an articulation of what the surfer knows "implicitly," by way of "constructive interpretation" of what all or most surfers seem to understand. 3. One who rides waves. See Surfing.

Surfer's contribution: Working less and surfing more, in order to emit less in leisure than one would if one were working. Helps to make the climate change problem less terrible than it would otherwise be. Can be made by anyone in working less if leisure is spent in relatively less consumptive activities (for example, chatting over coffee with friends or visiting the elderly). When instituted as a shorter workweek, the basis for an eminently sensible way to adapt to our more fragile global ecology (along with other equally or even more urgent measures, for example, carbon taxes and cap and trade). A way of continuing the leisure revolution within capitalism with new vigor (see Ecological scarcity; Efficiency; Leisure capitalism; Leisure revolution).

Surfer utility function: The surfer's willingness to trade time for enough money to have meaningful leisure, after which great and increasing weight is placed on the value of time relative to money. The preference for time versus money is a measure of objective goods or, if you prefer, idealized preferences instead of actual preferences (see Objective list theory; Preference satisfaction).

Surfer wage equity: The same wage is paid for less time at work. The more efficiently the person works, the more time he or she has to surf (or garden and so on). See also Leisure capitalism; Time efficiency.

Surfing: 1. Riding waves, often with aid of a surfing board. 2. To be attuned to a changing natural phenomenon, so as to be carried along by its propulsive forces by way of bodily adaptation, where this is done purposefully and for its own sake. See also Adaptive attunement; Play; Sports.

The Look (Sartre): 1. A person's gaze as a source of shame (for example, for being caught unawares peeping into a keyhole). 2. A glare of contempt or doubtful questioning. 3. How we could find it intelligible to suppose that others exist. See also Stink eye.

Three types of being (Sartre): 1. Being a mere object (an "in-itself"). 2. Being a conscious subject (a "for-itself"). 2. Being a conscious being who sees him- or herself through the gaze of another ("being-for-others"). See also Consciousness; Freedom (Sartre); Self-consciousness; The Look.

Time efficiency: Never wasting time in work for money, unless the money will go to an especially worthy or fine cause. Opposite of "money efficiency" (see Money efficiency). A feature of leisure capitalism (see Leisure capitalism). See also Efficiency; Surfer's utility function.

Transcendence: To go beyond something. See also Self-transcendence.

Tube: A cylinder formation some waves create as they advance. The wave's curl pitches out in front of the wave's face, landing in the wave's trough, creating open space inside the wave. Riding inside of the tubular formation is a pinnacle of the surfing experience. See Curl; Pitching; Tube ride; Wave face.

Tube ride: Surfing inside a tubing wave (see Tube). Also called getting "barreled," "shacked," "piped," "locked in," "time in the green room," "kegged," "slotted," "drained," "packing it."

Utilitarianism: The right action or just institution is the one that promotes the greatest overall welfare. Any means are justified if they advance this end.

Wave etiquette: The worldwide practice whereby all surfers are subject to public rules for sharing waves. Each has powers of enforcement; each has standing to speak up for his or her rights and demand a justification when there is cause for suspecting an infraction of right-of-way or courtesy. Each is rightly held accountable for his or her conduct, being prepared to give an account of it should anyone ask, on terms others could accept in good faith. "Localism" carves out special privileges for residents; see Asshole; Localism.

Wave face: The open front of an advancing wave, after a swell mounts, but before it breaks. Contrasts with a breaking wave's bottom or trough, its curl, and its whitewash (see Curl; Whitewash).

Whitewash: The turbulent, foaming water created after part of a wave has broken.

Work: 1. Market labor, or labor for money. 2. Toil, drudgery, tedium. 3. The exercise of skill, with the aim of learning or excellence, for example, while surfing. May or may not feel effortful, and may or may not be "leisure" (see Leisure).

Workaholic: 1. One who loves one's market labor and makes it central to one's life and identity at the expense of leisurely activities. 2. The person who can't dial back remunerated work below some (low) workweek average, without being miserable. 3. One who makes the climate change problem worse than it has to be. For comparison, see Surfer's contribution; Surfer's utility function; Surfer wage equity; Time efficiency.

Index